Edwin M. Yamauchi is Assistant
Professor of History at Miami University
Oxford, Ohio. He gained his PhD at
Brandeis University where he
specialized in ancient Near Eastern
languages. He has studied at the
American Institute of Holy Land
Studies in Jerusalem, and took part in
excavations at Jerusalem and at Tel
Anafa in Northern Israel.

PRE-CHRISTIAN GNOSTICISM

PRE-CHRISTIAN GNOSTICISM

A SURVEY OF THE PROPOSED EVIDENCES

by

Edwin M. Yamauchi

Associate Professor
Department of History
Miami University
Oxford, Ohio

WM. B. EERDMANS PUBLISHING COMPANY
Grand Rapids, Michigan

© TYNDALE PRESS

First edition May 1973

ISBN 0 85111 732 5
USA ISBN 0 8028 3429 9
Library of Congress Catalog Card No. 72–94668

To my son BRIAN

*Printed in Great Britain by
Richard Clay (The Chaucer Press), Ltd.,
Bungay, Suffolk*

FOREWORD

'It all depends what you mean . . .' was a gambit which
listeners came to associate with the late Cyril Joad when he
answered questions as a member of the BBC Brains Trust in
the early years of World War II. A number of people found its
constant repetition mildly amusing, but of course he was
absolutely right. There cannot be rational discussion of any
subject unless the participants are agreed on the meaning of
the terms they use, and this is as true in New Testament
studies as it is everywhere else.

The necessity of clear definition is particularly important
when such terms as 'Gnosis' and 'Gnosticism' are used. New
Testament interpreters will tell us that the 'human tradition'
against which Paul warns the Christians of Colossae was a
form of Gnosticism, or they may qualify it as 'incipient
Gnosticism'. Others, pre-eminently Rudolf Bultmann, will
tell us that what we are given in the Gospel of John is a
demythologized and Christianized version of a pre-Christian
Gnostic source. How are we to evaluate these and similar
accounts of our first-century Christian literature?

First, by definition. If we stick closely to the etymology of
'Gnostic' and related terms, then every form of religion which
makes the true knowledge of God fundamental has a claim to
be called 'Gnostic'. But we know that the meaning of terms is
decided by their use, not their etymology, and the use of
'Gnostic' and related terms is more restricted than that.
When, however, we examine the actual use of these terms, we
find a wide variation. There is indeed a general agreement to
limit the terms to those schemes which reflect the myth of the
Redeemed Redeemer (sometimes also identified with Primal
Man) who descends to the prison-house of matter to deliver
from it, by revealing the true knowledge, the heavenly essence

v

which is held in thraldom there since it fell from the upper world of light. But to what degree, or in what form, this myth must be reflected in a scheme if that scheme is to be called 'Gnostic', is something on which there is no unanimity. Hence the need for definition.

Second, by studying the evidence. For the most part, our surviving evidence for Gnosticism is considerably later than the New Testament period – so much so that the protagonists of pre-Christian Gnostic influence on the New Testament are countered by others who maintain that the distinctive features of Gnosticism in the narrower sense are best accounted for in terms of Christian influence. When two such directly opposed positions can be held, we may suspect that the evidence is ambiguous, or that powerful *a priori* factors are at work. In any case, the complicated problem can be resolved only by a dispassionate and comprehensive study of all the available evidence. The available evidence continues to increase in volume as more of the Nag Hammadi documents are published. It may be that some of these documents, when they have been carefully examined, will give clearer answers than have been possible thus far to questions of the existence and nature of pre-Christian Gnosticism. Unfortunately, we get the impression at times that existing presuppositions are unconsciously allowed too much weight in the interpretation of new material as it comes to light.

In this situation Dr Yamauchi, who has already established his reputation as an authority in the field of Mandaean studies, helps us greatly both in defining our terms and in evaluating the evidence. He surveys the whole range of Gnosticism and gives us an up-to-date assessment of the present state of the question. With this 'Guide to the Per-plexed' many New Testament students will be able to grasp and to judge more intelligently authoritative but conflicting assertions about Gnostic influence which they would otherwise be unable to control. It is a pleasure to welcome and recom-mend Dr Yamauchi's work.

F. F. BRUCE

CONTENTS

PREFACE

The following monograph is an expansion of the Tyndale Lecture for Biblical Archaeology presented before the Tyndale Fellowship for Biblical and Theological Research in July 1970, at Cambridge. I would like to express my warm thanks for the hospitality shown to me by Alan Millard of the University of Liverpool, Gordon Wenham of the University of Belfast, and Derek Kidner, the Warden, during my stay at Tyndale House.

I am indebted to Professor David Scholer of Gordon-Conwell Theological Seminary for allowing me to have a pre-publication copy of his *Nag Hammadi Bibliography 1948–1969* (E. J. Brill, Leiden, 1971), which was of inestimable help. My warm thanks go also to Professor Malcolm Peel of Coe College, who permitted me to examine the unpublished portion of his Yale dissertation, 'The Epistle to Rheginos: A Study in Gnostic Eschatology and Its Use of the New Testament' (1966).

This work would not have been possible without the whole-hearted co-operation of Mr Leland S. Dutton, Research Resources Librarian of Miami University, and of his staff in securing inter-library loans.

My research has benefited from grants from the Rutgers University Research Council, and the Miami University Research Council. A grant from the discretionary fund of the provost of Miami University helped to pay for travel expenses to England. Also of assistance was a grant from the American Philosophical Society, which was primarily used to examine unpublished Mandaic manuscripts in the Bodleian Library in Oxford. The publishers and I are grateful for a subvention grant from the provost of Miami University, which has helped to make the publication of the manuscript possible.

I am especially appreciative of the suggestions which were made by Professor F. F. Bruce of Manchester University, Alan Millard of Liverpool University, and Andrew Helmbold of Tidewater College, who were kind enough to read the manuscript.

Last but not least I am thankful to my wife, Kimie, for her help as I wrote this manuscript.[1]

[1] The manuscript was completed at the end of 1971; a few additions were incorporated in June 1972. An important work which I obtained too late to incorporate into the manuscript is L. Schrotroff, *Der Glaubende und die feindliche Welt* (1970). The author subscribes in part to Schmithal's thesis and seeks to prove that the Gospel of John is a Gnostic document.
Papers on the Nag Hammadi texts have been contributed by P. Perkins, *Society of Biblical Literature, Seminar Papers* (1971), I, pp. 165–177, and by D. M. Parrott, *idem*, II, pp. 397–416; by G. W. MacRae, C. W. Hendrick, P. Perkins and F. Wisse in *Society of Biblical Literature, Proceedings* (1972), II, pp. 573–607.

ABBREVIATIONS

BiOr	*Bibliotheca Orientalis*
CBQ	*The Catholic Biblical Quarterly*
CG	*Cairensis Gnosticus, i.e.* the Nag Hammadi texts
ET	English Translation
GEMO	Yamauchi, *Gnostic Ethics and Mandaean Origins*
GL	Left *Ginza*
GR	Right *Ginza*
HTR	*Harvard Theological Review*
JAOS	*Journal of the American Oriental Society*
JBL	*Journal of Biblical Literature*
JTS	*The Journal of Theological Studies*
NovTest	*Novum Testamentum*
NTA I	Hennecke and Schneemelcher, *New Testament Apocrypha* I
NTA II	Hennecke and Schneemelcher, *New Testament Apocrypha* II
NTS	*New Testament Studies*
OG	Bianchi, *Le Origini dello Gnosticismo*
OLZ	*Orientalistische Literaturzeitung*
RB	*Revue Biblique*
RechSR	*Recherche de Science Religieuse*
RevSR	*Revue des Sciences Religieuses*
RGG³	*Die Religion in Geschichte und Gegenwart*, 3rd edition
RThPh	*Revue de Théologie et de Philosophie*
SSR	Bianchi, *Studi di Storia Religiosa della tarda antichità*
StTh	*Studia Theologica*
ThLZ	*Theologische Literaturzeitung*
ThR	*Theologische Rundschau*
Trajectories	Robinson and Koester, *Trajectories through Early Christianity*
VigChr	*Vigiliae Christianae*
ZNW	*Zeitschrift für die neutestamentliche Wissenschaft und die Kunde der älteren Kirche*
ZRGG	*Zeitschrift für Religions- und Geistesgeschichte*
ZThK	*Zeitschrift für Theologie und Kirche*

CHAPTER ONE

INTRODUCTION

One of the most important issues facing New Testament scholarship today is the issue of Gnosticism. The publication in 1969–1971 of English translations of Wilhelm Bousset's *Kyrios Christos*, of Walter Bauer's *Rechtgläubigkeit und Ketzerei im ältesten Christentum*, of Rudolf Bultmann's *Das Evangelium des Johannes*, and of Walter Schmithals's *Das Kirchliche Apostelamt* and *Die Gnosis in Korinth*, and the ongoing publication of Qumran, Mandaic, and Coptic texts make this a most appropriate time for considering the broad questions concerning the relationships between Gnosticism and the New Testament.

Was there a pre-Christian Gnosticism? How fully developed was Gnosticism in the first century? Did Gnosticism directly or indirectly influence nascent Christianity? How have new texts and new studies affected the situation today? What methodological assumptions undergird the work of scholars who accept a pre-Christian Gnosticism?

I. PROBLEMS IN DEFINING GNOSTICISM

One of the immediate problems facing us is the definition of 'Gnosticism' and of 'Gnostic'. On the one hand, we have those who would define Gnosticism very narrowly and, on the other hand, we have those who would define the phenomenon quite broadly. Thus one man's Gnosticism may be simply another man's Mysticism, Esoterism, Docetism, or Encratism. Those who will accept only a 'narrow' definition of Gnosticism do not find any conclusive evidence of pre-Christian Gnosticism, whereas those scholars who operate with a 'broad' definition of Gnosticism find it not only in the New Testament but in many other early documents as well.

To begin with, van Baaren, who thinks that it is not possible to give 'a short definition' of Gnosticism, lists sixteen characteristics of mature Gnosticism:

1. 'Gnosis considered as knowledge is not primarily intellectual, but is based upon revelation and is necessary for the attainment of full salvation.'

2. 'There is an essential connection between the concept of gnosis as it appears in gnosticism and the concept of time and space that is found there. . . .'

3. 'Gnosticism claims to have a revelation of its own which is essentially secret. . . .'

4. 'The Old Testament is usually rejected with more or less force. If not fully rejected it is interpreted allegorically. The same method of exegesis is as a rule chosen for the New Testament.'

5. 'God is conceived as transcendent. . . . God is conceived as beyond the comprehension of human thought and at the same time as the invariably good. . . . Nearly always evil is inherent in matter in the manner of a physical quality. The cosmological opposition between God and matter is correlated with the ethical opposition of good and evil. God's transcendence may be qualified by the appearance of various beings intermediate between God and the Cosmos, usually called aeons. These beings are as a rule conceived as divine emanations.'

6. 'The world is regarded with a completely pessimistic view. The cosmos was not created by God, but, at most, it is the work of a demiurge who made the world either against God's will, or in ignorance of it. . . .'

7. 'In the world and in mankind pneumatic and material elements are mixed. The pneumatic elements have their origin in God and are the cause of the desire to return to God. . . .'

8. 'Human beings are divided into three classes, according to whether they have gnosis or not. The pneumatics, who possess full gnosis, are by their nature admitted to full salvation. Those who have only pistis ("faith"), may at least attain a certain degree of salvation. Those who are fully taken up with the material world have no chance of salvation at all.'

9. 'Gnosticism makes a clear difference between pistis and gnosis.'

10. 'The essentially dualistic world-view leads as a rule to an extremely ascetic system of ethics, but in some cases we find an "Umwertung aller Werte" expressed in complete libertinism.'

11. 'Gnosticism is a religion of revolt.'

12. 'Gnosticism appeals to the desire to belong to an elite.'

13. 'In connection with the basic dualism there is a strong tendency to differentiate between the Heavenly Saviour and the human shape of Jesus of Nazareth. This has led to varying solutions of which docetism is the most prominent one.'

14. 'In most systems Christ is regarded as the great point of reversal in the cosmic process. As evil has come into existence by the fall of a former aeon, so Christ ushers in salvation because he proclaims the unknown God, the good God who had remained a stranger until that moment.'

15. 'In connection with the person of the saviour we often find the conception of the salvator salvatus or salvandus (the "redeemed redeemer").'

16. 'In connection with the basic dualism salvation is usually conceived as a complete severing of all ties between the world and the spiritual part of man. This is exemplified in the myth of the ascension of the soul.'[1]

Now how many of these elements are truly essential, since it is obvious that not all of these items will be found in any given system of Gnosticism? Goedicke suggests four basic propositions:

'*First*, the postulation of an Absolute outside of the immanent world which is the source of Gnosis.'

'*Second*, man as an intellectual immanent being partaking of the Gnosis.'

'*Third*, the partaking as the way to overcome the material world, and as such, Gnosis as salvation.'

'*Fourth*, Gnosis as understanding of the spiritually structured cosmos.'[2]

Most scholars would agree that quite essential to Gnosticism is a radical ontological dualism between the divine and the created, inasmuch as the creation of the world and matter has resulted from ignorance and error. According to Daniélou, 'It is this radical dualism, therefore, which is the properly Gnostic element, not the various images through which it is expressed.'[3] This dualism also implies an anticosmic enmity against the material world and its creator-demiurge.[4] Jonas draws the distinction between mysticism and Gnosticism on the basis of this dualism:

'A Gnosticism without a fallen god, without benighted creator and sinister creation, without alien soul, cosmic captivity and acosmic

---

[1] T. P. van Baaren, 'Towards a Definition of Gnosticism', in U. Bianchi (ed.), *Le Origini dello Gnosticismo* (hereafter abbreviated *OG*; 1967), pp. 178–180.

[2] H. Goedicke, 'The Gnostic Concept – Considerations about Its Origin', in U. Bianchi (ed.), *Studi di Storia Religiosa della tarda antichità* (hereafter abbreviated *SSR*; 1968), pp. 67–68.

[3] J. Daniélou, *The Theology of Jewish Christianity* (1964), p. 73.

[4] U. Bianchi in *OG*, p. 3. *Cf.* U. Bianchi, 'Le problème des origines du gnosticisme et l'histoire des religions', *Numen* 12 (1965), p. 176.

salvation, without the self-redeeming of the Deity – in short: a Gnosis without divine tragedy will not meet specifications.'[5]

Scholars who accept a 'high' or 'narrow' definition would distinguish a developed system of Gnosticism from merely 'gnostic' elements. Daniélou, however, when he speaks of a pre-Christian 'gnosticism', is speaking of esoteric Jewish knowledge which was later incorporated into mature Gnosticism.[6] His Jewish 'gnosis' refers to cosmological speculations based on an esoteric exegesis of Genesis.[7] Likewise when he speaks of 'gnosis' in Paul's writings he is referring to the knowledge of eschatological secrets rather than to the developed Gnosticism assumed by Bultmannian scholars. He writes:

> 'Gnosis in Jewish Christian writings belongs to the same complex of ideas. It is the knowledge of eschatological secrets, with an especial emphasis, already examined, on the exegesis of Cosmic mysteries in the opening of *Genesis*; but it is also more than this, it is the knowledge of the fulfilment of these eschatological events in Christ.'[8]

On the other hand, a scholar such as Pétrement would not regard 'gnosis' or 'knowledge' in such a Jewish sense as 'Gnosticism'. She writes, 'Gnosticism does not consist merely of the use of the word "gnosis"; it is a teaching that is concerned with the relations of God, man, and the world, and this teaching is nowhere found, it seems, before Christianity.'[9] She points out that in no alleged reference to Gnosticism in the New Testament is there any statement which places the Creator God, the God of Genesis, in the ranks of inferior powers.[10]

Those who recognize a development of Gnosticism roughly synchronous with Christianity but attested only in its incipient stages in the later books of the New Testament wish carefully to distinguish between what may be 'gnostic' in a broad sense and what can be proven to be 'Gnostic' in a developed sense. Wilson, who represents the more cautious British and Ameri-

---

[5] H. Jonas in J. P. Hyatt (ed.), *The Bible in Modern Scholarship* (1965), p. 293.

[6] J. Daniélou, *op. cit.*, p. 369.

[7] *Ibid.*, p. 69.

[8] *Ibid.*, p. 366.

[9] S. Pétrement, 'Le Colloque de Messine et le problème du gnosticisme', *Revue de Métaphysique et de Morale* 72 (1967), p. 371.

[10] *Ibid.*, p. 347.

can approach to the issue of Gnosticism and the New Testament, expounds this position:

'To sum up, while the gnostic movement in the broader sense is certainly wider than Christianity, and while we may reasonably speak of "gnostic" or "gnosticising" tendencies in the pre-Christian period, it is dangerous in the extreme to attempt too rigid a drawing of the lines, or to attempt to find anything like the developed Gnosticism of a later period at this early stage. In particular there are dangers in a loose and ill-considered use of the label "gnostic" in relation to concepts and terminology, for some "gnostic" concepts only become gnostic in the context of the Gnostic systems, and may be entirely neutral in other contexts.'[11]

German scholars in particular, however, have been accustomed to use the terms 'Gnostic' and 'Gnosticism' in a much broader and looser sense. Bultmann, for example, discerns an early type of Gnosticism in the prologue of John's Gospel, the *Odes of Solomon, etc.*, which is so reduced or denatured that there is no tragic split in the Godhead. He has been able readily to detect Gnostic elements in Philo, the Hermetica and the New Testament. The Dutch scholar, G. Quispel, by using a psychological approach is able to discern modern Gnostic types of religiosity in the Rosicrucians, the Freemasons, and in Carl Jung.[12] Gnostic elements in the broadest sense have been found even among Buddhists and the Aztecs![13] It is apparent, as C. H. Dodd notes, that:

'The terms "Gnostic" and "Gnosticism" are used by modern writers in a confusing variety of senses. If they refer, as by etymology they should refer, to the belief that salvation is by knowledge, then there is a sense in which orthodox Christian theologians like Clement of Alexandria and Origen, on the one hand, and Hellenistic Jews like Philo, and pagan writers like the Hermetists, on the other, should be called Gnostics; and in this wide sense the terms are used by many recent writers, especially in Germany.'[14]

[11] R. McL. Wilson in *OG*, p. 525. *Cf.* R. McL. Wilson, 'Gnostics – in Galatia?' in *Studia Evangelica* IV. 1 (1968), p. 362: 'Numerous terms employed in the New Testament are current in the later Gnostic systems, and for that reason may be legitimately characterised as "gnostic"; but are they in the New Testament used in the Gnostic sense? And when we trace in a New Testament document ideas of a "gnostic" character, are we to assume the existence of a fully-developed Gnostic *system*?'

[12] G. Quispel, *Gnosis als Weltreligion* (1951).

[13] *OG*, pp. 651ff., 676ff.

[14] C. H. Dodd, *The Interpretation of the Fourth Gospel* (1953; repr. 1968), p. 97.

Because of such divergent and confusing uses of these terms, the congress on 'The Origins of Gnosticism', held at Messina in 1966,[15] attempted to secure an agreement among scholars to use the terms 'pre-Gnostic' and 'proto-Gnostic'. 'Pre-Gnostic' would be used to designate elements in existence in pre-Christian times which were later incorporated into Gnosticism proper; 'pre-Gnostic' elements do not constitute 'Gnosticism' in the strict sense. On the other hand 'proto-Gnostic' would designate the early or incipient forms of Gnosticism which preceded the fully developed Gnosticism of the second century.[16]

Not every scholar would subscribe to such distinctions without a murmur. J. Munck, who wrote before the Messina conference, wished to reserve the term 'Gnosticism' for the fully developed phenomenon of the second century and to use the term 'syncretism' for earlier phenomena. He objected that a term such as 'proto-Gnostic' implies too many overtones of the developed system.[17]

On the other hand, K. Rudolph, who prefers a broader use of the term, argues that every form of 'gnosis' as a form of knowledge for an élite as 'soteriologisches Mittel' presupposes a system, and is therefore not merely 'gnosis' but 'Gnosticism'. Like Bultmann, Rudolph designates trends of heterodox Judaism as 'Gnostic', where others would call them 'pre-Gnostic'.[18] In a similar fashion Kümmel, in speaking of the Colossian heresy, describes it as a form of Jewish Gnosticism: 'The preference for the term "Prägnosis" . . . is only a terminological difference.'[19]

---

[15] Most of the papers have been printed in *OG*; a few have been printed in *SSR*.

[16] G. W. MacRae, 'Gnosis in Messina', *CBQ* 28 (1966), p. 332; H. J. W. Drijvers, 'The Origins of Gnosticism as a Religious and Historical Problem', *Nederlands Theologisch Tijdschrift* 22 (1968), pp. 327–328.

[17] J. Munck, 'The New Testament and Gnosticism', in W. Klassen and G. Snyder (eds), *Current Issues in New Testament Interpretation* (1962), pp. 236–237.

[18] K. Rudolph, 'Randerscheinungen des Judentums und das Problem der Entstehung des Gnostizismus', *Kairos* 9 (1967), pp. 106–107. *Cf.* Drijvers, *op. cit.*, p. 325.

[19] P. Feine, J. Behm, and W. G. Kümmel, *Introduction to the New Testament* (14th ed., 1966), p. 240.

Most recently, H. Koester seems to have despaired of establishing any clear-cut definitions:

> 'No less ambiguous and vague is the use of the term *gnostic* as a convenient tag for early Christian heresies. There may be different opinions about the origins of Gnosticism, whether it antedated Christianity . . . or whether it was an inner-Christian development in the second century A.D. Such questions are secondary. More important is the recognition of the indebtedness of Christianity as a whole to a theological development that bears many marks of what is customarily designated as "gnostic." The line between heretical and orthodox cannot be drawn by simply using the term *gnostic* for certain developments customarily designated in such fashion.'[20]

But surely this is going too far in the direction of blurring all lines of differences. Though it is true that there is a great danger of extrapolating backwards into the first century connotations of later 'orthodoxy', 'heresy', and 'Gnosticism', and granted that certain indeterminate borderline cases did exist, there is none the less an essential difference between the core of Christianity and the core of Gnosticism which cannot be melded together.

Our own position follows closely that of Wilson's in distinguishing between pre-Gnostic elements and a fully developed Gnosticism. Where the cosmological dualism is not explicit but may be inferred, we would accept the possibility of proto-Gnosticism with the qualification that one cannot build elaborate hypotheses from ambiguous evidence.

Our primary task in this study is descriptive and analytical rather than expositional. In the chapters that follow we will first survey the attempts which have been made to interpret the New Testament on the basis of an assumed pre-Christian Gnosticism, and then examine the evidences which have been adduced to support the thesis of pre-Christian Gnosticism. We shall then conclude with a chapter criticizing some of the methodological fallacies which have been involved in the use of such evidences.

Before proceeding further, however, we shall need to give a brief outline of the history of research which has led to the opposition between the traditional view of post-Christian Gnosticism and the critical view of pre-Christian Gnosticism.

[20] H. Koester in J. M. Robinson and H. Koester, *Trajectories through Early Christianity* (hereafter abbreviated *Trajectories*; 1971), pp. 115–116.

II. POST-CHRISTIAN GNOSTICISM

Until the twentieth century the traditional view of Gnosticism had been that presented in the writings of the Church Fathers who viewed Gnosticism as a Christian heresy. Among scholars who have affirmed this position are: A. Harnack, G. Kretschmar, H. Leisegang, F. C. Burkitt, J. Duchesne-Guillemin, T. W. Manson, E. Percy, H.-Ch. Puech, C. Schmidt, E. de Faye, R. P. Casey, J. Munck, and A. D. Nock.[21]

The most vigorous contemporary advocate of a post-Christian Gnosticism which developed only as a parasite upon Christianity is Simone Pétrement. She views even the non-Christian or pagan forms of Gnosticism as posterior to Christianity.

Mlle Pétrement argues that the Church Fathers were the contemporaries of Gnostics, and knew them at least as well as we do! Their view that Gnosticism was a post-Christian phenomenon would explain why we do not have a single pre-Christian Gnostic text. This would also be in accordance with the evidence that Gnosticism seems to have developed but gradually in the first century and seems not to have come into full bloom until the second century.

Non-Christian varieties of Gnosticism would have resulted from the progressive paganization of Christianity, as it was dispersed in various countries.[22] This would explain the difficulty of pin-pointing an area for the origin of Gnosticism. It was not *from* Egypt, Iran, Syria, or Mesopotamia that Gnosticism originated, but *to* these areas that Gnosticism was dispersed. The various local elements would be 'pre-Gnostic', but would not attest a 'proto-Gnostic' development in these areas, inasmuch as these elements would have been assimilated only after the rise of Christian Gnosticism.

There is nothing in the Pauline Epistles, whether in the

[21] In an article which was published posthumously, A. D. Nock, 'Gnosticism', *HTR* 57 (1964), p. 276, Nock commented on some of the initial publications of the Nag Hammadi Coptic texts as follows: 'The relation of these and other new texts to the New Testament seems to me to vindicate completely the traditional view of Gnosticism as Christian heresy with roots in speculative thought.' Nock's judgment is in turn cited by Raymond E. Brown, *The Gospel according to John I–XII* (1966), p. LV, as reaffirming the patristic picture of Gnosticism.

[22] S. Pétrement, 'Le Colloque de Messine', p. 362.

Letters to the Corinthians or to the Colossians, which can be said indubitably to attest a developed Gnosticism.[23] Contrary to Reitzenstein and Bultmann, Christianity is quite independent of Gnosticism. It is true that Christianity and Gnosticism appeared at about the same time, but it is the latter which is derived from the former.[24]

III. PRE-CHRISTIAN GNOSTICISM

As opposed to the long-accepted tradition of a post-Christian Gnosticism, W. Anz in 1897 first proposed a pre-Christian origin of Gnosticism. This was a view which was widely expounded by members of the Religionsgeschichtliche Schule or 'History of Religions' School. The two leading spokesmen were Wilhelm Bousset (1865–1920), a New Testament scholar who examined the early church as a Hellenistic–Jewish phenomenon, and Richard Reitzenstein (1861–1931), a philologist who studied the role of mysticism in Hellenism and sought to trace the origins of Gnosticism in Iranian and Mandaean traditions.

In his work, *Hauptprobleme der Gnosis* (1907), Bousset explained the Gnostic teachings reported by the Church Fathers as the result of a transformation of older oriental myths by Hellenistic philosophy. He sought to prove the pagan character of the Gnostic Redeemer by referring to Mandaean materials. He held it as self-evident that Gnosticism was prior to Christianity. 'Gnosticism is first of all a pre-Christian movement which has its roots in itself. It is therefore to be understood in the first place in its own terms and not as an offshoot or a by-product of the Christian religion.'[25] As evidence for the pre-Christian nature of Gnosticism Bousset cited Philo, the Hermetic literature and the Chaldean Oracles.[26] But above all he emphasized the combination of Babylonian and Persian traditions.[27]

---

[23] *Ibid.*, p. 367.
[24] S. Pétrement, 'La notion de gnosticisme', *Revue de Métaphysique et de Morale* 65 (1960), pp. 405ff.
[25] W. Bousset, *Kyrios Christos* (1st ed. 1913; 2nd ed. 1921 after Bousset's death; English translation, 1970), p. 245.
[26] *Ibid.*, p. 17.
[27] W. Bousset, 'Gnosticism', *Encyclopedia Britannica* XII (1910), p. 155.

Of far-reaching significance and influence have been the numerous works of Richard Reitzenstein: (1) *Poimandres: Studien zur griechisch-ägyptischen und frühchristlichen Literatur* (1904); (2) *Die hellenistischen Mysterienreligionen* (1910; 3rd ed. 1927); (3) *Das iranische Erlösungsmysterium* (1921); (4) *Die Vorgeschichte der christlichen Taufe* (1929); and (5) with H. H. Schaeder, *Studien zum antiken Synkretismus* (1926). Though these works have not been translated into English, all except *Das iranische Erlösungsmysterium* have recently (1965–1967) been reprinted by the Wissenschaftliche Buchgesellschaft of Darmstadt. Reitzenstein's interests were wide indeed. In the words of an unfriendly critic:

'The evolution of Reitzenstein's thought parallels in many respects that of the Viennese historian of art, Strzygowski. Both flitted over the Oriental landscape, pausing now in one country, now in another contemplating the cultural scene of each and attempting to detect its contribution to Hellenistic civilization. Reitzenstein's field of investigation was Egypt: Philo, the *Corpus Hermeticum*, the magical papyri, and Egyptian Gnosticism, but he soon turned his attention thence to Syria, Babylonia and Persia.'[28]

In his first major work, *Poimandres* (1904), Reitzenstein tried to prove the pre-Christian origin of the Gnostic myth of the Primal Man by using: (1) the Naassene sermon in Hippolytus, *Refutatio* V (third century AD); (2) book omega of the alchemist Zosimos (fourth century AD); (3) book 8 of the Neoplatonist Jamblichus (fourth century AD); and (4) especially the Hermetic tract of Poimandres. He deleted the Christian references in the Naassene sermon and expounded it as a non-Christian and pre-Christian source.

The Hermetica are Greek texts from Egypt issued under the name of Hermes Trismegistus, who represented the Egyptian god of wisdom, Thoth. They are extant in Greek manuscripts of the fourteenth century. Reitzenstein held, however, that they contained teachings which were the culmination of a long development in pre-Christian Egypt. He maintained that the doctrine of the *Anthrōpos* or Primal Man found in the Hermetic tract *Poimandres* was pre-Christian, and that this tract was the oldest extant Gnostic text. In the *Poimandres* the

[28] R. P. Casey, 'Gnosis, Gnosticism and the New Testament', in W. D. Davies and D. Daube (eds), *The Background of the New Testament and Its Eschatology* (1956), p. 53.

Primal Man sinks into nature from heaven but is given a saving revelation and re-ascends to his celestial sphere. Reitzenstein claimed that this teaching was borrowed from the Persian Avestan teaching of the Gayomart. He suggested that the teaching of the Son of Man in the Gospels was a reflection of this myth.[29] His exposition of this teaching was the first of what became known as the Gnostic Redeemer myth.

Reitzenstein sought to show that a very early salvation mystery existed among the Zoroastrians of Iran. Just before World War I he was in contact with Carl Andreas, who was working on recently discovered documents from Chinese Turkestan. For his book, *Das iranische Erlösungsmysterium* (1921), he used notes on these Parthian texts sent to him in 1918 by F. W. Müller.[30] At first Reitzenstein did not realize that these documents were Manichaean. When this was discovered, he and his followers argued that Mani (third century AD) must have transmitted earlier pre-Christian Iranian materials.

In the early twentieth century Mark Lidzbarski published a number of important texts of the Mandaeans, a Gnostic community which has survived in southern Iraq and southwestern Iran. In 1905 he published the text of *Das Johannesbuch der Mandäer*, and in 1915 its translation and a commentary.[31] This narrative describes John the Baptist as a Mandaean and Jesus as a false Messiah. In 1920 Lidzbarski published some Mandaean liturgies.[32] Then in 1925 he published the *Ginza*,[33] the major Mandaean work on cosmology. Lidzbarski believed in a western, pre-Christian origin of the Mandaeans. The publication of these texts had a tremendous impact, especially on and through Reitzenstein.

Even before Lidzbarski's translation of the *Ginza*, Reit-

[29] R. Reitzenstein, *Poimandres: Studien zur griechisch-ägyptischen und frühchristlichen Literatur* (1904; repr. 1966), p. 81.

[30] Mary Boyce, *The Manichaean Hymn-Cycles in Parthian* (1954), p. 1.

[31] M. Lidzbarski, *Das Johannesbuch der Mandäer* (I, 1905; II, 1915; both reprinted in 1966). An English translation of parts of Lidzbarski's German translation was made by G. Mead, *The Gnostic John the Baptizer* (1924).

[32] M. Lidzbarski, *Mandäische Liturgien* (1920; repr. 1962). This has been superseded by the more comprehensive translation of E. S. Drower, *The Canonical Prayerbook of the Mandaeans* (1959).

[33] M. Lidzbarski, *Ginza: Das grosse Buch der Mandäer* (1925).

zenstein was able to make use of an earlier edition of the text, published by H. Petermann in 1867, for his provocative essay, *Das mandäische Buch des Herrn der Grösse und die Evangelienüberlieferung* (1919). In portions of the Right *Ginza* Reitzenstein thought that he could recover a 'little apocalypse' – 'the Book of the Lord of Greatness' – which he believed gave him information about the early pre-Christian proto-Mandaeans. He held that Enosh-Uthra, the Mandaean messenger from heaven, who appears as a judge to destroy Jerusalem, was the prototype of the New Testament doctrine of the Son of Man.[34] Reitzenstein further suggested that his reconstructed 'little apocalypse' with parallels with Matthew 23:34–39 was no more and no less than the basis for the Gospel source 'Q'.[35] He concluded that John the Baptist and his followers had originated the earliest Mandaean doctrines and rituals. His collaborator, H. H. Schaeder, proposed that the prologue of John's Gospel was a Mandaic hymn taken over from Baptist circles.[36]

It was Rudolf Bultmann who distilled the classic model of the Gnostic Redeemer myth from the works of Bousset, Lidzbarski, and Reitzenstein. As far as Bultmann was concerned, Reitzenstein had proved the antiquity of the Redeemer myth. According to Meeks, 'Bultmann, therefore, never appears to doubt that the "redeemer myth" in all its essential parts existed long before the Hellenistic Age.'[37] On the assumption that the existence of such a Redeemer myth had been established, Bultmann in an important article published in 1925 sought to prove that this myth underlies the Gospel of John by adducing parallels from Mandaean and Manichaean texts, the *Odes of Solomon,* and the apocryphal *Acts of the Apostles.*[38] The fact that these proof texts are them-

---

[34] Reitzenstein's formulation impressed O. Cullmann, who in *Le problème littéraire et historique du roman pseudo-Clémentin* (1930), p. 202, expressed regret that G. Dupont in his work, *Le fils de l'homme* (1924), had not used Reitzenstein's materials.

[35] R. Reitzenstein, 'Iranische Erlösungsglaube', *ZNW* 20 (1921), p. 3: 'Dieser Schluss aber wird durch einen Vergleich der Evangelienquelle Q mit der alten mandäischen Apokalypse weiter gesichert. . . .'

[36] R. Reitzenstein and H. H. Schaeder, *Studien zum antiken Synkretismus aus Iran und Griechenland* (1926; repr. 1965), pp. 306–341.

[37] W. Meeks, *The Prophet-King* (1967), p. 8.

[38] R. Bultmann, 'Die Bedeutung der neuerschlossenen mandäischen

selves much later than John, Bultmann regarded as irrelevant since the myth to which they attest was, in his conviction, indubitably older.[39] The parallels between the Mandaean texts and John showed Bultmann that the simpler, fragmentary pattern of John must be derivative.[40] Furthermore, the prominence accorded John the Baptist in the Mandaean sources, notably in *Das Johannesbuch*, confirmed for Bultmann his hypothesis of a Baptist origin for the Johannine prologue. The so-called *Offenbarungsreden* or 'revelation discourses' in John, which have stylistic similarities to the prologue, were also believed to have been originally documents of the followers of John the Baptist who had exalted John and originally given to John the role of a Redeemer sent from the world of light. Therefore a considerable part of the Gospel of John was not originally Christian in origin but resulted from the transformation of a Baptist tradition.[41] Such are the guiding assumptions which control Bultmann's exposition of John in his famous commentary.[42] Furthermore Bultmann argued that the conflation of the mystery religions' myth of a dying and rising deity, the Gnostic myth of a Redeemer who comes to earth to save man, and the Jewish apocalyptic myth of a heavenly Son of Man was embodied in Paul's Christology, and was to prove determinative for Christianity.

A succession of able and influential students taught by Bultmann have well-nigh dominated German New Testament

---

und manichäischen Quellen für das Verständnis des Johannesevangeliums', *ZNW* 24 (1925), pp. 100–146; reprinted in E. Dinkler (ed.), *Exegetica: Aufsätze zur Erforschung des Neuen Testaments* (1967), pp. 55–104.

[39] Even in later years Bultmann has remained convinced of the pre-Christian nature of Gnosticism. R. Bultmann, *Primitive Christianity in Its Contemporary Setting* (1956), p. 162: 'Further research has, however, made it abundantly clear that it (Gnosticism) was really a religious movement of pre-Christian origin, invading the West from the Orient as a competitor of Christianity. . . . Gnostic sects . . . arose partly in the form of "baptist" movements in the region of the Jordan.'

[40] R. Bultmann, 'Johanneische Schriften und Gnosis', *OLZ* 43 (1940), cols 150–175; reprinted in Dinkler, *Exegetica*, pp. 230–254.

[41] W. Eltester, 'Der Logos und sein Prophet: Fragen zur heutigen Erklärung des Johanneischen Prologs', in *Apophoreta: Festschrift für Ernst Haenchen* (1964), pp. 109–134.

[42] R. Bultmann, *Das Evangelium Johannes* (1941; repr. 1968); ET *The Gospel of John: A Commentary* (1971).

scholarship. Hans Jonas, under the influence of Bultmann and Heidegger, provided a synthesis of Gnostic themes in 1934.[43] His study was based on a phenomenological approach and largely utilized Mandaean texts.

In 1939 E. Schweizer, working under Bultmann, published a work in which he attempted to prove the proto-Mandaean origin of the Good Shepherd discourse in John.[44] In 1956 Bultmann published posthumously the work of a student, H. Becker, who had died in the War in 1941.[45] Becker, using Mandaean parallels, attempted to show that the writer of the Fourth Gospel had expanded and transformed a pre-Christian Gnostic source.

In the 1950s and 1960s Pauline studies have been largely under the influence of students and followers of Bultmann who assume the pre-Christian existence of Gnosticism, e.g. G. Bornkamm, E. Haenchen, H. Schlier, U. Wilckens, D. Georgi, and W. Schmithals. There has, of course, been a great deal of varying degrees of commitment to the basic proposition. Schmithals, as we shall see in more detail, has been the most thoroughgoing and consistent in applying Gnosticism as the key to the Pauline Letters. Other Bultmannian students, such as H. Koester and the American, James Robinson, are much more careful in not going beyond the available textual evidence. And some of Bultmann's students have in fact defected. E. Käsemann, impressed by C. Colpe's criticism of the History of Religions School, has recently abandoned some of his earlier positions. K. G. Kuhn was convinced that the Dead Sea Scrolls do not support his teacher's thesis. Schweizer has come to doubt the existence of a pre-Christian Redeemer myth.

In recent years the renewed publication of Mandaic texts by Lady E. S. Drower, and studies based on these texts by R. Macuch and K. Rudolph, have been invoked as support for the pre-Christian and Palestinian origin of Gnosticism.[46]

---

[43] H. Jonas, *Gnosis und spätantiker Geist* I: *Die mythologische Gnosis* (1934).

[44] E. Schweizer, *Ego Eimi: Die religionsgeschichtliche Herkunft und theologische Bedeutung der joh. Bildreden* (1939; repr. 1964).

[45] H. Becker, *Die Reden des Johannesevangeliums und der Stil der gnostischen Offenbarungsreden* (1956).

[46] *Cf.* E. M. Yamauchi, 'The Present Status of Mandaean Studies', *Journal of Near Eastern Studies* 25 (1966), pp. 88–96.

Actually for those who maintain such a position, apart from the *Haran Gawaita* published by Lady Drower in 1953,[47] the most important Mandaean documents are still the *Ginza* and the liturgies originally published by Lidzbarski. (On the other hand, it has been increasingly recognized that *Das Johannesbuch*, which is the most important Mandaean document on John the Baptist, is a collection of late traditions.) Especially influential and increasingly cited are the two volumes of synthetic studies published by K. Rudolph in 1960–1961.[48]

The most significant developments contributing to the discussion of pre-Christian Gnosticism have been the spectacular discoveries at Qumran in 1946 of the Dead Sea Scrolls, and at Nag Hammadi in Upper Egypt in 1945 of Coptic Gnostic codices.[49] Among the latter, the treatises of Eugnostos, the *Apocalypse of Adam*, and the *Paraphrase of Shem* offer, according to some scholars, evidence of a non-Christian and possibly pre-Christian Gnosticism.[50] James M. Robinson of Claremont, the general editor of the Institute for Antiquity and Christianity's project to publish all of the Nag Hammadi treatises, writes:

'The persistent trend in the scholarship of the twentieth century has been carried one step further by the Coptic gnostic codices from near Nag Hammadi, which reflect in some of their tractates, such as the *Apocalypse of Adam* and the *Paraphrase of Shem*, what seems to be non-Christian Gnosticism, a gnostic or semignostic Judaism, in some cases localized in the Jordan region and interacting in some way with baptismal movements.'[51]

---

[47] E. S. Drower, *The Haran Gawaita and the Baptism of Hibil-Ziwa* (1953).

[48] K. Rudolph, *Die Mandäer I: Das Mandäerproblem* (1960); II: *Der Kult* (1961).

[49] For information on the latter, less well-known discovery, see J. Doresse, *The Secret Books of the Egyptian Gnostics* (1960); and A. Helmbold, *The Nag Hammadi Gnostic Texts and the Bible* (1967).

[50] K. Rudolph, 'Stand und Aufgaben in der Erforschung des Gnostizismus', *Sonderheft der wiss. Zeitschrift der Friedrich-Schiller-Universität Jena* (1963), p. 98: 'I am also of the opinion that the new texts will make it easier for us to prove the pre-Christian origin of the Gnostic redeemer myth.'

[51] *Trajectories*, p. 264. *Cf.* James M. Robinson, 'The Coptic Gnostic Library Today', *NTS* 14 (1968), pp. 356–401; 'The Institute for Antiquity and Christianity', *NTS* 16 (1970), pp. 185ff.

IV. THE PRESENT SITUATION

We are at present in a situation where we find scholars at three stages of conclusions regarding the possibility of pre-Christian Gnosticism: (1) There are those who are satisfied that the researches of Reitzenstein, Bultmann, *etc.* have established the thesis of a pre-Christian Gnosticism. The Catholic church historians Lebreton and Zeiller, for example, assume that Gnosticism was anterior to Christianity.[52] Kümmel writes, 'Today we know that there were Gnostic, syncretistic groups and propaganda already at the time of Paul, and that Gnosticism was a pre-Christian movement. . . .'[53] (2) On the other hand, there are scholars who have never accepted the arguments of Reitzenstein and Bultmann, and others who are impressed with the criticisms of the History of Religions School, especially as expressed by Colpe. They consider that the thesis of a pre-Christian Gnosticism is dubious or unsettled at best. In a recent work on the Gospel of John, D. M. Smith expressed himself as follows:

> 'In dealing with the hypothetical Offenbarungsreden I have put the problem of pre-Christian Gnosticism to one side. That problem is still being vigorously investigated and debated, and I am in no position to decide it here. Few scholars any longer doubt that most of the so-called Gnostic motives are pre-Christian, but there is real disagreement about the existence of a pre-Christian Gnostic redeemer or revealer myth.'[54]

(3) Finally there are those who like Rudolph and Robinson are seeking additional support for pre-Christian Gnosticism in the new Mandaic and Coptic texts.

In the following chapters we shall first of all examine the attempts at interpreting the New Testament on the basis of pre-Christian Gnosticism, and then examine the evidences adduced for this basis. In the sections on the various evidences we shall set forth first the positive attempts to use the texts as evidences of pre-Christian Gnosticism, and then relate the negative criticisms of such attempts by other scholars.

[52] J. Lebreton and J. Zeiller, *Heresy and Orthodoxy* (book III of *A History of the Early Church*; published in French in 1934–1935; ET 1942, 1947; paperback, 1962), p. 23.
[53] Feine–Behm–Kümmel, p. 241.
[54] D. M. Smith, *The Composition and Order of the Fourth Gospel: Bultmann's Literary Theory* (1965), p. 83.

CHAPTER TWO

NEW TESTAMENT EXEGESIS ON THE BASIS OF PRE-CHRISTIAN GNOSTICISM

I. THE GNOSTIC REDEEMER MYTH

As we have noted in the preceding chapter, Bultmann in his important article of 1925[1] drew on the researches of the History of Religions scholars[2] in gathering twenty-eight characteristics to form an outline of the Gnostic Redeemer myth. It was Bultmann's conviction that the origin of the Mandaeans lay ultimately with a group of the adherents of John the Baptist. Their texts have therefore preserved one of the purest extant forms of the early oriental Gnostic Redeemer myth.

The outlines of the Gnostic Redeemer myth as constructed by Bultmann have the following features:

1. In the cosmic drama a heavenly 'Urmensch' or Primal Man of Light falls and is torn to pieces by demonic powers. These particles are encapsuled as the sparks of light in the 'pneumatics' of mankind.

2. The demons try to stupefy the 'pneumatics' by sleep and forgetfulness so they will forget their divine origin.

3. The transcendent Deity sends another Being of Light, the 'Redeemer', who descends the demonic spheres, assuming the deceptive garments of a bodily exterior to escape the notice of the demons.

4. The Redeemer is sent to awaken the 'pneumatics' to the truth of their heavenly origins and gives them the necessary 'gnosis' or 'knowledge' to serve as passwords for their heavenly re-ascent.

---

[1] R. Bultmann, 'Die Bedeutung der neuerschlossenen . . . Quellen'.
[2] G. Widengren, 'Les origines du gnosticisme et l'histoire des religions', *OG*, pp. 28–60.

5. The Redeemer himself re-ascends, defeating the demonic powers, and thereby makes a way for the spirits that will follow him.

6. Cosmic redemption is achieved when the souls of men are collected and gathered upward. In this process the Redeemer is himself redeemed, *i.e.* the Primal Man who fell in the beginning is reconstituted.[3]

On the assumption that Gnosticism had developed before the rise of Christianity it is possible for Bultmann and other interpreters to view the New Testament itself as a stage in Gnosticism. That is, the New Testament in both its earliest as well as its latest writings manifests the absorption, transformation, and demythologization of the Gnostic Redeemer myth.

Those who approach the New Testament from a pre-Christian view of Gnosticism generally think in terms of a two-stage development. The first is a stage in which Gnostic ideas were utilized; the second is a stage in which Gnosticism was clearly opposed. These two stages are not chronologically distinguished and there is some overlap. In general, however, the later works of the New Testament betray a clear polemic against Gnosticism.

II. THE GOSPEL OF JOHN

According to Bultmann the writer of the Fourth Gospel was a convert from a Gnostic baptist sect. The Mandaeans represent a later stage of the Gnosticism prevalent among the disciples of John the Baptist, and hence preserve echoes of such a pre-Christian Gnosticism to which the writer once belonged. W. Schmithals, in a new introduction to the English translation of Bultmann's commentary on John, writes:

'On the one hand John manifests close contacts with the Gnostic conception of the world. The source of the discourses, which John takes over or to which he adheres, is Gnostic in outlook. It has its closest parallels in the Mandaean writings, the oldest strata of whose traditions go back to the time of primitive Christianity and to the region of

[3] R. Bultmann, *Theology of the New Testament* I (1952), pp. 166–183; *cf.* T. C. Oden, 'From Event to Language: The Church's Use of Gnostic Mythology', *Religion in Life* 36 (1967), pp. 92–99.

Syrian Palestine. In these Mandaean revelatory addresses are also to
be found parabolic sayings that characterise the Revealer as the good
Shepherd, the real Vine, etc.'[4]

The Fourth Evangelist has demythologized and Christianized his Gnostic source. His former Gnosticism was an early
oriental type of Gnosticism with a dualism of darkness and
light, but without any complicated theories of emanation.
The Evangelist both adopted and adapted the Gnostic
Redeemer myth, while at the same time refuting it by
reference to the earthly Jesus of Nazareth. In particular, the
prologue shows that Christ was a cosmic figure, who was
sent in the disguise of a man (Jn. 1:14). As in the Gnostic
Redeemer myth Christ comes as a 'messenger' (Jn. 10:36f.),
and reveals himself to his own in the great Gnostic Revealer
pronouncements: 'I am the light of the world' (Jn. 8:12), *etc.*
In the Gospel of John there is an 'eschatological shift' from the
Jewish futuristic expectations to the present realization of
the resurrection experience (Jn. 5:24–25; 12:31).[5]

In a dissertation carried out under Bultmann, E. Schweizer
argued for a proto-Mandaean origin of the Johannine Good
Shepherd discourse (Jn. 10:1–18), using a passage from the
Right *Ginza* (*GR* V.2). Later though he was to affirm his
belief that the Mandaeans had roots in pre-Christian Palestine, he was to express doubts that an exact *Vorlage* for the
Johannine formulation could be reconstructed. In his preface
to the 1964 reprinting of his 1939 work, Schweizer expressed
his opinion that the background against which the Evangelist
wrote was not necessarily Gnosticism proper but a teaching
which was probably already on the way to Gnosticism.[6] It is
interesting to note that in 1929 H. Odeberg had argued that
the same *Ginza* passage was dependent upon the Fourth
Gospel:

'In GR V 3 (*GR* 187.1–188.22 . . .) there is a relation of the spirits
of the Christian believers, kept in the Watchhouse of Christ. This
passage is important, since it shows familiarity with and dependence
upon thoughts and expressions occurring in the Fourth Gospel. Thus
there are allusions to Christ as the shepherd and his followers as the

[4] W. Schmithals in R. Bultmann, *The Gospel of John*, p. 8.
[5] R. Bultmann, *Theology of the New Testament* I, pp. 173–180; II (1955),
pp. 15–32.
[6] E. Schweizer, *Ego Eimi* (1964 repr.), p. viii.

herd (Jn 10.11, 14), as the giver (or, at least, promiser) of "water" to
the thirsty (Jn 4.10, 14, 7.31, 38), as the one, who said: "all has been
given into my hands" (Jn 3.35, 6.37 . . .). . . . The context in which
these allusions occur shows, further, that the Fourth Gospel with which
the Mandaeans were confronted belonged to the holy scriptures of the
Christian circles to which they were in opposition.'[7]

As noted before, Bultmann in 1956 published posthumously
the work of his pupil, H. Becker.[8] Becker sought to reconstruct
a typical archetype of the Gnostic Revealer discourse, mainly
from Mandaean texts as well as the *Odes of Solomon*, the
Hermetica, and the pseudo-Clementines. According to Becker
there were three basic elements in such a discourse: (1) the
self-predication of the Revealer; (2) the invitation or call to
decision; and (3) a promise for those who accept the invitation
often coupled with a warning against those who refuse. The
typical discourse would have had the following form:

> 'I am the Revealer, who has come from Heaven.
> I am of God, you are of the World.
> God is Light, the world is darkness.
> I proclaim to you salvation from the world.
> Leave the darkness, draw near to the light.
> Abandon the works of the world, and do the works of God.
> I am the helper sent from God.
> Whoever hears me, will see the light.
> Whoever hears me not, will sink in the darkness.'[9]

Becker concluded that he has shown that the author of the
Gospel of John has used such a non-Christian Gnostic source,
and thus has confirmed as a whole Bultmann's earlier
analysis.[10]

The interpretation of John's Gospel by Bultmann and his
students on the basis of Mandaean parallels has been accepted
in some circles,[11] but it has also provoked considerable oppo-

---

[7] H. Odeberg, *The Fourth Gospel* (1929; repr. 1968), p. 163. Scholars
such as Rudolph explain parallels in the Mandaean texts to the New
Testament as prototypes rather than allusions. Eric Segelberg, a Mandaean
scholar, in 'Old and New Testament Figures in Mandaean Version', in
Sven S. Hartman (ed.), *Syncretism* (1969), p. 239, in opposition to Rudolph
asks: 'But what are we to do if we find New Testament quotations?'

[8] H. Becker, *Die Reden des Johannesevangeliums*.

[9] *Ibid.*, p. 57.

[10] *Ibid.*, pp. 123–124.

[11] *Cf.* Feine–Behm–Kümmel, p. 160; R. Stahl, *Les Mandéens et les origines
chrétiennes* (1930), p. 11.

sition. As early as 1939 E. Percy had argued that John's Gospel was not influenced by Gnosticism either in language or in thought.[12] C. H. Dodd devoted an entire section of his work, *The Interpretation of the Fourth Gospel* (1953), to examine and refute the Mandaean parallels offered by Reitzenstein and Bultmann. In a *Festschrift* offered to Dodd, W. F. Albright emphasizes the confirmation of the historical nature of the Gospel of John, especially in the light of the Dead Sea Scrolls, in opposition to Bultmann's interpretation.[13] Elsewhere Albright has written: 'All the concrete arguments for a late date for the Johannine literature have now been dissipated, and Bultmann's attempts to discern an earlier and later form of the Gospel have proved to be entirely misleading, as both of his supposed redactions have similar Jewish background.'[14] That is, Bultmann had posited a first redaction by the Evangelist, an ex-Gnostic, of three sources: (1) the Sign Source, (2) Revelatory Discourse Source, and (3) the Passion and Resurrection story. Later an ecclesiastical redactor tried to harmonize the Gospel of John with the Synoptics.

Casey in the Dodd *Festschrift* remarked, 'No one, I fancy, would nowadays take seriously the notion that the Fourth Gospel arose as a Christian adaptation of a Mandean account of John the Baptist.'[15] The most recent commentary on John, the massive work in the Anchor Bible series by Raymond E. Brown, has this to say about Bultmann's theory:

> 'In summation, one cannot claim that the dependence of John on a postulated early Oriental Gnosticism has been disproved, but the hypothesis remains very tenuous and in many ways unnecessary. We hope to show below that OT speculation about personified Wisdom and the vocabulary and thought patterns of sectarian Judaism, like the Qumran community, go a long way toward filling in the background of Johannine theological vocabulary and expression. Since these proposed sources of influence are known to have existed, and the existence of Bultmann's proto-Mandean Gnostic source remains dubious, we have every reason to give them preference.'[16]

[12] E. Percy, *Untersuchungen über den Ursprung der johanneischen Theologie* (1939).

[13] W. F. Albright, 'Recent Discoveries in Palestine and the Gospel of St John', in W. D. Davies and D. Daube (eds), *The Background of the New Testament and Its Eschatology*, pp. 153–171.

[14] W. F. Albright, *New Horizons in Biblical Research* (1966), p. 46.

[15] R. P. Casey, 'Gnosis, Gnosticism and the New Testament', p. 54.

[16] R. E. Brown, *The Gospel according to John I–XII*, p. LVI.

Colpe has argued that the Johannine Christ is not to be compared with the concept of the Gnostic Primal Man-Redeemer.[17]

One need not subscribe to Bultmann's theory to recognize that the author of the Gospel of John used concepts which occur in Gnostic literature and that the Gospel was popular among Gnostics. Indeed, the first known commentary on John was written by the Gnostic Heracleon. In opposition, however, to Käsemann's view that the Fourth Gospel is clearly heretical in its portrait of Jesus as 'God walking on the face of the earth', and that John was a document which originated in a 'conventicle with gnosticizing tendencies',[18] S. Smalley has recently argued that the Gospel of John illustrates diversity and development rather than any conscious heterodoxy or orthodoxy. It is a Gospel which could be and was used by both the orthodox and the heterodox.[19] In a similar vein, Corwin writes: 'The author of the Fourth Gospel could not have foreseen that his emphasis on the otherworldly source of the life of Christ could be used to undermine its reality in the world of men, but the subsequent popularity of the gospel among gnostics bears witness to its ambiguity.'[20]

There is none the less still a great gulf between both the concepts and the language used by John and the Gnostic texts as recovered in the Nag Hammadi library.[21] The Nag Hammadi texts do provide us with new materials for the investigation of the Fourth Gospel, which should enable us to understand better the 'gnosticizing' trend of this book.[22]

---

[17] C. Colpe, 'New Testament and Gnostic Christology', in J. Neusner (ed.), *Studies in the History of Religions* XIV (1968), pp. 234–236.

[18] E. Käsemann, *The Testament of Jesus* (1968), pp. 6ff., 73.

[19] S. S. Smalley, 'Diversity and Development in John', *NTS* 17 (1971), pp. 276–292.

[20] V. Corwin, *St. Ignatius and Christianity in Antioch* (1960), p. 271.

[21] *Cf.* S. Laeuchli, *The Language of Faith: An Introduction to the Semantic Dilemma of the Early Church* (1962), pp. 75ff.; C. K. Barrett, 'The Theological Vocabulary of the Fourth Gospel and of the Gospel of Truth', in W. Klassen and G. Snyder (eds), *Current Issues in New Testament Interpretation*, pp. 210–223, 297–298.

[22] J. M. Robinson, 'The Johannine Trajectory', in *Trajectories*, pp. 232–268. *Cf.* G. W. MacRae, 'The Fourth Gospel in *Religionsgeschichte*', *CBQ* 32 (1970), pp. 13–24; 'The *Ego*-Proclamation in Gnostic Sources', in E. Bammel (ed.), *The Trial of Jesus* (1970), pp. 122–134.

III. THE SYNOPTIC GOSPELS AND ACTS

Reitzenstein had suggested that his 'apocalypse' extracted from the Mandaean *Ginza* lay behind the Gospel source Q. He also held that the Mandaean Enosh or Primal Man was the prototype of the designation of Jesus as *bar nasha*, 'the Son of Man'. Bultmann also suggested that the 'Son of Man' in the Synoptic traditions may betray fragmentary traces of the Redeemer myth.[23] In other words, the Gnostic doctrine of the Urmensch-Redeemer is supposed to be the root of the Jewish apocalyptic Son of Man expectations.[24]

Be that as it may, Bultmann and Haenchen recognize Matthew 11:27 and its parallel Luke 10:22 as the only Synoptic passages which 'sound Gnostic'.[25] Davies, however, has sought to trace this passage back to a Jewish, specifically Qumranian, background.[26]

James Robinson has recently isolated a *Gattung* (German for a specific literary genre), the *logoi sophōn*, which he believes to be one of the oldest and most primitive of the Gospel traditions.[27] According to Koester the 'gnosticizing proclivity' of the *logoi sophōn* became acceptable to the orthodox church after a radical alteration. This 'was achieved by Matthew and Luke through imposing the Marcan narrative-kerygma frame upon the sayings tradition represented by Q'.[28] Contrary to other scholars who hold that the Nag Hammadi *Gospel of Thomas* represents only a later Gnostic or Encratite transformation of canonical traditions, Koester holds that the

[23] R. Bultmann, 'Die Bedeutung der neuerschlossenen . . . Quellen', pp. 143–144.
[24] *Cf.* F. H. Borsch, *The Christian and Gnostic Son of Man* (1970), pp. 116ff.
[25] R. Bultmann, *Gnosis* (ET of the article from Kittel's *Theologisches Wörterbuch zum Neuen Testament*, V; 1952), p. 50; E. Haenchen, 'Gnosis und Neue Testament', in *RGG*[3], col. 1653.
[26] W. D. Davies, 'Knowledge in the Dead Sea Scrolls and Matthew 11:25–30', *HTR* 46 (1953), pp. 113–139.
[27] J. M. Robinson, 'LOGOI SOPHON: On the Gattung of Q', in *Trajectories*, pp. 71–113; this appeared originally as 'LOGOI SOPHON: Zur Gattung der Spruchquelle Q', in E. Dinkler (ed.), *Zeit und Geschichte: Dankesgabe an Rudolf Bultmann zum 80. Geburtstag* (1964), pp. 77–96.
[28] H. Koester in *Trajectories*, pp. 134–135. *Cf.* J. M. Robinson, 'Basic Shifts in German Theology', *Interpretation* 16 (1962), p. 82: 'The Q material may be used to illustrate the kind of tradition the Corinthians could have speculated upon in developing their heresy.'

Gospel of Thomas preserves some early and independent Palestinian traditions. 'Thus, Thomas does not use Q, but he does represent the eastern branch of the gattung, *logoi*, the western branch being represented by the synoptic *logoi* of Q, which was used in western Syria by Matthew and later by Luke.'[29]

Most scholars have been unable to recognize any references to Gnosticism in Acts. Bultmann finds two references to the Gnostic Redeemer in Acts 3:15; 5:31. Kümmel detects an anti-Gnostic polemic in Acts 20:29f. Most significant is the fact that Simon Magus, whom the Church Fathers considered as the arch-Gnostic, is not described as a Gnostic but only as a magician.[30]

Recent studies by C. Talbert, however, have argued that the purpose of both Luke and Acts is anti-Gnostic.[31] Luke's emphasis upon the authenticity of the apostolic witness, the legitimacy of the church's interpretation of Scripture and the succession of tradition are to be understood as defences against Gnosticism. But even Schmithals with his great facility to sense Gnostic elements where others fail to perceive them is unable to support a case for an anti-Gnostic polemic in Luke-Acts. He writes: 'Other than Mark and Matthew, no New Testament writer shows so little connection with Gnosticism as does Luke. In other words, it appears impossible to interpret the Lucan image of Paul as anti-Gnostic, as I myself at an earlier time had considered possible.'[32]

IV. THE PAULINE CORPUS

1. *The Early Epistles*

Wilhelm Bousset maintained that:

> 'It is the form which *Paul* gave to Christianity that drew the Gnostic circles to it as would a magnet. It was most of all the pattern of Christ-

[29] Koester in *Trajectories*, p. 136.

[30] E. Fascher, 'Christologie und Gnosis im vierten Evangelium', *ThLZ* 93 (1968), col. 722: '. . . denn ein Magier ist nicht ohne weiteres ein Gnostiker, und von "Gnosis" wie sie heute weithin als vorchristlich gesehen wird, ist m.E. in der ganzen Apostelgeschichte noch nirgends die Rede.'

[31] C. Talbert, *Luke and the Gnostics* (1966); 'An Anti-Gnostic Tendency in Lucan Christology', *NTS* 14 (1967–1968), pp. 259–271.

[32] W. Schmithals, *The Office of Apostle in the Early Church* (1969), p. 271. This is the ET of his *Das Kirchliche Apostelamt* (1961).

ianity as a one-sided religion of redemption and the connection of the redeemer myth with the figure of Jesus of Nazareth which, introduced by Paul into Christianity, exerted this great drawing power.'[33]

More recent studies have held that it was the so-called pre-Pauline Hellenistic church which was most responsible for the church's dialogue with Gnosticism. Even so, the results of this syncretism are best documented in the Pauline Letters. According to Oden, the following Gnostic elements were re-adapted by Paul:

'The gnostic dichotomy of body/spirit is resolutely denied by Paul, ... But he borrows gnostic language in his description of man's predicament.

'The Adam myth is recast in terms of the gnostic view of the two aeons. Although the corporate bondage of humanity under the prototype Adam is thoroughly in keeping with gnostic anthropology, Paul avoids a thoroughgoing gnostic determinism with his view of mankind as corporately responsible with Adam for its plight.

'. . . In the initiation rite of the mystery religions, the participant shares in the mystery divinity's death and renewal. Paul gave this structure more comprehensive meaning by coalescing to it the non-gnostic elements of the humiliation, passion and crucifixion of Jesus of Nazareth.'[34]

W. Schmithals is one of the few scholars who is able to find Gnosticism combatted in the two *Thessalonian* Epistles. Paul's admonition against fornication (1 Thes. 4:3–6) is considered to be an admonition against Gnostic licentiousness. His reassurances regarding the future resurrection of the faithful who have died before Christ's return (1 Thes. 4:14ff.) are interpreted as a corrective of the 'gnosticized' believers who deny a future resurrection. According to Schmithals, some of the Gnostics (rather than Paul himself as the text of 2 Thes. 2:2 would seem to indicate) were saying 'The day of the Lord is here'; this is the clearest evidence for the Gnostic spiritualization of the parousia expectation.[35] Schmithals further argues that the situation faced at Thessalonica was the same that was faced in the Letters to the Corinthians, the Philippians, and the Galatians.[36]

[33] W. Bousset, *Kyrios Christos*, p. 254.

[34] T. C. Oden, 'From Event to Language', pp. 97–98.

[35] W. Schmithals, *Paulus und die Gnostiker: Untersuchungen zu den kleinen Paulusbriefen* (1965), p. 120: 'Diese Behauptung, die im Sinne von 2. Tim. 2, 18 zu verstehen ist, ist der deutlichste Beleg für die gnostische Spiritualisierung des Parusiegedankens.'   [36] *Ibid.*, p. 127.

Contrary to the usual view that Paul's opponents at *Galatia* were Judaizers, Schmithals argues that they were Jewish Gnostics. His arguments are as follows: (1) Paul's appeal in Galatians 1:12 that he had received his apostolic authority by direct revelation is a 'genuin gnostisch' argument.[37] Schmithals assumes that the church's apostolate was derived from a prior Gnostic apostolate.[38] (2) The stress upon circumcision (Gal. 5:2–3) on the part of the false teachers in Galatia is not a necessary proof that they were Jews, as this circumcision could have referred to a symbolical release from the flesh on the part of Jewish-Christian Gnostics.[39] (3) The fact that it was Paul who pointed out the connection between circumcision and the obligation to keep the Mosaic law (Gal. 5:3) demonstrates that Paul's opponents were not Judaizers. (4) The reference to days and months, *etc.* (Gal. 4:10) is not to be understood in the light of Pharisaic practice but in the light of 'gnostisierende' Essene practice.[40] (5) The libertinism which is condemned by Paul (Gal. 5:1, 13) was characteristic of the Gnostics.[41]

According to Bultmann, a large number of 'transformed features of Gnosticism' are to be found in Paul's Letter to the *Romans*: (1) The connection of Adam's fall with the involvement of mankind in sin and death (Rom. 5:12–21) is Gnostic in origin.[42] (2) Baptism into the body of Christ (Rom. 6:5 and 12:4ff.) is compared with the inner unity of believers and the Gnostic Redeemer. (3) Paul's teaching on the fall of creation (Rom. 8:20ff.) alludes to Gnostic cosmology. (4) The reference to the powers of this age (Rom. 8:38ff.) is to the demonic powers which seek to frustrate the ascent of the pneumatics. (5) Exhortations to awake out of sleep and to be

---

[37] *Ibid.*, p. 19. Schmithals had earlier set forth his views in 'Die Häretiker in Galatien', *ZNW* 47 (1956), pp. 25–67.

[38] *Cf.* W. Schmithals, *The Office of Apostle.*

[39] Schmithals, *Paulus und die Gnostiker*, pp. 27, 41.

[40] *Ibid.*, p. 32, n. 93.

[41] Schmithals's extremely forced arguments have failed to convince many that Paul's opponents in Galatia were Gnostics rather than Judaizers. *Cf.* especially, R. McL. Wilson, 'Gnostics – in Galatia?'; Feine-Behm–Kümmel, pp. 194–195; H. Koester in *Trajectories*, pp. 144–145.

[42] *Cf.* C. Colpe, *Die religionsgeschichtliche Schule: Darstellung und Kritik ihres Bildes vom gnostischen Erlösermythus* (1961), p. 61, for a criticism of Bultmann's identification of Adam's fall with the fall of the Urmensch.

sober (Rom. 13:11–13) are reminiscent of Gnostic terminology.[43] Romans 16:17–20, which is taken by Schmithals to be part of a letter to Ephesus, is interpreted by him as referring to Gnostics who cause divisions and serve their bellies.[44]

It is at *Corinth*, in particular, that many scholars find evidence of Gnosticism. In 1908 W. Lütgert, *Freiheitspredigt und Schwarmgeister in Korinth*, first suggested that Paul's opponents were Gnostics. The list of those who have accepted this position includes Bousset, Reitzenstein, Bauer, Bultmann, Schniewind, Haenchen, Bartsch, and Dinkler among others.[45] In 1959 U. Wilckens devoted a full-scale monograph to the subject.[46] His main thesis is his contention that the Christology of the Gnostic heretics developed out of a Jewish personification of *Sophia* or Wisdom. Wilckens considers Paul's use of the word *psychikos* as a 'gnostischer Terminus technicus'. His reference to 'the deep things of God' (1 Cor. 2:10) is also 'typisch gnostisch'. Indeed the mention of *gnōsis* in 1 Corinthians 8:1ff. is an unmistakable allusion to Gnosticism.[47]

It is Schmithals who has provided the most thoroughgoing exposition of Paul's opponents in both 1 and 2 Corinthians as Jewish Gnostics.[48] Schmithals analyses the two canonical Epistles into no less than six different letters: two in 1 Corinthians and four in 2 Corinthians. Paul is faced with but one group of opponents who are especially prominent in 2 Corinthians 10–13. Assuming that Paul's opponents were full-fledged Gnostics, Schmithals concludes from the fact that Paul did not attack cosmic dualism that Paul himself shared certain elements of Gnostic belief. But in spite of Paul's use of Gnostic terminology, Paul betrays little exact knowledge of

---

[43] R. Bultmann, *Theology of the New Testament, passim*.

[44] W. Schmithals, 'Die Irrlehrer von Röm. 16, 17–20', *StTh* 13 (1959), pp. 51–69; reprinted in *Paulus und die Gnostiker*, pp. 159–174.

[45] For a history of the scholarship on Paul's Corinthian opponents, see D. Georgi, *Die Gegner des Paulus im 2. Korintherbrief* (1964), pp. 7–16.

[46] U. Wilckens, *Weisheit und Torheit* (1959).

[47] For a detailed criticism of Wilckens's work, see K. Prümm, 'Zur neutestamentlichen Gnosis – Problematik: Gnostischer Hintergrund und Lehreinschlag in der beiden Eingangskapiteln von 1 Kor?' *ZThK* 87 (1965), pp. 399–442; 88 (1966), pp. 1–50.

[48] W. Schmithals, *Gnostics in Corinth* (1971), which is a translation of *Die Gnosis in Korinth* (1956; 2nd ed. 1965); pp. 326–412 include supplementary material and responses to his critics.

the Gnostic myth. Indeed he is not even aware that he had to deal with Gnostics. Like Bultmann, Schmithals maintains that Paul had misunderstood his opponents when he wrote 1 Corinthians 15, thinking that they were completely sceptical about any form of life after death. Later when he realized that they were actually stressing their perfectionism in the present and were rejecting the realistic and futuristic aspects of eschatology, he wrote 2 Corinthians 5:1–10.

The Gnostics at Corinth were characterized by their pride in their knowledge and by their libertine behaviour. Their superiority is manifested by their speaking in tongues (1 Cor. 14). Their cursing of the 'earthly' Jesus in 1 Corinthians 12:3 is due to the fact that they honoured the 'heavenly' Christ.[49] The Gnostic presence at Corinth is also detected indirectly in the use that Paul made of his opponents' terminology and concepts. When Paul uses the antithesis of *psychikos-pneumatikos* (1 Cor. 2:14f.; 15:44–46), this is viewed as one of the clearest evidences for Paul's dependence upon Gnosticism.[50] When Paul says, 'Am I not an apostle? Have I not seen Jesus our Lord?' (1 Cor. 9:1), he is making a 'typisch gnostisch' claim. Paul's figure of the church as the 'body of Christ' is the Gnostic concept of the inner unity between believers and the Redeemer.[51]

The most extreme example of Schmithals's Gnostic exegesis is his interpretation of 1 Corinthians 10:16ff. as a Jewish Gnostic rite rather than as the Christian communion. 'The broken bread symbolizes the scattered Pneumatics in the one form of the Christ-Urmensch.'[52] In a rather incredible manner Schmithals explains verses 16b–17, 'The bread which we break, is it not the communion of the body of Christ?', as

[49] *Cf.* B. Pearson, 'Did the Gnostics Curse Jesus?' *JBL* 86 (1967), pp. 301–305.

[50] This antithesis has been considered a Gnostic technical phrase since Reitzenstein. Against such a Gnostic interpretation of the phrase, see J. Dupont, *Gnosis: la connaissance religieuse dans les épitres de St Paul* (1949); B. A. Pearson, 'The *Pneumatikos-Psuchikos* Terminology in 1 Corinthians: A Study in the Theology of the Corinthian Opponents of Paul and Its Relation to Gnosticism'. PhD dissertation, Harvard University (1968).

[51] For a criticism of this typically Bultmannian interpretation, *cf.* M. Barth, 'A Chapter on the Church – the Body of Christ. Interpretation of I Corinthians 12', *Interpretation* 12. 2 (1958), pp. 131–156.

[52] W. Schmithals, 'Das Verhältnis von Gnosis und Neuem Testament als methodisches Problem', *NTS* 16 (1970), p. 377.

not a Christian rite inasmuch as there is no reference to Jesus and as the word 'Christ' can mean simply the Jewish Messiah. And is this a model of how one should practise the exegesis of the New Testament?

Schmithals's methods have been criticized even by those who are in favour of a pre-Christian Gnosticism. Georgi, for example, scores the way in which he simplifies complex historical data. He is especially critical of Schmithals's reconstruction of a Jewish–Gnostic Redeemer myth.[53] Robinson writes, 'Unfortunately Schmithals, like Baur before him, overdoes his case and thus tends to discredit the truth in his position.'[54] Others are even more critical. Colpe notes that Schmithals is largely ignorant of the last thirty years of Iranian research.[55] Most scornful is Munck, who writes:

'The author of this book lacks historical training. He forces his a priori opinions upon the texts with offensive boldness. . . . Schmithals' book is a striking proof of the decline of exegetic research since the 1930's.'[56]

In contrast to Bultmann and Schmithals, some scholars would distinguish between Paul's opponents in 2 Corinthians and those in 1 Corinthians. In particular, D. Georgi has argued that the opponents in 2 Corinthians were not Gnostics but Hellenistic Jewish-Christian missionaries.[57] It is largely from evidence from 2 Corinthians that Schmithals has argued his case for Gnostics at Corinth.

Barrett in a recent article has suggested that Paul's opponents at Corinth were liberal Jews – the 'false apostles' – who were in turn the agents of the 'superlative apostles', the conservative Jewish Christian pillars at Jerusalem. These liberal Jews were willing to adopt 'a gnostic framework of thought . . .'.[58]

---

[53] Review of W. Schmithals, *Die Gnosis in Korinth*, by D. Georgi in *Verkündigung und Forschung* (1960–1962), pp. 90–96.

[54] J. M. Robinson, 'Basic Shifts', p. 80.

[55] C. Colpe, *Die religionsges. Schule*, pp. 140, 147, n. 5.

[56] J. Munck, 'The New Testament and Gnosticism', p. 152.

[57] *Cf.* also H. Koester, 'Häretiker im Urchristentum', in *RGG*[3], III, cols 17–21; and J. M. Robinson in *Trajectories*, p. 61, n. 68.

[58] C. K. Barrett, 'Paul's Opponents in II Corinthians', *NTS* 17 (1971), pp. 233–254; *cf.* J. W. Fraser, 'II Corinthians V. 16 Once More', *NTS* 17 (1971), pp. 293–313.

A number of scholars question whether a clear-cut mature type of Gnosticism can be proven for Corinth. Wilson is willing to speak of 'opponents of a more Gnostic type at Corinth' than the Judaizers in Galatia.[59] But MacRae questions whether the Corinthian heretics can properly be called Gnostics.[60] Grant is quite circumspect in his discussion of the heresy at Corinth:

> 'Though the ability of modern scholars to recover Paul's opponents' ideas may be over-estimated, it would appear that a movement like the one which later became Gnosticism was probably present in Corinth. . . . It is not so clear, however, that the Gnosticizing tendency present among them involved their setting forth a Gnosticizing or Gnostic myth. . . . It is true that such notions appear again among the Gnostics, but it need not be held that Paul himself has gone beyond apocalyptic toward, or into, Gnosticism. His interpretation of the Gospel in apocalyptic terminology, however, may have encouraged converts whose acquaintance with Judaism was minimal to understand him in a semi-Gnostic manner.'[61]

Other scholars deny that Gnosticism was involved at Corinth. Turner points out that the libertinism at Corinth need not have been Gnostic libertinism: 'A strict sexual morality does not usually characterize the life of a great port. Immorality may as easily be "unprincipled" as "principled".'[62] Conzelmann argues that the fact that Paul presupposed that the Corinthians shared his confession of faith refutes the thesis that the Corinthians had a Gnostic Christology. 'They are not gnostics but spirit enthusiasts.'[63] As to whether their use of the term *gnōsis* in 1 Corinthians 8:1 means that Paul's opponents were Gnostics, Pearson answers in the negative: '. . . Paul's opponents in Corinth were not "Gnostics" in the technical sense. Indeed, the affirmation – as part of the Corinthian *gnōsis* – that there is "one God", of whom

---

[59] R. McL. Wilson, *Gnosis and the New Testament* (1968), p. 54. *Cf.* 'How Gnostic Were the Corinthians?' *NTS* 19 (1972), pp. 65–74.

[60] G. W. MacRae, 'Gnosis, Christian', in the *New Catholic Encyclopedia* VI (1967), p. 522. *Cf.* his review of W. Schmithals, *Gnosticism in Corinth* in *Interpretation* 26 (1972), pp. 489–491.

[61] R. M. Grant, *Gnosticism and Early Christianity* (1959; 2nd ed. 1966), pp. 157ff.

[62] H. E. W. Turner, *The Pattern of Christian Truth* (1954), p. 69.

[63] H. Conzelmann, 'On the Analysis of the Confessional Formula in I Corinthians 15:3–5', *Interpretation* 20 (1966), p. 24.

all things exist, excludes this possibility.'[64] Nock concluded:

> 'The plain truth is that you could not have found anyone in Corinth
> to direct you to a Gnostic church: the overwhelming probability is that
> there was no such thing. It is at most possible that here (as certainly
> happened in Colossae) individual Christians came from or came into
> contact with esoteric Judaism.'[65]

2. *The Prison Epistles*

Schmithals again finds that the opponents at Philippi are not
Jews, but Jewish-Christian Gnostics.[66] Though the reference
to circumcision in Philippians 3:2ff. might seem to indicate
Jews, the insulting term 'dogs' must indicate that these are
those who are sensual in behaviour (Phil. 3:19). 'The only
libertine movement within the Christian community known to
us from early Christian times, however, is the Gnostic movement.'[67]

Koester would agree to the extent that he would characterize the movement at Philippi as the teaching of 'a law propaganda with gnosticizing tendencies'.[68] In an article written
a decade before, he had been more explicit. He had argued
that those at Philippi were Gnostics of Jewish origin whose
message was perfection through fulfilment of the law. 'Typically gnostic is the reinterpretation of all future apocalyptic
expectations as spiritual possessions of the individual in the
present. . . .'[69] Koester concluded, 'This is what I would call
typical of Early Christian Gnosticism.'[70]

There has been considerable support for the view that the
famous *Carmen Christi* or 'Christ Hymn' of Philippians 2:5–11
is an independent composition based on a Gnostic prototype.
As early as 1845 F. C. Baur had suggested a possible Gnostic

[64] B. A. Pearson, 'The *Pneumatikos-Psuchikos* Terminology', p. 121; *cf.*
p. 229.
[65] A. D. Nock, 'Gnosticism', p. 277.
[66] L. Goppelt accuses Schmithals of a 'phantastischen Pangnostizismus',
a charge which is seconded by Colpe and Wilson.
[67] W. Schmithals, *Paulus und die Gnostiker*, p. 61. *Cf.* his earlier article,
'Die Irrlehrer des Philipperbriefes', *ZThK* 54 (1957), pp. 297–341, which
has been reprinted with revisions in the preceding.
[68] *Trajectories*, p. 148.
[69] H. Koester, 'The Purpose of the Polemic of a Pauline Fragment
(Phil. 3)', *NTS* 8 (1961–1962), p. 324.
[70] *Ibid.*, p. 331.

background and the use of the Anthropos myth as a prototype. E. Lohmeyer in 1928 was the first to work out the full implications of this theory. He suggested that the model of the hymn was an Iranian myth of the Gayomart or Primal Man.[71]

After Lohmeyer the most important studies were by the Bultmannian scholars Bornkamm[72] and Käsemann.[73] The latter sees the hymn as an Urmensch myth in the context of a Gnostic cosmic drama of redemption. There are no traits of the personality of the human Jesus involved. The Redeemer descends, accomplishes his work on earth, and reascends to gain control over the celestial powers.[74] Jervell likewise assumes for at least verses 6–8 a Gnostic *Vorlage* which had developed in a Hellenistic Jewish environment.[75]

Martin emphasizes the important new factors which appear in the Christian version of the hymn, but concedes that it is evident that some use was made of a current 'myth'. He does not think that it is possible or important to decide exactly which category – whether pagan, Hellenistic-Jewish, Iranian, or Gnostic – has provided *the* background to the hymn.[76] On balance, however, Martin agrees with the criticisms of Percy and rejects the fully Gnostic interpretation of Käsemann and others. The cumulative effect of his exegesis is an exposition of the hymn in Jewish terms.[77]

Late in the nineteenth century J. B. Lightfoot had suggested

[71] E. Lohmeyer, *Kyrios Jesus: Eine Untersuchung zu Phil. 2, 5–11* (1928; 2nd ed. 1961). *Cf.* J. T. Sanders, *The New Testament Christological Hymn* (1971), for the hymns in Philippians, Colossians, *etc.*

[72] G. Bornkamm, 'Zum Verständnis des Christus-Hymnus, Phil. 2.6–11'. in *Studien zu Antike und Urchristentum: Gesammelte Aufsätze* II (1959), pp. 177–187.

[73] E. Käsemann, 'Kritische Analyse von Phil. 2, 5–11', *ZThK* 47 (1950), pp. 313–360; reprinted in *Exegetische Versuche und Besinnung* I (1960).

[74] For a criticism of Käsemann's use of the Gnostic Redeemer myth, see D. Georgi, 'Der vorpaulinische Hymnus Phil 2, 6–11', in E. Dinkler (ed.), *Zeit und Geschichte*.

[75] J. Jervell, *Imago Dei: Gen. i. 26 f. im Spätjudentum, in den paulinischen Briefen* (1960).

[76] R. P. Martin, *Carmen Christi: Philippians ii, 5–11 in Recent Interpretation and in the Setting of Early Christian Worship* (1967), p. 297.

[77] For a critical review of Martin's work, see I. Howard Marshall, 'The Christ-Hymn in Philippians 2:5–11', *Tyndale Bulletin* 19 (1968), pp. 104–127.

that the *Colossian* heresy was an incipient 'Gnostic' movement with links with the Essenes. He wrote:

'Yet still we seem justified, even at the earlier date, in speaking of these general ideas as Gnostic, guarding ourselves at the same time against misunderstanding with the twofold caution, that we here employ the term to express the simplest and most elementary conceptions of this tendency of thought, and that we do not postulate its use as a distinct designation of any sect or sects at this early date.'[78]

In our day the identification of the Colossian error as a Jewish Gnosticism is widely accepted. According to Kümmel:

'Concerning the nature of the Colossian heresy, views formerly varied widely. Today there are hardly any differences in basic opinion. Paul, with obvious correctness, sees in the heretical teaching Gnosticism, secret wisdom of a syncretistic sort (2:8, 18), Jewish ritualism and Jewish speculation about angels.'[79]

According to Bornkamm, 'Of the fact that behind the Colossian heresy there stands a Jewish or Judaistic Gnosis, strongly infected by Iranian ideas, there can scarcely be any doubt.'[80] He believes that he can trace the influence of Gnosticism in the 'eschatological shift' found in Colossians 1:5, 23, and 27, where 'hope' is no longer understood in the Jewish-Christian sense of a future eschatology but is conceived as a present possession.[81] Other Gnostic characteristics detected by Bornkamm, Bultmann, and Haenchen include: (1) the warning against 'philosophy' (Col. 2:8); (2) the emphasis upon the *plērōma* or 'fullness' of the Godhead (Col. 1:19); and (3) the reference to the church as the 'body' of Christ (Col. 1:18, 24), which gives a cosmic character to the church in keeping with Gnostic concepts. Thus in the Epistle to the Colossians Gnostic motifs are not only combatted but also absorbed. According to Käsemann, 'We thus arrive at the peculiar fact that heresy in Colossians is combatted by a confession of faith, the formulation of which has itself been very strongly conditioned by heterodox views.'[82]

[78] J. B. Lightfoot, *Saint Paul's Epistles to the Colossians and to Philemon* (1897), p. 113.
[79] Feine–Behm–Kümmel, p. 67.
[80] G. Bornkamm, *Das Ende der Gesetzes: Paulusstudien* (1958), p. 150; *cf.* p. 153.
[81] *Ibid.*, pp. 139ff.
[82] E. Käsemann, *Essays on New Testament Themes* (1964), p. 164.

In opposition to the foregoing, some scholars would maintain that the Colossian heresy lacked essential features of developed Gnosticism and would argue that Paul was not dependent upon Gnosticism for his conceptions. E. Percy, for example, argued that the Colossian heresy did not betray important characteristics of Gnosticism.[83] His view has been seconded recently by Hegermann, who holds that mere worship of the elemental spirits (Col. 2:8) is not Gnosticism. Gnosticism would have degraded the world elements into spirits of darkness.[84]

At the conference at Messina on Gnostic origins, S. Lyonnet contended along with Percy and Dupont that Paul was not dependent upon the Gnostics in the Letter to the Colossians.[85] He argued that Paul had no need of an Iranian myth or Gnostic speculations – if such had indeed existed – in order for him to attribute to Christ a role in the creation of the universe. To exalt Christ in the Letter to the Colossians Paul made use of Old Testament expressions which attributed a cosmological role to divine Wisdom, and also certain popular philosophic words as *sōma* and *plērōma*.[86]

Finally, Koester in describing the Colossian heresy has contented himself with writing that the antagonists at Colossae were the same as the Judaizing missionaries at Galatia. 'As various references in Paul's letter reveal (*e.g.* Gal. 4:9–10), these Judaizers must have emphasized the spiritual implications and the cosmic dimensions of the observance of the ritual law of the Old Testament in particular.'[87] Furthermore, Koester continues: 'It should be added that the heresy of Colossae was perhaps a more limited local phenomenon than is generally assumed. Its roots must lie in the particular form

---

Cf. H.-M. Schenke, 'Der Widerstreit gnostischer und kirchlicher Christologie im Spiegel des Kolosserbriefes', *ZThK* 61 (1964), p. 403: 'Der gnostischen Christologie der Häretiker wird hier mit einer radikalisierten gnostischen Christologie (*i.e.* of the author of Colossians) begegnet. . . .'

[83] E. Percy, *Probleme der Kolosser- und Epheserbriefe* (1946).

[84] H. Hegermann, *Die Vorstellung vom Schöpfungsmittler im hellenistischen Judentum und Urchristentum* (1961), p. 163.

[85] S. Lyonnet, 'Saint Paul et le gnosticisme: L'épitre aux Colossiens', in *OG*, pp. 538–551.

[86] *Cf.* P. Benoit, 'Corps, tête et pleroma dans les Épitres de la captivité', *RB* 63 (1956), pp. 5–44.

[87] *Trajectories*, pp. 144–145.

of Jewish syncretism which was prevalent in Lydia and Phrygia at that time. . . .'[88]

As in Colossians so also in *Ephesians* Gnostic terminology and imagery have been detected. The major contributions to a Gnostic understanding of Ephesians have come from H. Schlier[89] and from E. Käsemann.[90] The latter has examined in detail the image of the church as the body of Christ, and has concluded that this figure is Gnostic in origin. Schlier detects the following traces of Gnostic thought: (1) the descent and ascent of the heavenly Saviour (Eph. 4:8–10); (2) the 'dividing-wall' of Ephesians 2:14–16 is understood as the opposition of the hostile powers to the ascent of the souls to the divine pleroma; (3) the figure of the Heavenly Man who appears in Ephesians 2:15 as a 'new man' and in 4:13 as a 'perfect man'; (4) the 'heavenly marriage' (Eph. 5:22ff.) between Christ and the church.[91]

More recently P. Pokorný, taking into account studies which have emphasized the Jewish background of the Anthropos myth, has explained the figure of the Head-Member imagery as the result of an interaction with Jewish Gnosticism. The writer of Ephesians, a follower of Paul about AD 80–90, has combined the Gnostic concept of the heavenly body with Old Testament and Christian ideas and applied them in a concrete manner to the church.[92] As an example of a group in which Old Testament concepts and Iranian dualism could be combined he cites the Mandaeans.[93] Pokorný in his exposition is able to detect a Gnostic background even in the writer's exhortation to the slaves (Eph. 5:5–8). He believes that this warning has been uttered lest the slaves should allow themselves to be led by a Gnostic ecstasy into an illusionary flight from their daily cares![94]

---

[88] *Ibid.*, p. 145, n. 86. *Cf.* A. Kraabel, 'Judaism in Asia Minor', ThD dissertation, Harvard University (1968).

[89] H. Schlier, *Christus und die Kirche im Epheserbrief* (1930).

[90] E. Käsemann, *Leib und Leib Christi* (1933).

[91] *Cf.* R. A. Batey, 'Jewish Gnosticism and the *hieros gamos* of Eph. V, 21–33', *NTS* 10 (1963–1964,) pp. 121–127.

[92] P. Pokorný, *Die Epheserbrief und die Gnosis: Die Bedeutung des Haupt-Glieder-Gedankens in der entstehenden Kirche* (1965), p. 70.

[93] *Ibid.*, pp. 170f.

[94] *Ibid.*, p. 122. *Cf.* also his earlier 'Epheserbrief und gnostische Mysterien', *ZNW* 53 (1962), pp. 160–194.

Alternatives to a thoroughgoing Gnostic exposition of the various passages in Ephesians have been offered. Daniélou points out that the ascent and descent motif was a common symbolism of Jewish origin, adopted both by Christianity and by Gnosticism.[95] Most English-speaking commentators explain Ephesians 2:14 'the middle wall of partition' as a reference to the balustrade at the temple in Jerusalem which separated the area restricted to Jews only from that where Gentiles were allowed. Percy vigorously opposes a Gnostic explanation of the body imagery, and favours parallels from the Old Testament ideas of the community and Jewish speculations on the heavenly Adam.[96] Feuillet argues for an Old Testament background for the *plērōma* concept in Ephesians and Colossians.[97]

The striking parallels which have been provided by the Dead Sea Scrolls have caused K. G. Kuhn to abandon the Gnostic interpretation of his teacher Bultmann in favour of an interpretation of Ephesians based on Qumranian parallels. The so-called 'baptismal hymn' of Ephesians 5:14, which has been interpreted as Gnostic since Reitzenstein, is now seen by Kuhn to be 'not a question of knowledge about the nature of the actual self, but more a question of a decision of the will, *a change in one's walking*, away from sinful action towards action which is pleasing to God. That is something quite different from the Gnostic awakening.'[98]

Likewise F. Mussner concludes:

'It should now be evident that the Scrolls throw much light on Eph, not only with respect to various individual themes, but also to a whole series of connected concepts, especially in the central section formed by Eph 2. We find here a thematic association of ideas, which is also in evidence in the Scrolls. This intensifies the belief that the thematic

[95] J. Daniélou, *The Theology of Jewish Christianity*, pp. 206ff.; *cf.* J. Daniélou, 'Judéo-christianisme et gnose', in *Aspects du judéo-christianisme* (1965), p. 156 and *passim*.
[96] *Cf.* E. Schweizer, 'Die Kirche als Leib Christi in den paulinischen Homologumena', *ThLZ* 86 (1961), cols 161–174.
[97] A. Feuillet, 'L'église pleroma du Christ d'après Ephes. I, 23', *Nouvelle Revue Théologique* 88 (1956), pp. 593–610.
[98] K. G. Kuhn, 'The Epistle to the Ephesians in the Light of the Qumran Texts', in J. Murphy-O'Connor (ed.), *Paul and Qumran* (1968), p. 127; Kuhn's important article first appeared as 'Der Epheserbrief im Lichte der Qumran-texte', *NTS* 7 (1960–1961), pp. 334–346.

material of Eph has its roots in a tradition that is also represented at Qumran, and which is far removed from later Gnosticism.' [99]

Mussner stresses the fact that the dualism of Ephesians is ethical and not the metaphysical–cosmic dualism of Gnosticism. He also rejects the Schlier–Käsemann Gnostic interpretation of the 'body of Christ' imagery of Ephesians. He holds that its background is to be sought in Old Testament ideas of corporate personality.[100]

3. The Pastoral Epistles

When we come to the Pastoral Epistles and other later documents of the New Testament, there is near agreement between those who maintain that Gnosticism was a pre-Christian phenomenon and those who maintain that Gnosticism was a largely post-Christian phenomenon that the heresy which was combatted in these books was some form of Gnosticism. The former hold that by this time Christians no longer entertained Gnostic concepts but banned them with but few exceptions – e.g. Bultmann and others see a modified form of the Gnostic Redeemer myth in 1 Timothy 3:16. More conservative scholars would argue that the heresy cannot in every case be irrefutably identified as Gnosticism, and further that if it was Gnosticism, it was an incipient form of Gnosticism.

The following are just a few of the passages which deal with false teaching in the Pastorals: there are warnings against 'senseless controversies' (1 Tim. 6:4; 2 Tim. 2:23; Tit. 3:9f.), against speculative 'myths and genealogies' (1 Tim. 1:4; 2 Tim. 4:4; Tit. 1:14; 3:9), and against the *gnōsis*, which is falsely called 'knowledge' (1 Tim. 6:20). The false teachers have come from within the church and have fallen from the faith (1 Tim. 1:6, 20; 2 Tim. 2:17). Among their teachings we may infer the following from the warnings directed against the heresy: (1) the belief that the 'resurrection is already past' (2 Tim. 2:18); (2) an injunction to avoid marriage and certain foods (1 Tim. 4:3); and apparently (3) a dualistic

[99] F. Mussner, 'Contributions Made by Qumran to the Understanding of the Epistle to the Ephesians', in Murphy-O'Connor, p. 178.
[100] F. Mussner, *Christus des All und die Kirche: Studien zur Theologie des Epheserbriefes* (1955).

understanding of the world which gave rise to the ascetic rules (1 Tim. 4:3–5; Tit. 1:14–15).

Some scholars who recognize Gnosticism in these letters at the same time maintain that the Pastorals are non-Pauline and quite late. Grant writes, 'Surely those Church Fathers were right who believed that in these letters the Gnostic systems of the late first or early second century were under fire.'[101] Cullmann associated the heresy in the Pastorals and in Colossians with the Jewish Gnosticism opposed in the letters of Ignatius, who died c. AD 117.[102] In a recent article Ford has suggested that the Pastoral heresy was not Gnosticism but a 'Proto-Montanism'.[103] Even if one should not wish to bring down the Pastorals to AD 126 – the earliest possible date for the outbreak of Montanism in Phrygia – the fact that Ford could make such a proposal indicates that the Gnostics are not the only candidates who can be put forward to fit the characteristics of the heresy.

Quispel, for example, suggests that those who wished to abandon marriage at Corinth and in the Pastorals were not ascetic Gnostics but Encratites:

'Perhaps it (Encratism) was present in Corinth, where Paul exhorts the Encratites not to give up marriage in spiritually overrating their all too human frames. Certainly it is there too in the pastoral letters, where Jewish Encratites proclaim that the resurrection has already taken place and that marriage should be abolished.'[104]

Lyonnet has suggested that the polemic against marriage in 1 Timothy may have been directed against something like Qumranian asceticism, which also emphasized celibacy.[105]

Wilson also asks: 'The description in 1 Tim. iv. 3 of people who forbid marriage and enjoin abstinence from certain foods would fit some Gnostics; but were these Gnostics the only people to practise such asceticism?'[106] He concludes that the

[101] R. M. Grant, *Gnosticism and Early Christianity*, pp. 161–162; cf. C. Colpe, *Die religionsges. Schule*, p. 67; G. W. MacRae, 'Gnosticism and New Testament Studies', *Bible Today* 38 (1968), p. 2629.

[102] O. Cullmann, *Le problème . . . du roman pseudo-Clémentin*, pp. 172–173.

[103] J. M. Ford, 'A Note on Proto-Montanism in the Pastoral Epistles', *NTS* 17 (1971), pp. 338–346.

[104] G. Quispel, 'Gnosticism and the New Testament', in J. P. Hyatt (ed.), *The Bible in Modern Scholarship* (1965), p. 255.

[105] *OG*, p. 551.

[106] R. McL. Wilson, *Gnosis and the New Testament*, p. 41.

'cumulative effect of a number of features shared with the later Gnostics by the opponents attacked in these documents . . . makes us think of an incipient Gnosticism as the heresy in view. But there is nothing . . . to suggest that this incipient Gnosticism had as yet advanced very far in the direction of later developments.'[107] Cerfaux concluded that in the Pastorals the allusions to gnosis are so vague and the Gnosticism described so amorphous that one need not date these letters after Paul's time.[108]

V. HEBREWS

E. Käsemann has sought to show that the background of certain conceptions in the Letter to the Hebrews is Gnostic.[109] He finds the following Gnostic concepts: (1) the Gnostic 'heavenly journey' is the idea behind the migration of the people of God and their search for rest (Heb. 3:11, 18; 4:1, 3, 5, 10f.); (2) the Gnostic myth of the Primal Man is behind the description of the Son of God as an 'Anthropos' (Heb. 1–2); (3) the gathering of the godly seed is behind the idea that the Son of God brings the people of God to perfection (Heb. 2:10; 5:9; 7:19; etc.); and (4) the Gnostic Anthropos myth is combined with Jewish messianic expectations in the speculations in Hebrews concerning the heavenly high priest.

In contrast to Käsemann's approach, other scholars have emphasized the striking parallels between the Dead Sea Scrolls and the Letter to the Hebrews.[110] One specific example of a document from Qumran which is of great importance for our understanding of Hebrews is a text from Cave XI which describes Melchizedek as a heavenly deliverer similar to the archangel Michael. This may help to explain why the author of Hebrews stressed not only Christ's superiority to the Aaronic priesthood but also to the angels (Heb. 1–2). Hebrews 7:3

---

[107] *Ibid.*, p. 42.

[108] L. Cerfaux, 'Gnose préchrétienne et biblique', in *Dictionnaire de la Bible*, Supplément III (1938), col. 692.

[109] E. Käsemann, *Das wandernde Gottesvolk: Eine Untersuchung zum Hebräerbrief* (1952; 3rd ed. 1959).

[110] *E.g.* Y. Yadin, 'The Dead Sea Scroll and the Epistle to the Hebrews', *Scripta Hierosolymitana* 4 (1965), pp. 36–55.

which speaks of Melchizedek without parentage may now
be interpreted in the light that Melchizedek was regarded as
a supra-human being. M. de Jonge and A. S. van der Woude
conclude: 'It is no longer necessary to suppose that the conception of a heavenly high-priest in Hebrews was influenced
by Hellenistic Jewish, gnostic, and/or Philonic traditions.'[111]

VI. JAMES

The attempt of H. Schammberger, *Die Einheitlichkeit des Jk.
im antignostischen Kampf* (1936), to argue that the Letter of
James betrays signs of an anti-Gnostic struggle has not
received any support. The sole passage of a Gnostic type to
be identified by Bultmannians in James is the contrast between
'psychic-pneumatic' implied in James 3:15.[112] Pearson, on
the other hand, feels that the term *psychikos* in this verse is
used simply as a pejorative adjective and not as an anthropological term in a Gnostic sense.[113] Even Schmithals agrees:
'In any case, James shows no anti-gnostic tendency.'[114]

VII. THE PETRINE EPISTLES AND JUDE

Bultmann believes that the 'faction makers' of 2 Peter 2:1
were Gnostics. On the other hand, he finds that Gnostic
terminology has been transformed and used as follows:
(1) the exhortation to be sober (1 Pet. 1:13) is reminiscent of
the Gnostic 'terminology of parenesis'; (2) Christ's ascent to
heaven, subjecting the demonic powers (1 Pet. 3:22), is
borrowed from the framework of the Gnostic Redeemer myth;
(3) the reference to Christ's preaching to the spirits in prison
(1 Pet. 3:19ff.) is held to refer to the region of the air where the
stars kept the dead confined.[115]

  Käsemann holds that the references to the 'cunningly
devised fables' (2 Pet. 1:16) and to 'feigned words' (2 Pet. 2:3)

---

[111] M. de Jonge and A. S. van der Woude, '11 Q Melchizedek and the
New Testament', *NTS* 12 (1965–1966), p. 322.

[112] R. Bultmann, *Theology of the New Testament* I, p. 174; U. Wilckens,
Weisheit und Torheit, p. 91.

[113] B. A. Pearson, 'The *Pneumatikos-Psuchikos* Terminology', p. 34.

[114] W. Schmithals, *The Office of Apostle*, p. 258, n. 123.

[115] R. Bultmann, *Theology of the New Testament* I, pp. 175–176.

are polemical statements against the enthusiasm of Gnostics who ascribe their sayings to the Spirit.[116] On the basis of the alleged references to Gnosticism Käsemann would date 2 Peter as late as AD 150. Reicke would date 2 Peter about AD 90, inasmuch as 'References to Gnosticism and other movements are not conclusive, as these were already present in the first century.'[117] As a matter of fact, Reicke, who dates 1 Peter before Peter's death in AD 64,[118] is able to interpret 1 Peter 3:7 – 'Likewise, ye husbands, dwell with them according to *gnōsis*' – as a conscious polemic against the Gnostic contempt for women.[119]

Bultmann holds that the references in Jude 8–11, 19 refer to Gnostic false teachers. On the other hand, Wilson points out that 'idolatry and immorality in themselves' are not adequate criteria for the identification of Gnostics in this letter.[120]

VIII. THE JOHANNINE EPISTLES

Bultmann has advocated a pre-Christian Gnostic source for the first Johannine Epistle.[121] He has argued that the following examples show indebtedness to Gnosticism: (1) the 'seed' of God which remains in one and keeps one sinless (1 Jn. 3:9); (2) the separation of those 'of the devil' (1 Jn. 3:8) from those 'begotten of God' (1 Jn. 2:29; 3:9; *etc.*); (3) the Gnostic antithesis between 'truth-falsehood' (1 Jn. 2:21, 27), and between 'light-darkness' (1 Jn. 1:5); and (4) the view that the world is ruled by Satan and lies in wickedness (1 Jn. 5:19). At the same time the author attacks heretical Gnostic groups (1 Jn. 2:18ff.; 4:1–6; *etc.*). Most commentators, including

---

[116] E. Käsemann, 'An Apology for Primitive Christian Eschatology', in *Essays on New Testament Themes*, pp. 169–195; originally published in *ZThK* 49 (1952), pp. 272–296.

[117] B. Reicke, *The Epistles of James, Peter, and Jude* (1964), p. 144.

[118] *Ibid.*, p. 71.

[119] *Ibid.*, p. 103. *Cf.* his 'Die Gnosis der Männer nach I. Ptr. 3.7', in W. Eltester (ed.), *Neutestamentliche Studien für Rudolf Bultmann* (1954; 2nd ed. 1957), pp. 296–304.

[120] R. McL. Wilson, *Gnosis and the New Testament*, p. 40.

[121] R. Bultmann, 'Analyse des ersten Johannesbriefes', in *Festgabe für Adolf Jülicher* (1927), pp. 138–158; reprinted in Dinkler, *Exegetica*, pp. 105–123. *Cf.* W. Nauch, *Die Tradition und der Charakter des Johannesbriefes* (1957).

the Catholic scholar Wikenhauser, would agree that the polemic in 1 John seems to be directed against Gnosticism:
'. . . at the present day there is hardly any further doubt that
it was a Gnostic error.'[122]

Some scholars would like further to suggest that the type
of Gnosticism encountered here may have been that of the
teachings of Cerinthus, who taught in Asia Minor at the end
of the first century. Kümmel, however, points out that the
letter does not show any trace of Cerinthus's view that the
Christ was joined only temporarily with the man Jesus. None
the less he finds that 'it is nevertheless significant that here,
in contrast to Colossians, the Pastorals, Jude, and II Peter,
the enthusiastic Gnosticism also has Christological effects.
Hence we have to do here with a developed form of Gnosticism.'[123] On the other hand, Haardt holds that it is highly
questionable that 1 John contains polemics against early
Gnostics: 'The Gnostic Christology (cf. Cerinthus in Irenaeus,
Adv. Haer., I, 25, 1) reconstructed by some scholars with the
help of 1 Jn 5:6 in particular, is simply an interpretation,
which remains open to doubt.'[124]

W. Bauer had suggested that the Diotrephes mentioned in
3 John 9, 'who loved to have the pre-eminence', was a Gnostic
heretic.[125] E. Käsemann, who succeeded Bauer at Göttingen,
boldly reversed the roles of the elder and Diotrephes, and
suggested that it was Diotrophes who was the orthodox
bishop and the author of 3 John who was the Gnostic![126]
Robinson points out that, 'This was just the time when there
was talk in some church circles in Germany of a heresy trial
for Bultmann, so that Käsemann was casting the evangelist
in a role not too dissimilar from what Bultmann's might have
become.'[127]

[122] A. Wikenhauser, *New Testament Introduction* (1963), p. 523.

[123] Feine–Behm–Kümmel, p. 310.

[124] R. Haardt, 'Gnosticism', in *Sacramentum Mundi* II (1968), p. 377.

[125] W. Bauer, *Orthodoxy and Heresy in Earliest Christianity* (1971), p. 93;
originally *Rechtgläubigkeit und Ketzerei im ältesten Christentum* (1934; 2nd
ed. 1964).

[126] E. Käsemann, 'Ketzer und Zeuge; Zum johanneischen Verfas-
serproblem', *ZThK* 48 (1951), pp. 292–311; reprinted in *Exegetische
Versuche und Besinnung* I, pp. 168–187.

[127] J. M. Robinson, 'Basic Shifts', p. 77.

IX. THE APOCALYPSE

The polemic in Revelation 2 is directed against heretics who are known as 'Nicolaitans'. Haenchen feels that the rebuke against 'fornication' in Revelation 2:14, 20–23 is aimed against Gnostic libertinism. These heretics also engaged in daring interpretations of Scripture and claimed to have knowledge of the 'deep things of Satan' (Rev. 2:14). Koester would associate the heresy of the Nicolaitans with the Docetic adversaries of Ignatius of Antioch, who wrote to several churches in the same area of Asia Minor which is addressed in the letters to the seven churches in Revelation 2–3.[128]

According to the Church Fathers the Nicolaitans of Revelation 2 are named after Nicolaus, a proselyte from Antioch and one of the original deacons (Acts 6:5). Hippolytus (AD 160–235) cited 2 Timothy 2:18 and traced the heresy of baptismal resurrection to Nicolaus. Despite the fact that the patristic evidence from the days of Irenaeus and Clement of Alexandria (late second century) is unanimous in connecting the Nicolaitans with Nicolaus, Ehrhardt urges caution:

> 'Nevertheless, even this external attestation is unsufficient to prove this assumption beyond reasonable doubt. For none of the fathers shows any personal knowledge of the sect, which does not seem to have continued for very long. It can only be held as a possible hypothesis, therefore, that Nicolaus the Deacon was indeed the founder of the sect of the Nicolaitans.'[129]

[128] *Trajectories*, p. 148.
[129] A. A. T. Ehrhardt, *The Framework of the New Testament Stories* (1964), pp. 164f. Also expressing doubt about the association are R. McL. Wilson, *Gnosis and the New Testament*, p. 41, and R. Haardt, 'Gnosticism', p. 379.

CHAPTER THREE

THE PATRISTIC EVIDENCE

Until the nineteenth century we were almost entirely dependent for our knowledge of the Gnostics upon the polemical
writings of the Church Fathers of the second and third
centuries: Justin Martyr (d. 165), Irenaeus (d. *c.* 200),
Hippolytus (d. 235), Origen (d. 254), Tertullian (d. post-
200), and the later descriptions of Epiphanius (d. 403). Some
of the Fathers preserved extracts of primary Gnostic documents, but for the most part their accounts are highly polemical.

Thus scholars were not sure as to how accurate a picture of
the Gnostics we had in their writings. E. de Faye, writing
early in this century, was extremely sceptical.[1] He viewed any
information relating to movements earlier than Justin's
writing, the lost *Syntagma*, as completely legendary. He regarded the philosophical teachings of Valentinus, Basilides,
and Marcion of the second century as prior to the mythological systems of the Sethians, *etc.*, which he considered to
be later degenerations of Gnosticism.

Recent studies have placed more confidence in the patristic
information about the early development of Gnosticism in the
late first and the early second centuries.[2] The new information
from the Coptic codices found near Nag Hammadi has in
part confirmed some of the patristic materials:

'One has only to glance through the new writings to recognize, for
instance, the reliability of such an account as that given in the *Philo-
sophumena*. . . . We can also confirm the accuracy of *some* of the accounts

[1] E. de Faye, *Gnostiques et gnosticisme* (2nd ed. 1925).
[2] *E.g.* R. M. Grant in his convenient anthology of patristic references,
Gnosticism: A Sourcebook of Heretical Writings from the Early Christian Period
(1961).

of Epiphanius. . . . On the other hand, we are put somewhat upon our guard about what we were told of the great heretical teachers, not one of whom makes any explicit appearance in the writings from Chenoboskion.'[3]

Few scholars, however, are prepared with Pétrement to accept the patristic picture of Gnosticism as simply a Christian heresy.[4]

I. DOSITHEUS

According to some of the patristic accounts, the arch-Gnostic Simon Magus was taught by a Dositheus whom he later supplanted. Now Dositheus is not mentioned by Justin Martyr or by Irenaeus. The earliest reference to Dositheus can be traced back to the lost *Syntagma* of Hippolytus. The legendary Clementines claim that both Dositheus and Simon were followers of John the Baptist.

There is no indication that Dositheus himself was a Gnostic. The interesting suggestion has been made by Daniélou that Dositheus may have been a sort of Samaritan Essene who may have been the 'missing link' between the pre-Gnostic Dead Sea Scrolls and later Simonian Gnosticism.[5] The suggestion has been thoroughly discussed by Wilson, who supports the connection albeit with his wonted caution.[6]

Although the theory is intriguing, the evidence is far from clear. Caldwell has shown that there are actually two figures of Dositheus represented in the patristic traditions. As to whether the later Dositheus, who was an older contemporary of Simon's, can be considered a link between Qumran and the Gnosticism of the second century, Caldwell concludes that we can as easily affirm as deny the suggestion.[7] MacRae[8] and Schubert[9] remain sceptical.

---

[3] J. Doresse, *The Secret Books of the Egyptian Gnostics*, pp. 249–250.
[4] S. Pétrement, 'Le Colloque de Messine', p. 361.
[5] Daniélou, *The Theology of Jewish Christianity*, p. 72; *cf.* his *The Dead Sea Scrolls and Primitive Christianity* (1958), pp. 94–96.
[6] R. McL. Wilson, 'Simon, Dositheus and the Dead Sea Scrolls', *ZRGG* 9 (1957), pp. 21–30.
[7] T. Caldwell, 'Dositheos Samaritanus', *Kairos* 4 (1962), p. 117.
[8] G. W. MacRae, 'Gnosis, Christian', p. 529.
[9] K. Schubert, 'Jüdischer Hellenismus und jüdische Gnosis', *Wort und Wahrheit* 18 (1963), p. 456.

It is interesting that a sect called the Dositheans survived
perhaps to the sixth century. Theodore bar Konai identified
the Dostheans (*sic*) with the Mandaeans. Among the Nag
Hammadi texts is one which Doresse called *The Revelation of
Dositheus* or *The Three Stelae of Seth* (the latter is the
title adopted by the Coptic Gnostic Library project). Doresse,
however, points out that there were numerous figures called
Dositheus. There is no indication that this short Coptic work is
to be ascribed to the Dositheus who was the mentor of Simon.[10]

II. SIMON MAGUS

Our earliest source on Simon Magus is the eighth chapter of
Acts, where he is depicted not as a Gnostic but as a magician
who was superficially converted to Christianity. The word
magos does not actually appear in the story, but the participle
mageuōn 'practising as a magus' and the phrase *tais magiais*
'works of a magus' indicate his profession. Simon is reported
to have called himself 'the great Power of God' (Acts 8:10).

The earliest patristic writer on Simon is Justin, also himself
a native of Samaria, who mentions him in his *Apology* (chs 22
and 56) written at Rome in AD 154, and in the *Dialogue*
(ch. 120) written shortly thereafter. A lost work by Justin,
Against All Heresies, is believed to be the basis of Irenaeus's
Adversus Haereses i. 23–27. At a considerable remove in time
is the work of Hippolytus's *Refutation of All Heresies* from the
third century.

Justin tells us that Simon was a Samaritan magician from
Gitta. Was Simon a pagan from the area of Samaria or was
he a member of the Samaritans, who as quasi-Jews revere the
Pentateuch and still perform the Passover sacrifice on Mount
Gerizim? Cerfaux believes that Simon came from the pagan
milieu of Samaria. Quispel, on the other hand, believes that
Simon was a member of the 'heretical' Jewish sect of the
Samaritans. However, no unambiguous traces of Gnosticism
can be demonstrated in the later Samaritan documents such
as the *Memar Marqah* (fourth century AD) despite efforts to
discover them.[11]

[10] J. Doresse, *op. cit.*, pp. 188–190.
[11] R. Trotter, *Gnosticism and Memar Marqah* (1964), p. 17: 'It does not

According to Justin, Simon came to Rome under Claudius (AD 41–54) and was honoured as a holy god for his magical miracles by a statue on the island in the Tiber with the inscription SIMONI DEO SANCTO. It seems that Justin had been misinformed about what was actually an inscription to a Sabine deity, as in 1574 a fragment to Semo Sancus was found on the island with the inscription SEMONI SANCO DEO. In the apocryphal *Acts of Peter* (AD 190) and the Pseudo-Clementines (third century) Simon challenges Peter by his magical feats at Rome. The latter causes Simon to plummet from his flight in the air!

Justin reports that the Samaritans regarded Simon as a god 'above every principality and authority and power' (*cf.* Eph. 1:21). He also writes that Simon was accompanied by a certain Helen, an erstwhile prostitute from Tyre, who was called his *Ennoia* or First Thought. Justin and Irenaeus relate that Simon claimed that this Thought leaped forth from him in the beginning and generated angels by whom the world was made. These angels, however, seized her and held her captive. She was prevented from returning to him but was transmigrated from age to age, *e.g.* as Helen of Troy and as the lost sheep of the Gospels. It was to rescue her that Simon came disguised as a man, and also to offer men salvation through his knowledge. According to Irenaeus (*Adv. Haer.* i. 23) Simon taught that he was the one 'who was to appear among the Jews as Son, would descend in Samaria as Father, and would come among the other nations as Holy Spirit'. Since the Old Testament prophets were inspired by the evil angels, Simonians could disregard the law for 'by his (Simon's) grace men are saved, and not by just works' (*cf.* Eph. 2:8–9).

The Church Fathers from Irenaeus to Eusebius held that Simon was the one from whom all heresies originated. There

---

appear possible to discard entirely the suggestion that the writer of *Memar Marqah* knew about or was influenced by Gnostic thought. The belief, however, may be retained that the case for the existence of Gnostic ideas in *Memar Marqah* has been overstated, and even exaggerated.' Trotter's examples of possible Gnostic allusions are not convincing. J. Bowman, *Samaritanische Probleme* (1967), claims that the *Memar Marqah* contains a mixture of orthodox Samaritanism and the 'gnosis' of Dositheus.

is unanimous testimony that Simon is the first individual who was designated a Gnostic, and that Simonianism is the earliest form of Gnosticism recognized by the patristic sources. The questions which may be raised at this point are: (1) How much of the teachings ascribed to Simon by Justin and Irenaeus are teachings of the master himself and not later developments of his disciples? (2) Was Simon a Gnostic before his contact with Christianity? (3) If so, what kind of Gnosticism did he represent?

Haenchen, for one, has argued that Simon was a full-fledged Gnostic before he came into contact with Christianity.[12] He holds that if Helen were a historic figure, her appellation as Simon's *Ennoia* would have been based on a myth which must have been still earlier than Simon. The fact that the title 'the Great Power' has mythological connotations in Justin, Irenaeus, and Hippolytus must mean, according to Haenchen, that the title in Acts and in Luke's source must also have had such a connotation. Haenchen's view is supported by Schmithals,[13] and by Schenke.[14] Jonas is inclined to accept the testimony of the Church Fathers, though he does not believe that we can place 'the burden of having started the mighty gnostic tide on the frail shoulders of the very localized Samaritan group'.[15]

The main objection to viewing Simon as a representative of a fully developed Gnosticism is the fact that Acts, our earliest account, portrays Simon as a magician rather than as a Gnostic.[16] Haenchen argues that this only means that the New Testament tradition has degraded Simon from a divine

[12] E. Haenchen, 'Gab es eine vorchristliche Gnosis?' *ZThK* 49 (1952), pp. 316–349.

[13] W. Schmithals, *The Office of Apostle*, p. 137.

[14] H.-M. Schenke, 'Die Gnosis', in J. Leipoldt and W. Grundmann (eds), *Umwelt des Christentums* I (1965), p. 491. In fact, Haenchen's view has hardly been challenged in Germany until the penetrating criticisms of K. Beyschlag, 'Zur Simon-Magus-Frage', *ZThK* 68 (1971), pp. 395–426.

[15] *OG*, pp. 103, 108; and in J. P. Hyatt (ed.), *The Bible in Modern Scholarship*, p. 292.

[16] K. Beyschlag, *op. cit.*, p. 406: 'Niemand, der den Simon-Magus-Bericht in Apg 8 unbefangen liest, würde von sich auf den Gedanken kommen, hinter dem puren samaritanischen Magier auch nur die Andeutung jener gnostischen Erlösergottheit zu vermuten, wenn es nicht eben Irenäus und der Chor der antignostischen Väter seit dem 2. Jahrhundert ausdrücklich behaupten würden.'

redeemer into a mere sorcerer.[17] As Wilson points out, Haenchen's solution involves 'assumptions regarding the reliability of Acts which not every scholar would be prepared to entertain'.[18] Talbert disputes Haenchen's reading into the Acts passage a Gnostic or mythological sense to the designation of Simon as 'the Great Power'.[19] Pétrement notes that nothing in Acts indicates that Simon was a Gnostic, and that in any case nothing proves that he had been a Gnostic before his encounter with Christianity.[20]

Wilson, who unlike Haenchen does not eliminate the references to Christianity in the heresiologists' account of Simon, concludes:

'It is clear . . . that Simon's system is nothing more or less than an assimilation of imperfectly understood Christian doctrines to a fundamentally pagan scheme. Something is due to Stoicism, something to the Orient, something to Christianity, but the Christian elements play a relatively small part. Several features of later Gnostic thought are already present (unless they have been read back into the theory), such as the conception of emanations, the idea that the world is the creation of inferior powers, and that there is in it an element of the divine imprisoned and awaiting deliverance.'[21]

Daniélou believes that Simonian gnosis gives us an example of pre-Christian Jewish Gnosticism. In particular, the radical opposition between the world of the angels and the world of the Saviour – an ontological dualism foreign both to Judaism and to Jewish Christianity – is the properly Gnostic element.[22] Quispel, although he doubts whether Simon himself was fully a Gnostic, thinks that the heterodox Judaism represented by Simonian gnosis was the seedbed which produced Gnosticism. He points out that there are elements common to later Gnosticism in Simonianism and yet Simon's teaching is simpler than that found in the *Apocryphon of John* (second century).[23]

---

[17] E. Haenchen, *op. cit.*, p. 348: 'Simon is also nicht vom Zauberer zum göttlichen Erlöser aufgestiegen, sondern in der christlichen Tradition vom göttlichen Erlöser zum blossen Zauberer degradiert worden.'

[18] R. McL. Wilson, *Gnosis and the New Testament*, p. 49.

[19] C. H. Talbert, *Luke and the Gnostics*, p. 83.

[20] S. Pétrement, 'La notion de gnosticisme', p. 391, and 'Le Colloque de Messine', p. 367.

[21] R. McL. Wilson, *The Gnostic Problem* (1958), p. 100.

[22] J. Daniélou, *The Theology of Jewish Christianity*, p. 73.

[23] G. Quispel, 'Gnosis', *Vox Theologica* 39 (1969), p. 32.

Foerster notes the following points which distinguish Simon from the later Gnostics: (1) Simon himself claimed to be divine; (2) the followers of Simon were to be freed through the recognition of Simon and not through any self-knowledge.[24]

Cerfaux on the basis of his extensive studies of Simonianism concluded that the religion of Simon was in its beginnings not fundamentally Gnostic but was a 'gnosis of pagan myth and magic'. The Gnostic themes developed only later among his followers and were then attributed to Simon by the Church Fathers.[25]

Simon was followed by a fellow-Samaritan, Menander, who came from the village of Kapparetaia. He later taught at Antioch towards the end of the first century, and persuaded his followers that they would not die. Like Simon and unlike later Gnostic teachers, Menander himself claimed to be the saviour. In Justin's time (c. 150) it seemed that almost all the Samaritans had become followers of Simon, and there were still some devoted followers of Menander who believed that they would not die. But by the year 178 Celsus no longer attributed any importance to the Simonians, and Origen (185–254) knew only about thirty Simonians. As to the followers of Menander they did not continue very long. As Grant points out, 'The reason we hear little of this system at a later date is obvious; time and mortality conspired to refute it.'[26]

III. THE APOPHASIS MEGALE

In 1842 the Bibliothèque Royale received a group of fourteenth- to fifteenth-century manuscripts from Mount Athos in Greece. Among them was a manuscript published in 1851 by Emmanuel Miller under the title *Origenis Philosophymena* and ascribed by later writers to Hippolytus (AD 160–

---

[24] W. Foerster, 'Die "Ersten Gnostiker" Simon und Menander', in *OG*, p. 195: 'Es ist noch keine Gnosis im Sinne der Selbsterfassung als im Wesenskern göttlich.'

[25] L. Cerfaux, 'La gnose simonienne', *RechSR* 15 (1925), pp. 489–511; 16 (1926), pp. 5–20, 265–285, 481–503.

[26] R. M. Grant, 'The Earliest Christian Gnosticism', *Church History* 22 (1953), p. 87.

235) of Rome. Though the attribution to Hippolytus is disputed by some, it is generally regarded as his *Refutations* known from references by Eusebius and Jerome. The composition of the work is dated *c.* AD 230. Among the materials in the manuscript is a short notice on Simon and a collection of fragments known as the *Apophasis Megalē* ('the Great Revelation'), attributed to Simon. Hippolytus in book vi of his *Refutations* had included materials from a Simonian work cited as the *Apophasis Megalē*. From a literary analysis, Frickel has concluded that this material is not an excerpt but a reproduction of a paraphrase of the original *Apophasis*.[27]

Until recently most scholars, including G. Salmon, A. von Harnack, H. Stähelin, M. Nilsson, and L. Cerfaux, considered the Great Revelation to be a later work of Simon's disciples because of its strongly philosophic character. For example, Schenke regards the distinctly philosophic systems of Simon and of Basilides described by Hippolytus in books vi-vii of his *Refutations* to be 'quite obviously later and secondary'.[28]

In the past few years there has been an effort to rehabilitate the Great Revelation as a genuine work of Simon himself. Some even view it as evidence for a developed pre-Christian Gnosticism. Pokorný, for example, cites it as one of his evidences of a non-Christian Gnosticism.[29] Haenchen, by excising the three or four New Testament citations found in the fragments known to us, argues that the document is non-Christian. The fact that it is a philosophic system means for Haenchen that it presupposes an even earlier system which was mythological on the principle that the philosophical is always later than the mythological.[30] The fact that in the Great Revelation Simon appears only as a revealer and not as a redeemer and that Helen is no longer mentioned also points back to an original work of Simon which has been demythologized. Haenchen writes: 'However one must thereby not

[27] J. Frickel, 'Die Apophasis Megale, eine Grundschrift der Gnosis?' in *SSR*, pp. 37–49; *Die 'Apophasis Megale' in Hippolyt's Refutatio (VI 9–18)* (1968).
[28] H.-M. Schenke, 'Hauptprobleme der Gnosis', *Kairos* 7 (1965), p. 119.
[29] P. Pokorný, *Die Epheserbrief*, p. 41; *cf.* P. Pokorný, 'Gnosis als Weltreligion und als Häresie', *Numen* 16 (1969), p. 51.
[30] E. Haenchen, 'Gab es eine vorchristliche Gnosis?', pp. 336ff.

forget that the basic Gnostic understanding of man and the world, even if weakened, is still ever present in the Great Revelation.' Therefore as to the question of whether there was a pre-Christian Gnosticism one may answer: 'There was a pre-Christian Gnosticism. It was mythological.'[31]

Schmithals also argues that the system of the Great Revelation is the oldest handed down under the name of Simon, and that the legendary historization of Simon is a later development. The fact that the Great Revelation still shows 'no Christian influences' speaks for its antiquity. Schmithals concedes that the system of the Great Revelation knows nothing at all of a genuine dualism or of a heavenly Redeemer figure.[32] In his reconstruction of the mission of Simon he reads back into Simon's task the call of the Redeemer to gather all the pneumatics out of the world, which is a gratuitous assumption.[33]

A major attempt to demonstrate that the Great Revelation is a genuine work of Simon is a monograph by Salles-Dabadie.[34] Unlike Haenchen, however, Salles-Dabadie holds that the document is a witness to a primitive, philosophical Gnosticism, and not a demythologized witness to a developed pre-Christian Gnosticism. He notes that the Greek of the text is inexact, that many concepts are borrowed in an eclectic way from Stoicism without the technical vocabulary of the Stoics, and that the Old Testament is freely interpreted. The teachings of the Great Revelation differ from classical Gnosticism in several respects: (1) As a good disciple of Hellenistic philosophy the author finds that the cosmos is not evil but beautiful.[35] (2) As a corollary the author betrays no contempt for the body, which is considered to be as divine as the cosmos. (3) One does not find the usual concepts or the technical vocabulary of Gnosticism. Salles-Dabadie therefore concludes that the Great Revelation is a genuine work of Simon which contains 'la gnose archaïque et rudimentaire'.[36]

[31] Ibid., p. 349.
[32] W. Schmithals, The Office of Apostle, p. 160.
[33] Ibid., pp. 165–166.
[34] J. M. A. Salles-Dabadie, Recherches sur Simon le Mage, I: L'Apophasis Megalè (1969).
[35] Ibid., p. 109.
[36] Ibid., p. 143.

In a sharp criticism of Salles-Dabadie's analysis, which he regards as characterized by naïveté, Beyschlag holds that Simon's teaching is not Gnosticism.[37] The latter moreover rejects as misguided the recent attempts to resurrect Simon's reputation as an early Gnostic or as a representative of pre-Christian Gnosticism, and reconfirms Cerfaux's earlier judgment. The historical Simon is the magician portrayed in Acts and not the arch-Gnostic depicted by the Church Fathers. The patristic Simon represents a development which is dependent upon the Christian Gnosticism of the second century.[38]

Doresse has pointed out that there are two treatises in the Nag Hammadi corpus which seem to be apparently similar to the Great Revelation. They are: (1) *The Treatise on the Triple Epiphany, on the Prōtennoïa of Threefold Form*, which is also called *A Sacred Scripture Composed by the Father in a Perfect Gnosis* (IX. 34 according to Doresse's enumeration; according to the revised listing *CG* XIII. 1, and titled by the Coptic Gnostic Library project *Discourse of the Three Appearances*). (2) *The Sense of Understanding, the Thought of the Great Power* (VI. 22 according to Doresse; now *CG* VI. 4, and titled *The Concept of Our Great Power*). Both of these treatises are as yet unpublished.[39]

IV. IGNATIUS

Ignatius was the bishop of Antioch in Syria, who between AD 108–117 wrote seven letters – to Smyrna, to Polycarp, to

[37] K. Beyschlag, 'Zur Simon-Magus-Frage', p. 415: 'Und wenn sich der historische Simon wirklich in – sagen wir – "magischer Identifikation" mit dem höchsten Gott den Namen "die grosse Kraft" zugelegt haben sollte, so ist das noch lange kein Gnostizismus.'

[38] *Ibid.*, pp. 424–425: 'Das heisst: Weder war der historische Magus der Erzketzer, zu dem ihn die Kirchenväter und neuerdings wieder die moderne Wissenschaft gemacht haben, noch ist das, was wir bei Irenäus als älteste Form eines simonianisch-gnostichen Systems vor Augen haben, ein besonders ursprüngliches Gebilde, vielmehr ein sekundäres, auf Simon Magus überpflanztes Kunst und Konkurrenzprodukt zum gleichzeitigen christlichen Gnostizismus, wobei eine besondere Affinität zu den valentinianischen Gruppen bestehen dürfte. . . . Schliesslich aber gibt as auch keine "vorchristliche Christusgnosis" oder ähnliches.'

[39] J. Doresse, *The Secret Books*, pp. 329ff.; cf. 'The Coptic Gnostic Library', *NovTest* 12 (1970), pp. 83–85. Beyschlag, p. 414, who had access

the Ephesians, to Magnesia, to Philadelphia, to Tralles, and to the Romans – as he travelled through Asia Minor to Rome to be martyred there. Earlier critics had questioned the genuineness of these letters since they felt that the opponents depicted were representatives of a developed Gnosticism to be dated after the time of Marcion in the middle of the second century. Lightfoot, however, decisively demonstrated that the letters are quite genuine.

Still a disputed question is whether Ignatius was contending with one or two sets of opponents: (1) against Judaizers and (2) against Docetic Gnostics, or against a combined front of Judaizing Gnostics. Bartsch, Talbert, and Molland argue that only one set of opponents was involved.[40] Corwin, on the other hand, distinguishes between the Docetists, and Judaizers who emphasized the law and considered Christ primarily as a teacher.[41]

Of more interest to our study is the question of whether the opponents of Ignatius were representatives of a developed Gnosticism which had influenced the thinking of Ignatius himself. Scholars of the Religionsgeschichtliche Schule have since Bousset and Reitzenstein sought to demonstrate Gnostic influence in Ignatius's writings.

> 'In the opinion of all the scholars of the religious-historical school . . . there stands in the background of Ignatius' thought an Iranian myth that has resulted in a complex group of influences – a pre-Valentinian form of gnosis, the fully articulated myth of the Mandaean redeemer, and various sorts of Syrian-Christian gnosis, some of which have already penetrated the Christian world-view and preaching.'[42]

W. Bauer in his handbook (1920) on the letters of Ignatius believed that he could detect Gnostic elements in them. But it was in particular the full-length study of H. Schlier published in 1929 that was the major work which attempted to demonstrate the influence of pre-Valentinian and Mandaean-

---

to the unpublished English translation by C. J. de Catanzaro of *CG* VI. 4, finds nothing in the treatise which relates it either with Simon Magus or with Simonian Gnosticism.

[40] E. Molland, 'The Heretics Combatted by Ignatius of Antioch', *Journal of Ecclesiastical History* 5 (1954), pp. 1–6.

[41] V. Corwin, *St. Ignatius and Christianity in Antioch*, p. 60.

[42] *Ibid.*, p. 11.

type Gnosticism in Ignatius.[43] Schlier thought that he was able to detect a number of the motifs of the Gnostic Redeemer myth in the Letter to the Ephesians 19. In this passage he takes the word *aiōn* not in the temporal sense of 'ages' but in the sense of spiritual powers. By excising Ephesians 19:2b he is able to read the passage as the hidden descent, the manifestation to men, and then the ascent of the Gnostic Redeemer. Schlier further sees the various images Ignatius used not as mere metaphors but as reflections of the Redeemer myth. 'Thus since in the language of gnosticism a reference to "sweet odor" means gnosis or revealed knowledge, so Ignatius' declaration that Christ received the ointment on his head in order to "breathe incorruption" on the church should be read in that sense.'[44] A later work by H.-W. Bartsch was critical of the use made by Schlier of the Gnostic Redeemer myth as the key to Ignatius's thought, but also saw Gnostic influence involved in Ignatius's concept of the unity of God.[45] Bartsch attempted to distinguish between the Redeemer myth and church tradition which Ignatius had fused together.

A major study which has criticized the methods and the conclusions of Schlier and Bartsch is the previously cited monograph of V. Corwin. She criticizes the atomistic method of the History of Religions School in extracting figures of speech out of context and then reading later mythological meanings into them. She points out that, 'The test of meaning must be whether the gnostic meanings are consistent with *all* Ignatius says, and it is particularly difficult to see that his view of the church fits neatly into gnostic ideas.'[46] Corwin concludes that though Ignatius was indeed confronted with Docetic Gnostics, he himself was not directly influenced by Gnosticism. Instead Ignatius emphasized the historic elements of Christianity. She also concludes that his opponents do not betray a fully developed Gnosticism, but only a rudimentary form of the heresy:

'His own freedom, and what he reveals of the thought of his docetic opponents, suggests that in his time there was no clear-cut single move-

[43] H. Schlier, *Religionsgeschichtliche Untersuchungen zu den Ignatiusbriefen* (1929). [44] V. Corwin, *op. cit.*, p. 199.
[45] H.-W. Bartsch, *Gnostisches Gut und Gemeindetradition bei Ignatius von Antiochien* (1940). [46] Corwin, p. 215.

ment that could be defined as gnostic, certainly not of a Mandaean sort, but that there were, rather, varieties of thought which could more properly be called protognostic.'[47]

In agreement with Corwin's estimate of Ignatius are Grant,[48] Turner,[49] Barth,[50] and Neill, who writes: 'There is no trace in Ignatius of Gnosticism in its later and developed form, as we find it about the middle of the second century; he is concerned with docetism – the denial that Jesus had really come in the flesh – and with the idea that the humanity of the Redeemer was only an appearance.'[51]

[47] *Ibid.*, p. viii.
[48] R. M. Grant, 'The Earliest Christian Gnosticism', p. 96.
[49] H. E. W. Turner, *The Pattern of Christian Truth*, p. 59.
[50] M. Barth, 'A Chapter on the Church', p. 138, n. 16: 'H. Jonas' *Gnosis und spätantiker Geist*, H. Schlier's and H.-W. Bartsch's books on the Ignatian letters scarcely give satisfactory evidence for the contrary assumption (that the Gnostic redeemer myth existed before the second century).'
[51] S. Neill, *The Interpretation of the New Testament 1861–1961* (1964), p. 52.

CHAPTER FOUR

THE HERMETIC EVIDENCE

The Hermetica are Greek texts from Egypt preserved in manuscripts of the fourteenth century and later. In Roman times the ancient Egyptian god of wisdom, Thoth, was identified with Hermes Trismegistus. The Hermetica include materials which are astrological, magical, philosophical, and religious. The first tractate of the Hermetic Corpus is called *Poimandres* from the name of the god who reveals to his prophet the origin of the universe and the way of salvation.[1] The Hermetica were among the first sources to be mined for possible evidence of pre-Christian Gnosticism.

I. REITZENSTEIN'S POIMANDRES

In 1904 Reitzenstein published his work entitled *Poimandres: Studien zur Griechisch-ägyptischen und frühchristlichen Literatur.* In this he attempted to prove that the Poimandres sect represented a development which had been founded about the time of the birth of Christ.[2] From the tractate *Poimandres* he worked out a Gnostic Redeemer myth in which the *Anthrōpos* or Primal Man – a concept with roots in the Iranian Gayomart – functions as a redeemer.

Bousset supported Reitzenstein's early dating of the Hermetica. He wrote: '. . . Reitzenstein is still correct in his attempt to trace this literature in its foundations and oldest component parts back into the first century.'[3] He also sought

---

[1] For a detailed exposition of the teachings of Poimandres, see C. H. Dodd, *The Bible and the Greeks* (1935; repr. 1964).

[2] R. Reitzenstein, *Poimandres*, p. 248.

[3] W. Bousset, *Kyrios Christos*, p. 16.

to confirm Reitzenstein's presentation by reconstructing the myth of the Redeemer from the experience of the believer as described in the latter half of the tractate *Poimandres*. Cerfaux accepted the Hermetic writings as proof of the existence of a pre-Christian, pagan Gnosticism.[4]

C. Colpe has now written a devastating critique of the reconstructions of Reitzenstein and Bousset. He points out that the tractate *Poimandres* does not as a matter of fact present the Anthropos as a Redeemer.[5] Reitzenstein lamely explained this lack on the ground that the Egyptian author preferred to 'destroy the myth', and argued that since Christian Gnosticism connected Jesus and the Primal Man, the latter must have originally been a redeemer. Bousset's reconstruction is also shown to rest on the quite disputable presupposition that the heavenly Adam is to be identified with the *Nous*, that is, the Redeemer with what was to be redeemed.[6] Recent studies have suggested that the Primal Man myth in the Hermetica is not so much a refraction of Iranian thought as Reitzenstein thought, as it is of Jewish speculation.[7]

II. THE GNOSTICISM OF THE HERMETICA

Depending upon one's definition of Gnosticism, scholars are divided as to whether to grant the Hermetica a fully Gnostic status. Festugière has emphasized the eclectic Middle Platonic character of these texts. Van Moorsel has called them 'semi-Gnostic'. He points out that they have no saviour, and that they are only mildly dualistic.[8] Grant would hold that the Hermetica are not Gnostic.[9]

On the other hand, Quispel considers the Hermetica to be an example of 'vulgar Egyptian Gnosticism'.[10] They do reflect a saving *gnōsis* of the 'self' and their cosmogony leans in the direction of Gnosticism. The recent discovery of some

---

[4] L. Cerfaux, 'Gnose préchrétienne', col. 671.
[5] C. Colpe, *Die religionsges. Schule*, pp. 16ff.
[6] *Ibid.*, pp. 18ff.
[7] *Cf.* G. Quispel, 'Der gnostische Anthropos und die jüdische Tradition', *Eranos Jahrbuch* 22 (1953), pp. 195–234.
[8] G. van Moorsel, *The Mysteries of Hermes Trismegistus* (1955).
[9] R. M. Grant, *Gnosticism and Early Christianity*, p. 148.
[10] G. Quispel, *Gnosis als Weltreligion*, pp. 9–10, 28–29.

Hermetic tractates in the Nag Hammadi library proves, at any rate, that the Gnostics could and did make use of such writings.[11]

III. THE DATE OF THE HERMETICA

In contrast to the early date for the *Poimandres* championed by Reitzenstein, Bousset, and Kroll[12] most scholars would today date the composition of the Hermetica to the second century and later. Dodd, who notes striking parallels with the Gospel of John and who believes that the *Poimandres* antedates Valentinus, does argue that 'there is no evidence which would conflict with a date early in the second century or even late in the first century' for the composition of the *Poimandres*.[13]

Other scholars would date the Hermetica later. Pétrement, who would associate the Hermetica with the Chaldean Oracles and the teaching of the philosopher Numenius as similar examples of non-Christian Gnosticism, would attribute these documents to the period of Valentinus's stay in Rome (AD 138 to 165).[14] Ménard would date the *Poimandres* between AD 100 and 300.[15] The three greatest scholars of the Hermetica – W. Scott,[16] A.-J. Festugière,[17] and A. D. Nock[18] – agree that the present form of the material must be dated in the second to fourth centuries AD and that knowledge of the sect's earlier history is unavailable.

In consequence of this consensus regarding the late date of the Hermetica, Munck writes:

'There have in fact been attempts in the past to prove the pre-Christian nature of Gnosticism by dating gnostic writings in the period

---

[11] J. Doresse, 'Hermès et la gnose à propos de l'Asclepius copte', *NovTest* 1 (1956), pp. 54–69.

[12] J. Kroll, *Die Lehren des Hermes Trismegistos* (1914), p. 389.

[13] C. H. Dodd, *The Bible and the Greeks*, p. 209.

[14] S. Pétrement, 'La notion de gnosticisme', p. 418; 'Le Colloque de Messine', p. 370.

[15] J.-É. Ménard, 'Le "Chant de la perle" ', *RevSR* 42 (1968), p. 292, n. 5.

[16] W. Scott and A. S. Ferguson, *Hermetica* I–IV (1924–1936).

[17] A.-J. Festugière, *La révélation d'Hermès Trismégiste* I–IV (1944–1954).

[18] A. D. Nock and A.-J. Festugière, *Hermès Trismégiste* I–IV (1945–1954).

before the New Testament writings were composed. This was attempted, for instance, in the case of the Hermetic literature, which, however, was finally proved to be later.'[19]

[19] J. Munck, 'The New Testament and Gnosticism', p. 226.

CHAPTER FIVE

THE IRANIAN EVIDENCE

I. THE IRANIAN SOURCES

The problems involved in reconstructing from Iranian or Persian sources the religious concepts involved in Zoroastrianism and in Mithraism,[1] to say nothing of a hypothetical Iranian Redeemer myth, are notorious. The periods of Persian history which are of interest to us are: (1) the Achaemenid Empire (sixth century BC to Alexander's conquest in the fourth century BC); (2) the Parthian period (from 250 BC to AD 226); and (3) the Sassanian period (from AD 226 to the Muslim conquest of Iran in the year AD 652). As far as the development of Iranian religions are concerned, we have: (1) the pre-Zoroastrian Iranian polytheism; (2) Zoroaster's reforms (628–551 BC); (3) the uncertain Zurvanite heresy of the Parthian period; (4) the classical dualistic Zoroastrianism of the Sassanids; and (5) the later developments with the emigration of the Parsees to India after the Muslim conquest.

For the earliest period that concerns us, the Achaemenid Empire, we have primarily royal inscriptions in Old Persian cuneiform, which give us very little religious information apart from a suggestion that the Achaemenids after Darius accepted Zoroastrianism.[2] There are very few Iranian texts from the Parthian period as the Hellenized Arsacid dynasty used Greek for the most part. This means that for the key pre-Christian and early Christian period of the Parthians we have virtually no direct evidence. Zaehner writes: 'Of the fortunes

[1] For the Mithraic evidence, see below, ch. 7, III, 'The Apocalypse of Adam'.
[2] R. G. Kent, *Old Persian* (1950; 2nd ed. 1953). *Cf.* E. Herzfeld, *Archaeological History of Iran* (1935).

of the Zoroastrians during the centuries of Seleucid and Parthian dominion we know practically nothing. . . .'[3]

The Zoroastrian sources are for the most part preserved only in the late recensions of the Parsees. Of these, only the *Gathas* can be traced back to Zoroaster's time.[4] Most of the Zoroastrian texts are Pahlavi or Middle Persian texts dated to the ninth century AD. It is possible that parts of the *Avesta* may date back to the third or even the fourth century BC, but all the Pahlavi texts such as the *Bundahishn*, the *Denkart*, *Zadsparam*, *Arda-Viraf*, etc. have not only been contaminated by misunderstanding of the Parthian materials in the Sassanid period, but are also under the suspicion of deliberate apologetic changes made by the minority Parsee community in India after their migration from Iran in the seventh–eighth centuries AD.[5] Since the early Avesta is so amorphous that almost anything can be proved from it, Frye points out that 'the basic Iranian sources for deriving influences are the ninth century AD. Pahlavi books, the syncretistic nature of which can easily be imagined'.[6]

Under Iranian sources we may also include the Manichaean fragments found in Turfan in Turkestan in the early twentieth century. In addition to texts written in the native Uighur and in Chinese, texts were found in the Iranian dialects of Sogdian and Parthian.

II. REITZENSTEIN AND THE IRANIAN REDEEMER MYTH

Writing in the early twentieth century, Reitzenstein took seriously the classical tradition which emphasized the

[3] R. C. Zaehner, *The Dawn and Twilight of Zoroastrianism* (1961), p. 22; *cf.* J. Neusner, *A History of the Jews in Babylonia*, I: *The Parthian Period* (1969), p. 19: 'As to Parthian religion, evidence is very scanty indeed.'

[4] *Cf.* K. G. Kuhn, 'Die Sektenschrift und die iranische Religion', *ZThK* 49 (1952), p. 310, who recognizes this: 'For the Gathas of Zarathustra are the only parts, which the Iranologists agree, that go back with certainty to such an ancient time.' For a translation of the *Gathas*, see J. Duchesne-Guillemin, *The Hymns of Zarathustra* (1952; paperback 1963).

[5] For some of the problems in dating materials in the Pahlavi texts, see H. W. Bailey, *Zoroastrian Problems in the Ninth-Century Books* (1943), pp. 149–177.

[6] R. N. Frye, 'Reitzenstein and Qumrân Revisited by an Iranian', *HTR* 55 (1962), p. 262.

contributions of Zoroaster to Greek thought, in particular to Plato. A. Götze lent support to this supposition by comparing a fourth-century BC Greek text, the *peri hebdomadōn*, with ninth-century AD Iranian texts – the *Bundahishn* and the *Denkart* – and concluding that Iran had been the source of the Greek teaching in which each part of the human body corresponds to a part of the universe.[7] Though a few modern Iranian writers still subscribe to the idea that Iran influenced Greek thinking,[8] most scholars today feel that the researches of J. Kerschensteiner, *Platon und der Orient* (1945), and others such as W. Koster have refuted such romantic notions.[9]

Just before World War I Reitzenstein heard about the newly discovered documents from Turkestan from C. F. Andreas. In 1918 he received notes on the Parthian texts from F. W. Müller. Reitzenstein used these materials in his book, *Das iranische Erlösungsmysterium* (1921), in seeking to prove that there had been a salvation mystery religion in ancient Iran. At first he did not realize that these texts were Manichaean. Mani, of course, lived in the third century AD. When this fact became known, Reitzenstein and his followers claimed that the Manichaean texts must have preserved some very ancient Iranian traditions which were not indebted to post-Christian Gnosticism, but which must have been the foundations of a pre-Christian Gnosticism.

On the basis of the Manichaean documents and some Zoroastrian texts, Reitzenstein constructed his thesis of an ancient Iranian origin of Gnosticism. The Iranian concept of the Gayomart or Primal Man was held to be the prototype of the teaching of the Anthropos in the Hermetica, the Jewish apocalyptic Adam, the Son of Man in the Gospels, and the Manichaean Urmensch.[10]

Kraeling has argued for the antiquity of the Gayomart

[7] A. Götze, 'Persische Weisheit in griechischen Gewande', *Zeitschrift für Indologie und Iranistik* 2 (1923), pp. 60–98, 167–177.

[8] *E.g.* R. Afnan, *Zoroaster's Influence on Greek Thought* (1965).

[9] R. N. Frye, *op. cit.*, p. 265; J. Duchesne-Guillemin, *The Western Response to Zoroaster* (1958), pp. 72–78.

[10] Such a daring reconstruction from very late Iranian sources has been severely criticized. *Cf.* R. P. Casey, 'Gnosis, Gnosticism and the New Testament', p. 54; C. H. Dodd, *The Interpretation of the Fourth Gospel*, p. 128; S. Neill, *op. cit.*, p. 160; G. Quispel in F. L. Cross, *The Jung Codex* (1955), pp. 76ff.

concept, though the most extensive account is found in the Pahlavi *Bundahishn*. His line of reasoning is as follows: (1) The *Bundahishn* is based on a lost Avestan text, the *Damdat Nask*, known in Sassanid times.[11] (2) The appearance of the Gayomart in so many portions of the Sassanid *Avesta* 'demands' that 'he be regarded as an element of the tradition current in Parthian times'.[12] (3) He is mentioned by name 'if nothing more' in the Yashts of the 'Younger Avesta'. (4) 'Though there is no incontrovertible direct evidence in support of this view', it seems that the Gayomart concept antedates even the Parthian period.[13] (5) *Gatha* 3·6 = *Yasna* 30·6 is considered an allusion to Gayomart, and the soul of the ox who is identified in Pahlavi tradition as the animal counterpart of the Gayomart also appears in the *Gathas*. It may be seen that each step backward in time becomes a more tenuously supported extension of the argument.

The only contemporary scholar who has continued to follow Reitzenstein's basic Iranian thesis – and one of the few scholars who is equally at home in Iranian and Semitic studies – is G. Widengren of Uppsala, Sweden. He remains convinced of the Iranian origins of Gnosticism. 'Particularly the dualism of Gnosticism, the figure of the saviour who is at the same time Primordial Man, and who manifests himself as salvator salvatus, and the soul's ascent to heaven are regarded by him (Widengren) as authentic Iranian theologoumena.'[14] Widengren believes that he can locate this originally Iranian material in the Hymn of the Pearl in the Syriac *Acts of Thomas*, in the Mandaean texts, in the Dead Sea Scrolls, in the Coptic Nag Hammadi treatises, and in the Manichaean texts.

Drijvers has criticized Widengren's methodology by which he is able to isolate motifs, disregarding their contexts, and concluding that wherever there are parallels there is dependence upon Iranian sources.[15] Pétrement notes that Widengren was relatively isolated in his defence of Reitzenstein's formula-

---

[11] C. H. Kraeling, *Anthropos and Son of Man* (1927), p. 91.
[12] *Ibid.*   [13] *Ibid.*, p. 92.
[14] H. J. W. Drijvers, 'The Origins of Gnosticism', p. 335. For Widengren's views, see his 'Les origines du gnosticisme', *OG*, pp. 28–60; 'Der iranische Hintergrund der Gnosis', *ZRGG* 4 (1952), pp. 97–114; *Iranisch-Semitische Kulturbegegnung in parthischer Zeit* (1960).
[15] H. J. W. Drijvers, *op. cit.*, pp. 336–337.

tions at the conference on Gnostic origins at Messina. She points out that other Iranologists are not able to discover Gnostic ideas in pre-Christian Iranian materials.[16]

Reitzenstein himself was not an Iranologist. His collaborator in writing *Studien zum antiken Synkretismus* in 1926, H. Schaeder, who was an Iranologist, later retracted some of the views he had shared with Reitzenstein. In commenting upon Reitzenstein's theory, Professor Frye, the leading American Iranologist, writes: 'What we need, however, is evidence for an autochthonous, flourishing Iranian "saviour-mystery religion" from which influences radiated to Palestine and Greece. Such evidence has not been forthcoming.'[17] He is also highly sceptical of trying to reconstruct an earlier Iranian religion from the later syncretistic *mélange* of Manichaeism. The leading British Zoroastrian scholar is quite contemptuous; R. C. Zaehner writes, 'The Iranian *Erlösungsmysterium* is largely REITZENSTEIN's invention.'[18] In a review of the report on the congress at Messina, Quispel is caustic:

'He (Widengren) admits that Reitzenstein made a serious mistake when he built his enormous theories upon certain unpublished texts, which he held to be Iranian and which were in fact Manichaean; Widengren also has ruefully to admit that there is no consistent evidence in Iran for the myth of the saved Saviour. Yet he maintains that he was always right.'[19]

The most thoroughgoing criticism of Reitzenstein's theory of a Redeemed Redeemer myth has come from C. Colpe, who studied under H. Schaeder and J. Jeremias.[20] Colpe asserts that the dominance of Bultmann's synthesis based upon Reitzenstein's theories has made New Testament scholars complacently neglectful of the last thirty years of Iranian studies. Re-examining the Iranian sources themselves, he shows that Reitzenstein misunderstood certain texts, and that his formulation of the Redeemed Redeemer myth is built on a chain of unproven hypotheses. He concludes that there is no direct or indirect connection between the Iranian Gayomart of the *Avesta* and the later Gnostic views of the Redeemer.

[16] S. Pétrement, 'Le Colloque de Messine', p. 358.
[17] R. N. Frye, *op. cit.*, p. 277.
[18] R. C. Zaehner, *op. cit.*, p. 347.
[19] Review of U. Bianchi, *OG* by G. Quispel, *JAOS* 90 (1970), p. 321.
[20] C. Colpe, *Die religionsges. Schule*, pp. 10–57, and *passim*.

It is true that the Reitzenstein–Widengren school has made a recent convert of O. Huth. Huth, however, is very uncritical and simplistic in thinking that he can neatly tie together the Essenes, Mandaeans, and primitive Christians. He believes that the same baptismal ritual binds all three groups together.[21] His understanding of this rite is indebted to Reitzenstein and Widengren.

More serious attempts have been made to connect the dualism of Iran with the dualism of Qumran through allusions to the more monotheistic form of Zoroastrianism known as Zurvanism.[22] Zurvan was the Zoroastrian god of time, and according to some sources the father of the twin spirits of Ahura-Mazda (Ormazd) and Ahriman. Zaehner has theorized that Zurvanism spread in the latter half of the Achaemenian period and became the popular religion under the Sassanids.[23] On the other hand, Frye points out that Zaehner's reconstruction is for the most part dependent upon a late Syriac source (Bar Konai) and a late Armenian source (Eznik). He therefore concludes that, 'Presumably we can assert that the Essenes existed, but a separate religion of Zurvanism with organized followers is unattested and, in my opinion, consequently a myth.'[24]

In opposition to Winston, who takes seriously the parallels between Qumran and Zurvanism and argues for Essene dependence upon Iran,[25] Neusner suggests that the parallels may have arisen from independent developments.[26] Examining the later Talmudic evidence, Neusner is not very sanguine about theories of purported Iranian influence upon Judaism:

'If we must make premature hypotheses, let me here hypothecate that Iranian "influences" on the culture and religion of Babylonian

[21] O. Huth, 'Das Mandäerproblem – das Neue Testament im Lichte der mandäischen und essenischen Quellen', *Symbolon* 3 (1962), pp. 18–38.

[22] *Cf.* K. G. Kuhn, 'Die Sektenschrift und die iranische Religion'; H. Michaud, 'Un mythe zervanite dans un des manuscrits de Qumrân', *Vetus Testamentum* 5 (1955), pp. 137–146.

[23] R. C. Zaehner, *Zurvan, A Zoroastrian Dilemma* (1955).

[24] R. N. Frye, *op. cit.*, p. 258.

[25] D. Winston, 'The Iranian Component in the Bible, Apocrypha, and Qumran', *History of Religions* 5 (1966), pp. 183–216.

[26] J. Neusner, 'Jews and Judaism under Iranian Rule: Bibliographical Reflections', *History of Religions* 8 (1968), p. 160.

Jewry, and all the more so of Palestinian Jewry, have been for the most part exaggerated and overrated. Examining just what the Talmudic rabbis actually knew about Iranian culture, we can hardly be impressed by the depth of their knowledge. Some could understand Pahlavi when it was spoken but could not read it. The Talmud preserves a thoroughly garbled account of Persian festivals, and two of the three Mazdean holidays the rabbis mention were in fact days upon which taxes had to be paid, so their knowledge does not prove them to have been very profound.'[27]

III. MANICHAEISM

One of the fundamental issues which is raised by the use of the Manichaean texts by Reitzenstein and by Widengren is the question of the basic nature of Manichaeism. As it is a highly syncretistic religion, scholars have tended to regard it as either a form of Christian heresy, or as an oriental religion preserving pre-Christian Gnostic elements. Those who have favoured the first position include F. C. Baur, F. C. Burkitt, and A. D. Nock; those who have emphasized the second position have included K. Kessler, R. Reitzenstein, H. Nyberg, and G. Widengren.[28]

With the exception of the book *Shahburagan*, which was dedicated to the Sassanid king Shahpur I and written in Middle Persian, Mani himself wrote all his books in Syriac in a variant of the Palmyrene script. 'Apart from a few fragments which came to light in Egypt, all the texts in the Syriac original have disappeared.'[29]

Later Manichaean texts are found in various languages and bear varying degrees of Christian influence. They include: (1) the texts found at the beginning of the twentieth century in the oasis of Turfan in Chinese Turkestan (eighth–ninth century AD), written in Arsacid and Sassanid Pahlavi, in Sogdian, in Uighur and in Chinese; (2) more than 3,000 leaves in Coptic found at Medinet Madi in the Faiyum in Egypt in 1930, dated *c.* AD 400, close to the time when Augus-

---

[27] *Ibid.*, p. 162.
[28] K. Rudolph, 'Gnosis und Manichäismus nach den Koptischen Quellen', in *Koptologische Studien in der Deutschen Demokratischen Republik*, ed. Institut für Byzantinistik (Halle, Universität; 1965–1966), p. 156.
[29] J. P. Asmussen, 'Manichaeism', in C. J. Bleeker and G. Widengren (eds), *Historia Religionum* I: *Religions of the Past* (1969), p. 584.

tine was a Manichaean auditor; these include the *Kephalaia*, a collection of the utterances of Mani, and a set of Homilies; (3) a Psalm-book in Coptic, composed by Mani's disciple, Thomas.

Mani was born in 216 and lived until about 275. It seems that he was born near Seleucia – Ctesiphon in Babylonia. According to the Arabic writer an-Nadim (tenth century), his father Patik came from Ecbatana (Hamadan) in Media. It is possible that Mani was of princely Arsacid (Parthian) origin.

Mani's father was a member of a sect known in Arabic as the *Mughtasilah* or 'those who wash themselves'. Most writers have identified this baptizing sect with the Mandaeans, despite the fact that an-Nadim stressed the ascetic nature of the Mughtasilah. The Mandaeans are far from ascetic.[30] For example, Widengren writes: 'Our conclusion is therefore the same as that of modern research: Mani grew up in a southern Babylonian gnostic, more explicitly Mandaean, baptist community and there received impressions crucial to his future.'[31] A few scholars suggested that the baptist group to which Mani belonged in his youth were followers of Bardaisan.[32]

These identifications, however, disregard the clear notice in an-Nadim's *Fihrist* that the leader of Patik's baptist sect was known as *al-Ḥasîḥ*, *i.e.* the Arabic form of the famous Elchasai. Elchasai, who is mentioned by Hippolytus and Epiphanius, seems to have come from a Jewish-Christian background, perhaps from Transjordan.[33] He flourished during the early second century during Trajan's reign.   -

The publication in 1970 of a very important Greek codex on the life of Mani from Cologne now explicitly confirms an-Nadim's statement.[34] The new codex is one of the tiniest

[30] See E. M. Yamauchi, *Gnostic Ethics and Mandaean Origins* (hereafter abbreviated *GEMO*; 1970), pp. 35ff., pp. 45ff.

[31] G. Widengren, *Mani and Manichaeism* (1965), p. 26; *cf.* K. Rudolph, *Die Mandäer* I, p. 239; E. S. Drower, *The Secret Adam* (1960), p. xiii.

[32] H. J. W. Drijvers, *Bardaiṣan of Edessa* (1966), p. 203.

[33] E. Hennecke and W. Schneemelcher, *New Testament Apocrypha* II (hereafter abbreviated *NTA* II; 1965), pp. 745ff.

[34] See A. Henrichs and L. Koenen, 'Eine alte griechische Mani Schrift', *Zeitschrift für Papyrologie und Epigraphik* 5 (1970), pp. 97–216, plates IV–VI. Professor Richard Frye called the attention of the American Oriental

codices ever known. Its pages are only 4½ centimetres high
and 3½ centimetres wide; none the less there are twenty-three
lines to a page! The parchment dates from the fifth century,
but is no doubt a translation of an early Syriac text.

The codex quite explicitly names the founder of the sect
against which Mani rebelled as Alchasaios. Against the
repeated baptisms in water of the Elchasaites, Mani emphasized the purification of the soul through gnosis.[35] Indeed,
Mani now appears to have been not so much the founder of
a new religion, but, at least at the beginning, a reformer of the
Elchasaites.[36] If the new codex proves anything, it shows that
the Christian elements in Manichaeism are not merely
secondary accommodations to the mission of the later Manichaeans. 'The Christian elements in Manichaism already go
back in essence to the Elchasaites.'[37] Heinrichs and Koenen
conclude that: 'One will not easily be able to overestimate
the influence which this Jewish-Christian baptist sect had on
the formation of the religious concepts of Mani.'[38]

Reitzenstein's and Widengren's estimate of Manichaeism
as essentially an Iranian religion enabled them to postulate the
survival of ancient pre-Christian Gnostic elements. This over-
looks the obvious fact that Manichaeism is a late post-Christian
form of Gnosticism. Is the Manichaean Urmensch more likely
the prototype of a pre-Christian Redeemer myth or the culmination of two centuries of Gnosticism before Mani? The fundamental debt which Mani is now shown to have owed to the
Jewish-Christian Elchasaites has tilted the balance in favour
of those scholars who have viewed Manichaeism as essentially
a further development of a Christian heresy.

Although they are extant in Coptic, the Manichaean
Psalms of Thomas may be discussed here. A. Adam has
attempted to demonstrate that some of the Psalms and the
famous Hymn of the Pearl (which we shall discuss in the
following chapter) contain Parthian mythology and may

---

[35] *Ibid.*, p. 150.
[36] *Ibid.*, p. 154.
[37] *Ibid.*, p. 159.
[38] *Ibid.*, p. 160.

therefore be taken as evidences for the development of pre-Christian Gnosticism.[39]

The Coptic Manichaean Psalm-book contains some twenty psalms of Thomas, the disciple of Mani.[40] These particular psalms were composed in Syriac in the last quarter of the third century AD. T. Säve-Söderbergh has demonstrated that they incorporate some earlier Mandaean materials.[41]

Adam's novel theory is based on the assumption that the origins of Gnosticism reach back to the wisdom speculations of Judaism. He speculates that Iranian influence affected the exiles from the northern kingdom of Israel after the Assyrian deportation of 722 BC. How he can suggest that Iranian influence was more likely among these deportees than among the Judean deportees after the Babylonian invasion of 587 BC is hard to follow.[42] His arguments connecting the northern kingdom of Israel with the rise of Gnosticism are highly speculative: (1) Bar Konai called the Mandaeans Dostheans; (2) Dositheus, the teacher of Simon, was a Samaritan; (3) the prominence of the Jordan river in the Mandaean texts reminds him of the Naaman story in the Old Testament, which in turn directs him to the northern kingdom.

Comparing *Psalm of Thomas* 1 with the *Wisdom of Solomon* 18:14–16, Adam concludes that the latter must be based on the former. He believes that the *Wisdom of Solomon* was composed in Mesopotamia by exiles from northern Israel in the first century BC.[43] Accordingly, the *Wisdom of Solomon* 'may be judged as the first document of developing Gnosticism on

---

[39] A. Adam, *Die Psalmen des Thomas und das Perlenlied als Zeugnisse vorchristlicher Gnosis* (1959).

[40] C. Allberry, *A Manichaean Psalm-book* (1938).

[41] T. Säve-Söderbergh, *Studies in the Coptic Manichaean Psalm Book: Prosody and Mandaean Parallels* (1949). Colpe would date them to AD 250–275.

[42] According to A. Adam, *op. cit.*, p. 31: 'Hier war der iranische Einfluss seit langer Zeit wirksam, im Gegensatz zu der babylonischen Exilantenschaft, wo solche Einwirkungen schlecht denkbar sind.'

[43] More credible but still highly speculative is Adam's more recent suggestion that Gnosticism was created by a *Weisheitsschule* of Aramaic scribes, who over the centuries combined traditions from Zurvanism in the Achaemenid period with Hellenistic philosophy after Alexander's conquest and with Jewish elements to create Gnosticism in the first century BC. A. Adam, 'Ist die Gnosis in aramäischen Weisheitsschulen entstanden?', *OG*, pp. 291–301.

the basis of its connection with the Psalm of Thomas'.[44] This would also mean that the first Thomas psalm must contain materials prior to *Wisdom* and dated to at least the end of the second century BC.

But as Klijn points out in his review:

'If we compare these two texts (Psalm of Thomas i and Wisdom of Solomon xviii. 14–16) it is obvious that they have nothing to do with each other. In Psalm 1 darkness attacks light, after which a young boy in full armament is sent into darkness to conquer the powers of darkness. It seems that he also brings back to their original abode parts of light being captured by darkness. In Sap. Sal. nothing similar can be found.'[45]

In other words, Adam's elaborate hypothesis is but a precarious structure based on extremely tenuous parallels which have led to even more dubious conjectures.[46]

[44] A. Adam, *Die Psalmen des Thomas*, p. 33.
[45] Review of A. Adam, *Die Psalmen des Thomas* by A. F. J. Klijn in *BiOr* 19 (1962), pp. 94f.
[46] *Cf.* the critical remarks of C. Colpe, 'Die Thomaspsalmen als chronologischer Fixpunkt in der Geschichte der orientalischen Gnosis', *Jahrbuch für Antike und Christentum* 7 (1964), pp. 83ff.

CHAPTER SIX

THE SYRIAC EVIDENCE

I. THE RISE OF SYRIAC CHRISTIANITY

In the Old Testament period the most important city in Syria was the caravan oasis of Damascus, only 70 miles north-east of Galilee. Though Paul was converted on the road to Damascus, the city did not play an important role in early Christianity.[1] The most important city in Syria in the early Roman Empire lay far to the north of Damascus – the city of Antioch on the Orontes river not far from the Mediterranean. It was a Hellenistic city founded under the Seleucids. Its importance stemmed from the fact that it was the western gate of the trade route which led through the northern tier of Mesopotamia through Media and eventually to China.

Some 150 miles north-east of Antioch lay the important city of Edessa (modern Urfa), the centre of the district of Osrhoene. It has been called the 'Athens of the Orient'.[2] There was a Jewish community at Edessa. But about 140 miles east of Edessa there was an even stronger Jewish community at Nisibis. The Jews were actively involved as traders along the caravan routes. A little more than 150 miles to the south-east of Nisibis was the city of Arbela, the centre of Adiabene, an area once known as Assyria. The ruling house of Adiabene was converted to Judaism in the first century AD.

The area of Syria as it extended along the trade routes upon the arc of the 'Fertile Crescent' was an important military buffer for the Romans against the powerful Parthians, whose centre of power lay at Ctesiphon in lower Mesopotamia. Trajan had temporarily succeeded in conquering upper and

[1] W. Bauer, *Orthodoxy and Heresy*, p. 232.
[2] See J. B. Segal, *Edessa 'The Blessed City'* (1970).

lower Mesopotamia early in the second century, but his successor, Hadrian, had to relinquish control of most of the area to the Parthians.[3] Edessa, which was captured by the Romans in 116, was fully incorporated into the Roman Empire in 216.

The date at which Christianity arrived in eastern Syria and the means by which it spread are subjects which are highly disputed. Our sources of information on this topic are quite late and obviously legendary. Eusebius (i. 13; ii. 1; fourth century AD) tells of the evangelization of Edessa by one of the seventy-two disciples of Jesus, a man called Thaddaeus, as the result of correspondence between Jesus himself and King Abgar V Ukkama ('the Black'), who reigned from AD 9 to 46. This legend is further amplified in a Syriac work called *The Doctrine of Addai*, which was probably composed at Edessa in the fourth century.[4] *The Chronicle of Edessa* (*c.* AD 550), which seems to be fairly reliable, says nothing about a correspondence between Abgar and Jesus. Its first notice is dated 201, a year in which a church was destroyed in Edessa. There is also a *Chronicle of Arbela* from the sixth century. In addition to these legendary-historical materials, there are texts which were presumably composed in Syria such as the *Odes of Solomon*, the *Acts of Thomas*, the *Gospel of Thomas*, and the writings of Bardaisan (AD 154–222).

Now the association of Abgar V with the conversion of Edessa is impossible; the first Christian king of Edessa was King Abgar IX, who ruled at the end of the second century.[5] On the other hand, the promise of Jesus in the Abgar legend that Edessa would be for ever independent suggests a date for the original development of the legend before 116, and certainly before 216 when Edessa was swallowed up into the Roman Empire. Christianity had therefore spread to eastern Syria at least by the second century. From whence Christianity spread to Edessa is contested. Three points of origin have been suggested: (1) Antioch, (2) Adiabene, and (3) Palestine.

It was from Antioch that Greek-speaking Christianity

---

[3] See F. Stark, *Rome on the Euphrates* (1966).
[4] See Bauer in E. Hennecke and W. Schneemelcher, *New Testament Apocrypha* I (hereafter abbreviated *NTA* I; 1963), pp. 437ff.
[5] *Cf.* L. W. Barnard, 'The Origins and Emergence of the Church in Edessa during the First Two Centuries A.D.', *VigChr* 22 (1968), pp. 161–175.

spread to eastern Syria, according to F. C. Burkitt.[6] As evidence for this thesis Burkitt cites the tradition that Palut of Edessa was consecrated bishop by Serapion, who was bishop of Antioch AD 190–212. He also notes Epiphanius's statement that Tatian, a disciple of Justin Martyr, went back to his native Assyria after his master's death in 165. Burkitt identified the legendary Addai with Tatian, as both shared in an ascetic outlook.[7] Syriac-speaking Christianity would then have developed from the second century on. Ehlers has recently supported this thesis of the origin of Edessan Christianity with marked Hellenistic characteristics from Antioch in the second half of the second century.[8]

Others suggest that it was from Adiabene that Christianity came to Edessa, as there are some explicit references to Christianity which appear earlier in Adiabene than at Edessa. The new converts to Judaism at Adiabene would have made a fertile seedbed for Christianity. Paul Kahle argued that Pequida, the first bishop mentioned in the *Chronicle of Arbela*, can be dated to *c.* AD 100. Neusner would date the first bishop of Arbela as early as AD 123.[9] Segal, who believes that Tatian returned to his native Adiabene, not to Edessa, would suggest that Christianity took root first in Adiabene.[10] The authenticity of the *Chronicle of Arbela*, upon which the priority of Adiabene is advanced, has recently been seriously questioned.[11] In any case, Christian missionaries would have had to pass through Edessa first before reaching Adiabene. It is interesting to note that Christianity made no headway at Nisibis, between Edessa and Arbela, until about 300 because of the very strong influence of Jewish Tannaitic teachers there.[12]

[6] F. C. Burkitt, *Early Eastern Christianity* (1904).

[7] *Cf.* J. C. L. Gibson, 'From Qumran to Edessa', *Annual of Leeds University Oriental Society* 5 (1963–1965), p. 28.

[8] B. Ehlers, 'Kann das Thomasevangelium aus Edessa stammen?' *NovTest* 12 (1970), p. 293.

[9] J. Neusner, *A History of the Jews* I, p. 182.

[10] J. B. Segal, *op. cit.*, p. 69. *Cf.* H. J. W. Drijvers, *Bardaiṣan*, p. 215: 'It is therefore generally assumed that Christianity in Edessa is of Jewish origin and came there from the East, from Adiabene.'

[11] H. J. W. Drijvers, 'Edessa und das jüdische Christentum', *VigChr* 24 (1970), pp. 30–31.

[12] J. Neusner, *op. cit.*, I, pp. 182–183.

Most recently a number of scholars, including Gibson, Koester, and Quispel, have advocated an early first-century derivation of Christianity directly from Jewish Christians in Palestine. The researches of A. Vööbus have underscored the Encratite nature of the early Syrian church. That is, these Christians believed that abstinence from marital relations was a condition for baptism. Their ascetic ideas are traced by Gibson and others to Essene refugees who may have survived the disaster of the destruction of their monastery at Qumran in AD 68 and who may have then been converted to Christianity.[13] The fact that Addai stayed at the house of a Palestinian Jew, Tobias bar Tobias, is held to be a genuine tradition in the Addai story, linking the Edessene mission with Palestine.

Drijvers, however, is critical of the thesis of an early Palestinian link for Christianity at Edessa. From the fact that we do not know of any Tannaitic teachers or teaching associated with Edessa, he argues that we must think instead of a Hellenistic Judaism there such as we have at Dura Europos some 200 miles south of Edessa.[14] As for the authenticity of the tradition of Tobias bar Tobias as a Palestinian Jew in the *Doctrine of Addai*, he would argue that this is an obvious fiction of the later orthodox church to provide itself with a link to the homeland of Christianity.[15] Ehlers moreover points out that the legend of Abgar is in fact marked by a strong anti-Jewish tendency, which would militate against a Jewish-Christian origin for the story.[16]

II. BAUER'S THESIS

The great lexicographer Walter Bauer[17] set forth a far-reaching thesis concerning the development of Christianity in

---

[13] J. C. L. Gibson, *op. cit.*, pp. 36–37.
[14] H. J. W. Drijvers, 'Edessa', p. 11.
[15] *Ibid.*, p. 31.
[16] B. Ehlers, *op. cit.*, pp. 304, 309.
[17] The standard Greek New Testament lexicon, sometimes misnamed Arndt and Gingrich after the English translators, is the result of Bauer's life's work. With some justifiable bitterness for the fact that this was not adequately recognized among English-speaking students, Bauer once said to James Robinson, 'I worked on it at least five hours a day, Sundays not excepted, for forty years. And the name of my life is Walter Bauer.' J. M. Robinson, 'Basic Shifts', p. 76.

Syria and elsewhere in his epochal work, *Rechtgläubigkeit nnd Ketzerei im ältesten Christentum*.[18] As opposed to the traditional picture of a development of orthodoxy from the beginning with heresies springing up at the fringes, Bauer suggested that the situation as late as the second century was fluid and that in most cases heterodoxy preceded orthodoxy, which was only imposed later by the church at Rome. Bauer did not retroject his hypothesis back to New Testament times, but Bultmann developed the implications of his thesis for the New Testament.[19]

Bauer's insights have been hailed by many German scholars. His impact on the English-speaking world has been less pronounced because of the long delay in translation.[20] Considerable criticisms of his methodology have been raised, however. The major critical examination in English was one of the Bampton lectures of H. E. W. Turner included in his book, *The Pattern of Christian Truth*, published in 1954. Turner argued that though there was a 'penumbra' between heresy and orthodoxy, there was always a recognizable core of orthodoxy – an orthodoxy which was more flexible and varied than Bauer would allow.[21] Many reviewers have criticized Bauer's excessive use of the argument from silence. For example, he argues from the silence of Eusebius regarding Asia Minor that 'only *one* answer is possible, namely, that there was no discernible "ecclesiastical" life in central and eastern Asia Minor in the second century'.[22] The fact that heretical writers were also 'silent' does not prevent him from postulating a

[18] This first appeared in 1934; a second edition edited by G. Strecker appeared in 1964. An English edition, *Orthodoxy and Heresy in Earliest Christianity*, translated by a team of scholars from the Philadelphia Seminar on Christian Origins under Robert Kraft and Gerhard Krodel was published in 1971 by Fortress Press.

[19] R. Bultmann, *Theology of the New Testament* II, p. 137. *Cf.* J. M. Robinson, 'Basic Shifts', pp. 77, 86; H. D. Betz, 'Orthodoxy and Heresy in Primitive Christianity: Some Critical Remarks on Georg Strecker's Republication of Walter Bauer's "Rechtgläubigkeit . . ."', *Interpretation* 19 (1965), pp. 299–311.

[20] For the reception accorded to Bauer's work, see Appendix 2, *Orthodoxy and Heresy*, pp. 286–316, which was written by G. Strecker and extensively revised by R. Kraft.

[21] Turner's view is seconded by S. S. Smalley, 'Diversity and Development in John', p. 292.

[22] W. Bauer, *Orthodoxy and Heresy*, p. 173.

heretical church in the same area. Bauer's suggestion that the Christians described in Pliny's correspondence with Trajan might have included some heretical Christians seems gratuitous to me.[23] Bauer points out that the first bishop of Alexandria in Egypt was Demetrius AD 189–231. But was there no 'orthodox' group there before a bishop was consecrated?

As for Syria, Bauer's investigations led him to conclude that Christianity at Edessa rested on an unmistakably heretical basis with the followers of Marcion. Orthodoxy prevailed only gradually in the fourth century. Bauer's view of the Syrian church has been accepted by a number of scholars.[24] On the other hand, his reconstruction has been rejected by Turner because of the scantiness of the details which are available and because of Bauer's excessive scepticism of the orthodox tradition.[25] Bauer's specific suggestion that the origin of the Edessene church was due to the Marcionites has recently been criticized by Koester and Quispel. Koester would suggest that the *Gospel of Thomas* represents a form of Christianity which antedated the beginnings of both Marcionite and orthodox Christianity.[26] Quispel criticizes Bauer's evidence, which is the statement of the *Chronicle of Edessa* that in the year 137–38 Marcion left the Catholic church. This cannot mean that there were Marcionites at Edessa in the second century, and there is no other evidence to support Bauer's suggestion.[27]

III. THE GOSPEL OF THOMAS

A major line of evidence used by the advocates of an early, Palestinian origin of Christianity at Edessa concerns the *Gospel of Thomas*, recently recovered in a Coptic version from near Nag Hammadi in upper Egypt. It has been argued by a number of scholars that the *Gospel of Thomas* – like the *Acts of Thomas* believed to be written in Syriac at Edessa in the

---

[23] *Ibid.*, pp. 90–91.

[24] K. Rudolph, 'Stand und Aufgaben', p. 98; H. J. W. Drijvers, 'Edessa', p. 12; A. F. J. Klijn, *The Acts of Thomas* (1962), p. 32.

[25] H. E. W. Turner, *The Pattern of Christian Truth*, p. 45.

[26] *Trajectories*, pp. 127ff.

[27] G. Quispel, *Makarius, das Thomasevangelium und das Lied von der Perle* (1967), p. 66.

third century – must have originated from Edessa.[28] Since Greek fragments from Oxyrhynchus prove that the *Gospel of Thomas* was already known in Egypt by AD 150, it is further argued that the *Gospel of Thomas* must have been written by about AD 140.[29] Koester and Quispel have, moreover, argued that the *Gospel of Thomas* has preserved some early traditions independent of the canonical Gospels. According to Quispel:

> 'Scholarly research has shown convincingly that Jewish Christianity in Palestine remained alive and active even after the fall of Jerusalem in A.D. 70 and was instrumental in bringing Christianity to Mesopotamia and further East, thus laying the foundations of Semitic, Aramaic speaking, Syrian Christianity.'[30]

If we may assume with Quispel, Koester, Puech, and others that the *Gospel of Thomas*, which we now have extant in Coptic, was originally composed in Greek in Syria *c.* AD 140, we may ask what kind of Christianity is represented by it. The answers which scholars have given to this question are quite varied.

Haenchen believes that the work is so completely Gnostic that there is not a non-Gnostic saying in it. Moreover, the *Gospel of Thomas* is evidence for an 'ausserchristliche' Gnosticism which is at least as old as Christianity.[31] Grant believes that the *Gospel of Thomas* is primarily an interpretation of the canonical materials in the light of Naassene gnosis.[32] Gärtner has interpreted the theology of the *Gospel of Thomas* as a Valentinian Gnosticism.[33] Koester holds that the *logoi* in the *Gospel of Thomas* are but potentially Gnostic:

> 'Of course, not all these sayings are gnostic by any definition. Nevertheless, the unbroken continuation of such a *logoi* tradition is endowed

---

[28] Ehlers has objected to this attribution of the *Gospel of Thomas* to Edessa. A. F. J. Klijn, 'Christianity in Edessa and the Gospel of Thomas', *NovTest* 14 (1972), pp. 70–77, has replied to her objection.

[29] *Cf.* H. Koester in *Trajectories*, pp. 126–143; this section originally appeared as 'GNŌNAI DIAPHOROI: The Origin and Nature of Diversification in the History of Early Christianity', *HTR* 58 (1965), pp. 279–318.

[30] G. Quispel, 'The Discussion of Judaic Christianity', *VigChr* 22 (1968), p. 81; *cf.* also his *Makarius, passim*, and '"The Gospel of Thomas" and the "Gospel of the Hebrews"', *NTS* 12 (1965–1966), pp. 371–382.

[31] E. Haenchen, *Die Botschaft des Thomas-Evangeliums* (1961), p. 70.

[32] R. M. Grant and D. N. Freedman, *The Secret Sayings of Jesus* (1960), pp. 105–111.

[33] B. Gärtner, *The Theology of the Gospel according to Thomas* (1961).

by nature with the seed of Gnosticism as soon as it falls under the spell of a dualistic anthropology.'[34]

On the other hand, Quispel, starting from his conviction that there is no evidence for Marcionites or any other Gnostics in second-century Edessa, has argued vigorously that the *Gospel of Thomas* is simply an Encratite work which was later adopted by the Gnostics.[35] He is supported in this position by Grobel,[36] and by Frend, who concludes: 'The tendency of the community that produced *Thomas* seems to be more towards Encratism than Gnosticism.'[37]

IV. THE ODES OF SOLOMON

One of the most important Syriac manuscripts is the *Odes of Solomon*, discovered at the beginning of this century. This was published initially by J. R. Harris in 1909, and then by Harris and Mingana in a later edition.[38] Five of the *Odes* are contained in the Coptic *Pistis Sophia*,[39] and one of the *Odes*, the eleventh, is available in Greek.

The question of the original language of the composition is difficult to decide.[40] Some such as M. Testuz, M. Philonenko, and A. Klijn have favoured the hypothesis of a Greek original.[41] Others, by comparing the Syriac edition to the Greek ode found among the Bodmer Papyri published in 1959, have been convinced that the Greek is the poorer version. Emerton concludes:

'On the whole, therefore, it is probable that the Greek is not original. That leaves the possibility that the Odes were composed either in Syriac

[34] *Trajectories*, p. 140.

[35] G. Quispel, 'Gnosticism and the New Testament', p. 257; *cf.* 'Das Thomasevangelium und das Alte Testament', in W. C. van Unnik (ed.), *Neotestamentica et Patristica* (1962), pp. 243–248.

[36] K. Grobel, 'How Gnostic is the Gospel of Thomas?' *NTS* 8 (1962), pp. 367–373.

[37] W. H. C. Frend, 'The Gospel of Thomas: Is Rehabilitation Possible?' *JTS* n.s. 18 (1967), pp. 13–26. On Encratism, see A. Baker, 'Early Syriac Asceticism', *Downside Review* 88 (1970), pp. 393–409.

[38] J. R. Harris and A. Mingana (eds), *The Odes and Psalms of Solomon* (1916–1920).

[39] W. Till, *Koptisch-Gnostische Schriften* I: *Die Pistis Sophia, die beiden Bücher des Jeû, unbekanntes altgnostisches Werk* (1954).

[40] H. J. W. Drijvers, *Bardaiṣan*, p. 210, remains undecided.

[41] *Cf.* A. F. J. Klijn, *op. cit.*, pp. 46–47.

or in some other Semitic dialect. . . . The most probable conclusion to
be drawn is that the Odes of Solomon were composed in Syriac.'[42]

Because of parallels with the Gospel of John and with the
writings of Ignatius, the *Odes* have been dated to the early
second century. Adam would date them between AD 110 and
150.[43] Gibson and Charlesworth think that a date as early as
about 100 would be feasible.[44] Drijvers thinks that the *Odes*
originated about 125 either at Antioch or Edessa.[45] Corwin
accepts the suggestion that Ignatius of Antioch was familiar
with some of the *Odes*, which would bring their date down to at
least AD 117. Grant has suggested the following hypothesis:
'the Odes of Solomon, composed in Syriac at Edessa, were
known to the bi-lingual Ignatius either there or at Antioch'.[46]

As early as 1910 H. Gunkel suggested that the *Odes* were a
Gnostic hymn-book.[47] Bultmann made extensive use of the
Odes to reconstruct his pre-Christian Redeemer myth.[48] He
considers the Gnosticism represented in the *Odes* to be a
modified form of early oriental Gnosticism, as was the case in
John's prologue. Commenting on John 1:1, Bultmann
writes:

> 'There is no reflection on the origin of darkness in a primeval fall, and
> even if later in the Gospel traces of the "Iranian" type occur, in which
> the darkness achieves the role of an active power hostile to God, the
> mythology has been pushed back so far – as in the Odes of Solomon –
> that the early oriental type is in fact present in a modified form. And
> as in the Odes of Solomon, this particular form will be due to the
> influence of the O.T. belief in God.'[49]

[42] J. A. Emerton, 'Some Problems of Text and Language in the Odes
of Solomon', *JTS* n.s. 18 (1967), p. 406.
[43] A. Adam, *Die Psalmen des Thomas*, pp. 58f.
[44] J. C. L. Gibson, 'From Qumran to Edessa', p. 33. J. H. Charlesworth,
'Qumran, John and the Odes of Solomon', in J. H. Charlesworth (ed.),
John and Qumran (1972), p. 109.
[45] H. J. W. Drijvers, *Bardaiṣan*, p. 210.
[46] R. M. Grant, 'The Odes of Solomon and the Church of Antioch',
JBL 63 (1944), p. 377.
[47] H. Gunkel, 'Die Oden Salomos', *ZNW* 11 (1910), pp. 291–328.
[48] R. Bultmann, 'Die Bedeutung der neuerschlossenen . . . Quellen'.
[49] R. Bultmann, *The Gospel of John*, p. 29. *Cf.* Feine–Behm–Kümmel,
p. 159, where the *Odes* are described as presenting a Gnosticism whose
dualism was softened through Jewish influence. Drijvers, 'Edessa', p. 14,
wonders if in the *Odes* an earlier text has been later censored by orthodox
interests. *Cf.* J. T. Sanders, *The New Testament Christological Hymn*,
pp. 37ff., 106ff.

Rudolph in an article dedicated to Bultmann on his eightieth birthday attempts to emphasize the Gnostic character of the *Odes* by comparing them to the Dead Sea Scrolls and the Mandaean texts.[50] From these comparisons Rudolph concludes that the *Odes* are a product of a Jewish-Christian Gnosticism while the Mandaean texts are a product of a non-Christian, and heretically Jewish Gnosticism.[51]

Daniélou, who considers the *Odes* to be 'the most precious document' after the *Didache* relating to Jewish-Christian liturgy, concludes that the *Odes* exhibit features of a Jewish-Christian 'gnosis' which was later adopted and profoundly modified by Gnosticism.[52] Sanders analyses the motifs in the *Odes* as resulting from a hypostatization which is independent of the New Testament and 'is in some respects logically prior in its development to the hypostasis of the Logos in the prologue of John'.[53] He considers the origin of the *Odes* in a Jewish sect which 'also apparently received some influence from emerging Christianity'.[54]

After the publication of the Dead Sea Scrolls, and in particular of the *Hodayot* or Thanksgiving Hymns, many writers were struck by the parallels between the *Odes* and the Qumranian writings. So impressed with the parallels was Carmignac that he concluded that the author of the *Odes* was an Essene who had become a Christian.[55] It was to refute Carmignac's thesis that Rudolph, who believes that the *Odes*' author was a Gnostic, wrote his article cited above. Carmignac's thesis has now been seconded by Charlesworth, who emphasizes the primary Christian orientation of the author.[56]

[50] K. Rudolph, 'War der Verfasser der Oden Salomos ein "Qumran-Christ"?', *Revue de Qumran* 4 (1964), pp. 523–555.

[51] *Ibid.*, p. 553.

[52] J. Daniélou, *The Theology of Jewish Christianity*, p. 369.

[53] J. T. Sanders, *op. cit.*, p. 119.

[54] *Ibid.*, p. 120.

[55] J. Carmignac, 'Un Qumrânien converti au Christianisme: l'auteur des Odes de Salomon', in H. Bardtke (ed.), *Qumran-Probleme* (1963), pp. 75–108.

[56] J. H. Charlesworth, 'Les Odes de Salomon et les manuscrits de la mer-morte', *RB* 77 (1970), p. 549: 'Au fond de ces Odes apparaît la foi chrétienne de leur auteur. Les Odes sont essentiellement chrétiennes et secondairement sous l'influence essénienne.'

In another article Charlesworth has set out to refute systematically Rudolph's arguments that the author of the *Odes* was a Gnostic.[57] Against Rudolph's claim that the Gnostic character of the *Odes* is established by the abundant use of the root YD^c 'to know', Charlesworth argues that the frequent use of the same verb in the *Hodayot* does not prove it to be Gnostic. In the *Odes* 'knowledge' is not the Gnostic idea of salvation through self-comprehension of the soul's heavenly origin; rather knowledge is of Christ, the Most High, and the Lord. Unlike Gnostic cosmology, the creator is not condemned but praised. Typically Gnostic language is lacking, and the Old Testament is the pattern for the expressions of the *Odes*. Revelation is not secret but proclaimed. 'There is no suggestion in the Odes of a divine Redeemer who has descended from above to release men's souls and lead them back to the realm of light.'[58] Rudolph's references to descent and ascent are with the exception of *Ode* xxii. 1 without a cosmic dimension; the ascent mentioned in *Ode* xxix. 4 is not a progression through the Gnostics' many spheres but a movement upward from the Hebraic Sheol. Finally, the fact that the author of the *Pistis Sophia* deemed it necessary to append a Gnostic targum to each of the *Odes* which he included indicates that the *Odes* were not transparently Gnostic to him. Charlesworth concludes:

'In retrospect it is safe to say that the Odes of Solomon are not gnostic. In prospect it appears probable that the Odes are a tributary to Gnosticism which flows from Jewish apocalyptical mysticism . . . to the full-blown Gnosticism of the second century. The Odes are not "heretical" . . . but rather a Jewish-Christian hymn book of the first century.'[59]

---

[57] J. H. Charlesworth, 'The Odes of Solomon – Not Gnostic', *CBQ* 31 (1969), pp. 357–369.

[58] *Ibid.*, p. 368. *Cf.* C. Colpe, *Die religionsges. Schule*, p. 181: 'In den Oden Salomos dürfen wir vom "Urmensch-Erlöser" deshalb nicht reden, weil der Begriff "Urmensch" nicht vorkommt und wir es ja zunächst in Frage stellen, dass die Erlöser-figuren der christlichen Gnosis für einen vorchristlichen Urmenschen eingetreten sind.'

[59] J. H. Charlesworth, 'The Odes of Solomon', p. 369. *Cf.* H. Chadwick, 'Some Reflections on the Character and Theology of the Odes of Solomon', in P. Granfield and J. Jungman (eds), *Kyriakon* (*Festschrift Johannes Quasten*) I (1970), p. 270: 'It would probably be less misleading to describe the theology of the Odes as archaic rather than gnostic, but the epithet

V. THE HYMN OF THE PEARL

The famous Hymn of the Pearl (HP) appears in the apocryphal *Acts of Thomas*, which was originally composed in Syriac. Of the Syriac and Greek manuscripts of the *Acts of Thomas* which we have, Bornkamm suggests that the Greek text may be closer to the original Syriac than the extant Syriac text which displays 'numerous catholicizing revisions'.[60] There are also Arabic, Armenian, Latin, Coptic, and Ethiopic versions which are secondary in character.

From the position between Bardaisan and Mani which the *Acts of Thomas* occupies Bornkamm would date the latter to the first half of the third century. Klijn also places the *Acts of Thomas* at the beginning of the third century on the basis of a comparison with other apocryphal *Acts*.[61] Quispel favours a date of AD 225.[62]

We shall not be concerned here with the *Acts* as a whole with its depiction of Thomas as the twin of Jesus and as the apostle to India, but only with the Hymn of the Pearl which appears in the ninth *Act*, chs 108–113.[63]

Scholars are agreed that the most likely place for the composition of the HP is Edessa. But the estimates regarding the date of its composition vary widely. Because of the patent references to the Parthian dynasty the *terminus ad quem* would be AD 226 when the Arsacid dynasty gave way to the Sassanians.[64] Bornkamm holds that the HP is at least pre-Manichaean.[65] Quispel favours a date in the second century before the composition of the *Acts of Thomas* and after the introduction of Christianity into Edessa by Jewish Christians at the

---

matters very little and is not worth disputing, provided that it is understood and accepted that the Odes were not written to be the vehicle of any overt or hidden deviation from the apostolic tradition of faith.'

[60] G. Bornkamm, *Mythos und Legende in den apokryphen Thomas-Akten* (1933); and in *NTA* II, pp. 425ff., especially p. 442.

[61] A. F. J. Klijn, *The Acts of Thomas*, p. 26.

[62] G. Quispel, 'Gnosticism and the New Testament', p. 258.

[63] For a translation of the HP based on the Syriac text, see Klijn, *op. cit.*, pp. 120–125; Bornkamm, who used the Greek text for his translation of the *Acts of Thomas*, did use the Syriac text for the Hymn of the Pearl, cf. *NTA* II, pp. 433, n. 2, 498ff.

[64] Klijn, *op. cit.*, p. 279; J.-É. Ménard, 'Le "Chant de la perle"', p. 298.

[65] *NTA* II, p. 435.

end of the first century.[66] Segal would place the HP, which he calls the 'Hymn of the Soul', not later than the first century AD.[67]

Adam has argued that the HP was composed in the first century AD before the introduction of Christianity to Edessa.[68] One of his arguments is the unlikely suggestion that the baptismal hymn in Ephesians 5:14 was dependent on the HP. Widengren goes even farther back in time. Noting that the geographic orientation of the Hymn presupposes a time when the centre of gravity was still in the east, before the Parthians had chosen Seleucia-Ctesiphon on the Tigris as their capital, he would hold that the HP was composed before 150 BC.[69] Indeed, he would further maintain that the Hymn is the result of the transformation of an ancient Indo-Iranian myth which celebrated the victory of a hero over a dragon.[70]

In its present setting Thomas is the ostensible speaker of the HP. The original speaker, however, was a prince who describes how as a child he enjoyed the wealth of his royal home. His parents then divested him of his splendid garments, and sent him on a mission to Egypt to bring back a single pearl guarded by a serpent in the midst of the sea. After travelling to Egypt, the prince is fed some food which causes him to forget his home and his mission. His parents send him a letter to remind him of his origins and of his task. Thus reawakened, the prince succeeds in snatching the pearl from the serpent and returns home where he is again invested with his splendid robes and honoured for his success.

Bousset and Hilgenfeld had at first maintained that the prince was Mani. Indeed, the *Acts of Thomas* were used by the Manichaeans at a later date. Reitzenstein then identified the young prince as a type of the pre-Christian Redeemed Redeemer and the pearl as a symbol of the collective souls whom he gathers to himself.[71] He is followed in this interpretation by Widengren.[72] Adam believes that the HP is a pre-Christian

---

[66] G. Quispel, 'Gnosticism and the New Testament', p. 258.
[67] J. B. Segal, *Edessa*, p. 31.
[68] A. Adam, *Die Psalmen des Thomas*, pp. 60, 75.
[69] *OG*, p. 52.
[70] G. Widengren, 'Der iranische Hintergrund', p. 113.
[71] R. Reitzenstein, *Das iranische Erlösungsmysterium* (1921), pp. 70ff., 117.
[72] G. Widengren, *op. cit.*, p. 112.

hymn which was originally recited in a cultic ceremony.[73] He suggests that the magical naming of the father's name by the prince to break the spell may very well have been the name of the highest God, Zurvan.[74]

Just as scholars differ as to the date of the HP, they differ as to its alleged Gnostic character. Rudolph, who is convinced of the pre-Christian origin of the Gnostic Redeemer myth, cites the HP along with segments from the Hermetica and the Mandaean texts as irreproachable evidences for the non-Christian character of Gnosticism.[75] Bornkamm holds that the HP is 'among the most beautiful documents of Gnosticism which have come down to us'.[76] Grant maintains that the HP reflects 'late Valentinian doctrine, perhaps that of Bardaisan'.[77] Drijvers considers the HP to be Gnostic, but not unambiguously so. It all depended upon who heard the text.[78] Ménard suggests that the HP may originally have been a Jewish-Christian composition, which was then reworded by Gnostics who introduced the prince who needed to be saved, and which was finally reworked again for use by the Manichaeans.[79] Contrary to Adam, Ménard does not believe that the HP can be used as an evidence of pre-Christian Gnosticism.[80]

Recently Köbert has denied the alleged Gnostic character of the HP.[81] The non-Gnostic nature of the HP has been most vigorously advocated by Klijn.[82] Quispel also denies the Gnostic view of the HP: '. . . the Hymn of the Pearl is not gnostic, let alone a document of pre-Christian, Parthian

---

[73] A. Adam, *op. cit.*, p. 61: 'Der ausserchristliche und vorchristliche Charakter des Hymnus steht fast.'

[74] *Ibid.*, p. 56.

[75] K. Rudolph, 'Stand und Aufgaben', p. 97.

[76] *NTA* II, pp. 433, 435.

[77] R. M. Grant, *Gnosticism, A Sourcebook*, p. 116.

[78] H. J. W. Drijvers, 'The Origins of Gnosticism', p. 337.

[79] J.-É. Ménard, *op. cit.*, p. 301.

[80] *Ibid.*, p. 290: 'Contrairement à A. ADAM, nous ne croyons pas que l'Hymne soit le témoin d'une gnose pré-chrétienne.'

[81] R. Köbert, 'Das Perlenlied', *Orientalia* 38 (1969), p. 448: 'Gnostisches kam nicht ins Blickfeld.'

[82] In addition to his monograph cited above, see A. F. J. Klijn, 'The Influence of Jewish Theology on the Odes of Solomon and the Acts of Thomas', in *Aspects du Judéo-Christianisme*, pp. 167–179, and 'Early Syriac Christianity – Gnostic?' in *OG*, pp. 575–579.

Gnosis'.[83] He argues that the HP is Christian in origin and is basically an amplification of the parable of the pearl, especially as it is reproduced in the *Gospel of Thomas*.[84]

Klijn takes special issue with the way in which Adam has read details of the hypothetical Iranian Redeemer myth between the lines of the HP. He asks: (1) What is the relation between the babe sent from his father's house and the Suffering Servant? (2) Is it possible to explain the babe as the 'Gesamtseele'? (3) Is it possible to identify the babe as a redeemer?[85] On close examination Klijn questions whether the HP actually deals with redemption, as nowhere is the word 'redemption' or 'redeemer' to be met, nor is there any word about the miserable situation in which the pearl was found.[86] Quispel and Klijn both interpret the pearl in the light of Jewish concepts as the soul which has to be reminded of its origin in Paradise. Quispel concludes: 'The *Hymn of the Pearl* is not gnostic at all, but rather an orthodox Christian hymn tinged with Judaistic colours.'[87]

VI. BARDAISAN

One of the most original personalities who figured in the history of early Syrian Christianity was the many-sided Bardaisan. He was born in 154 and died in 222. We know that he was a learned courtier of Abgar VIII, the Great, of Edessa. He wrote many works, including polemics against the Marcionites. After Caracalla had brought an end to Edessa's independence in 216, Bardaisan probably went to Armenia.

There is no question but that Bardaisan's teachings were regarded as heretical by St Ephrem Syrus (306–373), who wrote both hymns and prose refutations against the Bardaisanites. Bardaisan denied the resurrection of the body though he believed in the immortality of the soul. He tried to reconcile Christian beliefs with the Hellenized astrology of the

---

[83] Review of Bianchi, *OG*, by G. Quispel, *op. cit.*, p. 322; *cf.* his *Makarius, passim*, and 'Makarius und das Lied von der Perle', *OG*, pp. 625–644.

[84] Quispel, 'Gnosticism and the New Testament', p. 257.

[85] Review of A. Adam, *Die Psalmen des Thomas*, by Klijn, p. 95.

[86] A. F. J. Klijn, *The Acts of Thomas*, p. 277, and 'The so-called Hymn of the Pearl', *VigChr* 14 (1960), pp. 156–157.

[87] G. Quispel, *op. cit.*, p. 259.

'Chaldaeans'. Segal views him as more of a philosopher and astrologer than a theologian. Such, however, was his prestige and influence that it is possible that his followers may have outnumbered the more orthodox Christians at Edessa.[88]

What is in question is whether we can properly call Bardaisan a Gnostic or not. He is designated a Valentinian Gnostic by Hippolytus and Epiphanius. Haase, for one, believed that such a designation was and is justified.[89] Widengren, moreover, sees Bardaisan not only as a true Gnostic but also as a representative of the Iranian–Semitic culture which was the seedbed of Gnosticism.[90] He asserts that Bardaisan and his followers gave Christianity a distinctly Gnostic character. Widengren ranks him as a predecessor of Mani along with Basilides and Marcion – all of whom developed a Gnosticism which gave Christianity a veneer of the Iranian dualistic outlook.[91] As a Gnostic he derived his ideas from the Mesopotamian world and from Zurvanite theology.

Bardaisan has also been suggested as the author of at least some of the *Odes of Solomon*.[92] The fact that the *Odes* can now be dated to the early second century rules out Bardaisan as their author. The suggestion has also been made that the HP was written by Bardaisan. Burkitt at first accepted this theory but then rejected it. As we have already seen, Grant still suggests that the HP may reflect the ideas of Bardaisanite teaching. Drijvers, however, writes: 'The great differences of spiritual climate between Bardaiṣan and the Acts (of Thomas), which are ascetic, have no astrology and do not display any special cosmology, plead against the authorship of Bardaiṣan.'[93]

As to the more general question of whether Bardaisan can be called a Gnostic, Drijvers answers in the negative for the following reasons:

> '1. B.'s "gnosis" is not based on revelation, but is insight intellectually acquired. In his thought, time plays a greater part than space.

[88] J. B. Segal, *Edessa*, p. 45.
[89] F. Haase, *Zur bardesanischen Gnosis* (1910), p. 89.
[90] G. Widengren, *Mesopotamian Elements in Manichaeism* (1946), pp. 176ff.
[91] G. Widengren, *Mani and Manichaeism*, pp. 11, 139.
[92] W. R. Newbold, 'Bardaisan and the Odes of Solomon', *JBL* 30 (1911), pp. 161–204.
[93] H. J. W. Drijvers, *Bardaiṣan*, p. 211.

2. B. does not have a tradition of his own besides revelation, if one can speak of revelation in his case.

3. Matter is not evil for B. in a direct sense. Evil only arises from the commixture. Before that, matter was ordered harmoniously.

4. B. looks upon the world optimistically, as created by the Word of God's Thought. There is no question of a demiurge.

5. People are not divided into classes, somatics, psychics and pneumatics. Soma, psyche and pneuma indicate three levels in the life of every man.

6. Christ is not the great turning-point in the cosmic process. At creation, salvation already begins.

These differences are so deep-seated, that it must be regarded as a mistake to speak of the Gnosis of Bardaişan.' [94]

[94] *Ibid.*, p. 224. *Cf.* H. J. W. Drijvers, 'Die Bardaişaniten und die Ursprünge des Gnostizismus', in *OG*, pp. 308ff.

CHAPTER SEVEN
THE COPTIC EVIDENCE

I. THE NAG HAMMADI CORPUS

The spectacular discovery by accident in 1945 of thirteen Coptic codices near Nag Hammadi in upper Egypt must be ranked in importance with the more widely publicized discovery of the Dead Sea Scrolls at Qumran in 1946. The bibliography of articles, books, and reviews on these texts has already grown to an impressive size. The bibliography of studies from 1948 to 1969 by D. Scholer runs to nearly 2,500 items.[1] Articles relating the new finds to New Testament studies have been published by Schulz,[2] by Robinson,[3] and by Rudolph.[4] An international team of scholars under the editorship of M. Krause and J. Robinson anticipate not only the publication of all the Nag Hammadi treatises but of related monographs as well.[5]

The approximate date of the extant Coptic manuscripts from Nag Hammadi is the middle of the fourth century AD. They were buried about AD 400.[6] It is quite clear, however, that the date of the composition of the individual treatises,

---

[1] D. M. Scholer, *Nag Hammadi Bibliography 1948–1969* (1971); cf. *idem*, 'Bibliographia Gnostica Supplementum I', *NovTest* 13 (1971), pp. 322–336, to be continued by Professor Scholer.

[2] S. Schulz, 'Die Bedeutung neuer Gnosisfunde für die neutestamentlich Wissenschaft', *ThR* 26 (1960), pp. 209–266.

[3] J. M. Robinson, 'The Coptic Gnostic Library Today'.

[4] K. Rudolph, 'Stand und Aufgaben'; and 'Gnosis und Gnostizismus, ein Forschungsbericht', *ThR* 34. 2 (1969), pp. 121–175; 34. 3 (1969), pp. 181–231; 36. 2 (1971), pp. 89–124.

[5] 'The Coptic Gnostic Library', *NovTest* 12 (1970), pp. 81–85. For information on publications of Nag Hammadi texts which are either forthcoming or planned see J.-E. Ménard, 'Les origines de la gnose', *RevSR* 42 (1968), p. 24, n. 1.

[6] J. M. Robinson, 'The Coptic Gnostic Library Today', pp. 370–372.

many of them originally in Greek, must be set much earlier. For example, the *Apocryphon of John* was known to Irenaeus and was cited in his *Adversus Haereses* i. 29, written in AD 180.

Whether or not these new texts can provide us with evidence for pre-Christian Gnosticism in general, and for a pre-Christian Redeemer myth in particular is a question of the greatest interest. Neill, who is pessimistic about such possibilities, writes:

> 'This new Gnostic material may thus come to be highly important in connexion with the history of the Church in the second century, and with that of the tradition of the New Testament. It can hardly bring us nearer to an answer to the question as to whether there was or was not a pre-Christian Gnosticism, on which the Gentile Churches leaned heavily for the working out of their theology.'[7]

James Robinson, on the other hand, is more optimistic. In 1968 he wrote: 'But now the Coptic gnostic library may provide some of the documentation that bridges the gulf from Qumran to Christian Gnosticism, and thus contribute to our understanding of the context in which Christianity emerged.'[8] In a work published in 1971 he has repeated his conviction that the Nag Hammadi texts can provide us with evidences of non-Christian Gnosticism. After citing a long passage by Rudolph which affirms the pre-Christian and Palestinian roots of Mandaeanism, Robinson writes:

> 'This persistent trend in the scholarship of the twentieth century has been carried one step further by the Coptic gnostic codices from near Nag Hammadi, which reflect in some of their tractates, such as the *Apocalypse of Adam* and the *Paraphrase of Shem*, what seems to be non-Christian Gnosticism, a gnostic or semignostic Judaism, in some cases localized in the Jordan region and interacting in some way with baptismal movements.'[9]

Inasmuch as Robinson has worked more closely with the Coptic texts than Neill, he is in a better position to judge the possibilities.

Quispel, however, who has also worked very closely with

---

[7] S. Neill, *The Interpretation of the New Testament 1861–1961*, p. 175.
[8] J. M. Robinson, 'The Coptic Gnostic Library Today', p. 380.
[9] *Trajectories*, p. 264.

the Nag Hammadi texts, takes issue with Robinson's stated optimism:

'In the above mentioned article ("The Coptic Gnostic Library Today") James Robinson has made a dubious attempt to save honor: he argues that a number of writings found at Nag Hammadi, which for the greatest part have not yet been published and which might be non-Christian, are pre-Christian. But that is not the question at all. The question is whether in pre-Christian times there existed a very specific, coherent myth of the redeemed redeemer. And it appears that that question must be answered in the negative.'[10]

We are, of course, unable to discuss all the Nag Hammadi treatises which have been published. Many of them are not directly relevant to our problem as they are obviously documents of post-Christian Gnosticism. In our chapter on Syriac evidence we have already discussed the *Gospel of Thomas* inasmuch as it is the consensus of scholars that it was composed in Syria. Apart from Haenchen few have claimed to discover any evidence of an early non-Christian Gnosis in this document.[11]

The *Apocryphon of John*, which appears in three versions in the Nag Hammadi codices and which was known to Irenaeus, has been claimed as a representative of barely Christianized, pre-Valentinian gnosis.[12] Grant suggests with some hesitancy that it might even be the work of Saturninus at the beginning of the second century.[13] Quispel has suggested that the Gnosticism of the *Apocryphon*, which betrays but little Christian influence, might stem from a pagan, perhaps even a pre-Christian Gnosticism.[14]

As examples of works which may have originally been non-

[10] G. Quispel, 'Gnosis', p. 28. For the translation from the Dutch I am indebted to Professor Marten H. Woudstra of Calvin Theological Seminary.

[11] H.-J. Schoeps, 'Judenchristentum und Gnosis', *OG*, p. 528 does say, 'Das Thomas-Evangelium aus Nag Hamâdi in Ägypten gilt als ein Dokument früher Gnosis, wenn nicht praegnostischer Art.'

[12] *NTA* I, p. 331.

[13] R. M. Grant, 'The Earliest Christian Gnosticism', pp. 89–90.

[14] G. Quispel, *Gnosis als Weltreligion*, p. 5: 'Wenn man darauf achtet, wie gering und unbedeutend die christlichen Einflüsse sind, die im *Apokryphon Johannis* vorliegen, dann ist man wohl geneigt, zu denken, dass diese Gedankengänge, die mit dem Christentum innerlich kaum eine Berührung zeigen, einer heidnischen, vielleicht sogar vorchristlichen Gnosis entstammen.'

Christian but which may have been secondarily Christianized M. Krause suggests the following: (1) *The Hypostasis of the Archons* (*CG* II. 4),[15] which gives a cosmogony similar to that of the *Apocryphon of John* and similar to that ascribed to the Sethians and Ophites by the Church Fathers.[16] (2) *The Book of Thomas the Athlete* (*CG* II. 7), as yet unpublished. (3) *The Acts of Peter and the Twelve Apostles* (*CG* VI. 1), also unpublished. (4) *The Gospel of Mary*. This appears in the Codex Berolinensis 8502 (BG 8502), which has had an interesting history. It was purchased in 1896, but was published by W. Till only in 1955.[17] This codex also contains a recension of the *Apocryphon of John*, an *Acts of Peter*, and a *Sophia of Jesus*.

Those who seek support for evidence of a non-Christian Gnosticism in the Nag Hammadi texts have turned to three treatises in particular: (1) *Eugnostos*, (2) *The Apocalypse of Adam*, and (3) *The Paraphrase of Shem*. We shall attempt to discuss these treatises in some detail.

II. EUGNOSTOS AND THE SOPHIA OF JESUS CHRIST

It is only in the case of the *Letter of Eugnostos* (*CG* III. 3 and V.1) and the *Sophia of Jesus Christ* (BG 8502 and *CG* III. 4) that we have both Christian and non-Christian versions of the same basic text.

J. Doresse, who first called the works to the public attention, argued that *Eugnostos* was prior to the *Sophia*.[18] He has recently expressed himself on the appropriation of *Eugnostos* by the *Sophia* in this way:

'Not content with inventing entire apocryphal works in which Christ was given the characteristics of the imaginary Gnostic Saviour, the sectarians went so far as to disguise their earliest revelations under summary Christian travesties. It is in this way that the *Epistle of Eug-*

---

[15] *CG* stands for *Cairensis Gnosticus*, the official designation of the Nag Hammadi corpus. The Roman numeral designates the codex; the Arabic numeral indicates the treatise within a given codex.

[16] R. Bullard, *The Hypostasis of the Archons* (1970).

[17] W. Till, *Die gnostischen Schriften des koptischen Papyrus Berolinensis 8502* (1955).

[18] J. Doresse, 'Trois livres gnostiques inédits: Évangile des Égyptiens, Epître d'Eugnoste, Sagasse de Jésus Christ', *VigChr* 2 (1948), pp. 137–160; cf. *The Secret Books*, pp. 195ff.

nostos to his disciples was, later, cut up into slices offered to us as the substance of a dialogue between the Saviour and his disciples, the whole bearing the title *Sophia of Jesus*.'[19]

The most systematic exposition of the priority of *Eugnostos* has been presented by M. Krause.[20] It is agreed by all that both *Eugnostos* and the *Sophia* contain the same cosmogony. In *Eugnostos* this material is cast in an epistolary form, whereas in the *Sophia* it is put in the form of a dialogue between the resurrected Christ and his disciples. Krause, who had access to all the texts in question, examined: (1) the material common to both *Eugnostos* and the *Sophia*; (2) the material peculiar to *Eugnostos*; (3) the material peculiar to the *Sophia*. He concluded that the material peculiar to *Eugnostos* fits into the common material in an integrated fashion, whereas the narrative framework and dialogue form of the *Sophia* are poorly integrated with the common material. For example, the questions of the disciples are not always answered by Christ's response. *Eugnostos* was therefore the primary work, and the *Sophia* a secondary adaptation. Krause furthermore maintains that *Eugnostos* contains no Christian ideas although it has some Jewish elements. [21]

Some scholars have maintained the reverse position, however, that Eugnostos is a later de-Christianized version of the *Sophia*. Till, without giving any detailed reasons, wrote: 'It seems to me much more probable that SJC was the source of Eug. and not the contrary.'[22] H.-M. Schenke produced a detailed criticism of Doresse's arguments in an article published in 1962.[23] To Schenke it is hardly credible that anyone, even a Gnostic, would take a systematically ordered system of thought (as in *Eugnostos*) and then recast it into a question and answer format (as in the *Sophia*); whereas the reverse would be understandable, namely the systematization of the

[19] In Bleeker and Widengren, *Historia Religionum*, p. 548.
[20] M. Krause, 'Das literarische Verhältnis des Eugnostosbriefes zur Sophia Jesu Christi', in *Mullus (Festschrift, T. Klauser)* (1964), pp. 215–223.
[21] *Ibid.*, p. 216: 'Christliches Gedankengut ist in dieser Schrift nicht enthalten, wohl aber jüdisches.'
[22] W. Till, *Die gnostischen Schriften*, p. 54.
[23] H.-M. Schenke, 'Nag-Hamadi Studien II: Das System der Sophia Jesu Christ', *ZRGG* 14 (1962), pp. 263–278. It should be noted that Schenke had access only to BG 8502, and Till's critical apparatus with *CG* III. 4 and the parts of *CG* III. 3 which parallel BG 8502.3.

answers given in response to questions.[24] In opposition to
Doresse, Schenke claims that Christian motifs are firmly rooted
in the teachings of *Eugnostos*.[25] Unfortunately, he does not
detail what he considers such motifs.

R. McL. Wilson, who was able to check the same materials
which Krause used through the latter's kindness, notes the
following possible Christian or New Testament allusions in
Eugnostos:

> 'Codex III (77.20ff., cf. SJC 95.17ff. Till) refers to the creation of
> "gods and archangels and angels for service" . . . This recalls Heb.
> 1.14, although the Greek loan-word in the Coptic texts is not the one
> used in Hebrews. On the following page (96.10f. Till) the titles "God
> of gods" and "King of kings" may reflect knowledge of Rev. 17.14,
> 19.16, but here of course the Old Testament also has to be taken into
> account (cf. Deut. 10. 17, Dan. 2.47) . . . Finally, there is a reference
> to "the kingdom of the Son of man" (Codex III 81.13; SJC 101.6f.),
> and the title "Son of man" appears later in conjunction with the
> other title "Saviour" (Codex III 81.21ff.; SJC 102.15ff.). The phrase
> "from the foundation of the world" (SJC 80.7f., 83.11; common
> material) is common in the New Testament, and there is a passage in
> Codex V of Eugnostos (8.11) which with its reference to a "form" and
> a "name" may recall Phil. 2. . . .'[26]

As to the use of the title 'Son of Man' in *Eugnostos*, Borsch, who
has made exhaustive studies of the phrase, would suggest
that it may be the one work – but admittedly the only one –
in which Christian influence might be ruled out: 'If, however,
Krause is correct in maintaining that the Epistle of *Eugnostos*
represents non-Christian thought which only later came to be
Christianized, then we have at least one instance of a non-
Christian usage of the term in Gnosticism for which we might
well need to seek another source than Christianity.'[27]

In view of these considerations, Wilson makes the following
suggestion:

> 'At the very least, however, they (the possible New Testament
> allusions) demand a due measure of caution over against assertions that

[24] *Ibid.*, p. 265. Krause, who wrote to refute Schenke, argues that the
reverse seems to be true in the *Apocryphon of John* and in the late *Pistis
Sophia*, where presumably clear systems have become obscure. Krause,
op. cit., p. 217.

[25] H.-M. Schenke, *op. cit.*, p. 265: 'Christliche Motive sind in der Lehre
des Eug. fest verwurzelt.'

[26] R. McL. Wilson, *Gnosis and the New Testament*, p. 115.

[27] Borsch, *The Christian and Gnostic Son of Man*, p. 99.

Eugnostos is entirely non-Christian or shows no sign of Christian influence. There is nonetheless a further possibility: is the Epistle of Eugnostos itself a Christianised version of an earlier document?'[28]

Krause himself had suggested that the original basis of *Eugnostos* was a cosmogonical text designed to refute three different philosophical theories about the origin of the universe. Pétrement thinks that it is very probable that Eugnostos himself was a Christian or at least under the influence of Christianity. He is listed as the transcriber of the *Gospel of the Egyptians*, a Sethian work. Pétrement's suggestion was made from the incomplete citation of the colophon of the latter work by Doresse: '. . . Eugnostos the agapite, according to the spirit (i.e. his spiritual name); in the flesh, my name is Goggessos. . . .'[29] But the continuation of the colophon makes it even clearer that Eugnostos was a professing Christian. The Coptic text of 69, lines 12–15, reads: M̄N NA SHB̄ROUOEIN HN̄ OUAPHTHARSIA ĪS PEX̄S PSHĒRE M̄PNOUTE PSŌTĒR ĪXTHUS THEOGRAPHOS, which is to be translated: 'with my companions of light, in an incorruptibility, Jesus the Christ, the Son of God, the Saviour: ĪXTHUS, written of God'.[30]

In summary, it appears that Krause has been able to prove that *Eugnostos* was adapted by the *Sophia of Jesus Christ*. His second claim that Eugnostos is wholly without any Christian element is not so certainly established. In any case, final judgment must await the publication of the text of *Eugnostos*.[31]

III. THE APOCALYPSE OF ADAM

The *Apocalypse of Adam* (*CG* V. 5) is a revelation of Adam to Seth, which recounts the salvation of Noah from the Flood and

[28] R. McL. Wilson, *op. cit.*, p. 117.

[29] J. Doresse, *The Secret Books*, p. 180. She, of course, used the original French edition.

[30] J. Doresse, ' "Le Livre sacré du grand Esprit invisible" ou "l'Évangile des Égyptiens" ', *Journal Asiatique* 204 (1966), pp. 428–429.

[31] A German translation of *Eugnostos* was to have appeared in 1970 in M. Krause and K. Rudolph (eds), *Die Gnosis* II, which was to be published by Artemis Verlag of Zürich. I have not been able to obtain this volume; nor does the National Union Catalog of the Library of Congress yet list it. A synopsis of the Coptic texts of the *Sophia* and *Eugnostos* will appear in *Patristische Texte und Studien*, and a German translation in *Kleine Texte für Vorlesungen und Übungen* from de Gruyter in Berlin, according to Borsch, p. 94. An English translation of *Eugnostos* is being prepared for the Coptic Gnostic Library project by Douglas M. Parrot.

the salvation of Seth's seed from a destruction by fire.[32] After a period the *Phōstēr* or Illuminator appears. He will work signs and marvels by which he will debase the powers. But then the god of these powers will be troubled and angered at this man. The powers will not see him with their eyes. 'Then they will punish the flesh of the man upon whom the Holy spirit has descended. *Then they will use the name*, the angels and all the generations of the power, in an aberration, saying: "From whence has he come?" '[33]

Towards the end of the apocalypse is a long passage describing the origin of the Illuminator through thirteen kingdoms and a final 'generation without a king'. Throughout these successive generations the Illuminator's origin is placed in human beings, then in nature, then in gods, and finally in natural principles. It is only the last generation without a king, *i.e.* Gnostics, who know the true nature of the origin of the Illuminator, *viz.* God's choice of him as the agent of his gnosis.

The extraordinary importance of this document lies in the claim of the editor Böhlig that here we have a non-Christian and a pre-Christian presentation of a redeemer figure. He asserts:

> 'The text is undoubtedly Gnostic and also a Sethian writing. It must however strongly be doubted, whether it has been created only by Sethians in the strict sense; it points moreover to a pre-Christian origin out of Jewish–Iranian Gnosticism.'[34]

In view of parallels with Mandaean texts Böhlig would connect the origin of this tradition with a Palestinian baptist group, represented by the proto-Mandaeans. James Robinson has claimed that this text and the *Paraphrase of Shem* now supply the necessary evidence for Bultmann's hypothesis:

> 'The absence of the gnostic redeemer myth at Qumran did seem to diverge from what Bultmann had anticipated concerning Jordanian baptismal sects; but this omission would seem to have been filled in by such Nag Hammadi materials as the *Apocalypse of Adam* (*CG*, V. 5).'[35]

---

[32] A. Böhlig and P. Labib, *Koptisch-gnostische Apokalypsen aus Codex V von Nag Hammadi im Koptischen Museum zu Alt-Kairo* (1963).

[33] R. Kasser, 'Bibliothèque gnostique V: Apocalypse d'Adam', *RThPh* 16 (1967), p. 326.

[34] A. Böhlig, *Mysterion und Wahrheit* (1968), p. 149.

[35] *Trajectories*, p. 234, n. 4.

Rudolph in his review agrees with Böhlig's estimation, and writes: 'The importance of this document resides especially in the fact that it is obviously a *non-Christian*, indeed probably a pre-Christian product.'[36] Kasser likewise concurs, at least with respect to the work's components:

'One finds here nothing, in effect, which recalls Christianity, at least not directly or openly, so that this work, or one or the other of its principal components, could well go back either to pre-Christian times or to some non-Christian (heterodox Jewish) milieu contemporary with the most obscure periods of primitive Christianity.'[37]

MacRae would also agree in part with Böhlig's arguments. He would not agree that 'Iranian pre-Gnostic mythology found a receptive soil for growth in certain late-Jewish circles', but would suggest that 'the redeemer myth of the *Apocalypse of Adam* grew out of late Jewish speculations that were fostered by the syncretistic atmosphere of the Near East around the time when Christianity made its appearance'.[38] MacRae views the episode of the Illuminator as a sort of Gnostic midrash on the Deutero-Isaian Servant Songs. As to possible New Testament allusions he follows Böhlig in arguing:

'If one starts from the premise that the author knew the New Testament, then these and several other statements will be seen to contain traces of Christianity. But this is most improbable. To have borrowed Christian ideas or expressions and then eliminated any clear reference to Christ or some apostle or other New Testament personality would have gone completely against the grain of any second-century Gnostic.'[39]

But against the contention of MacRae and of Böhlig we may consider Pétrement's suggestion as to why there are no explicit references to Christianity if the work is in fact influenced by Christianity. Her suggestion is that the work contains no explicit Christian references because it is supposed to be a revelation to Adam, who lived long before Christ.[40] Böhlig's response that despite the Adam frame a Christian would have added a reference to the covenant is not convincing.

[36] Review of Böhlig and Labib, *Koptisch-gnostische Apocalypsen aus Codex V*, by K. Rudolph in *ThLZ* 90 (1965), col. 361.
[37] R. Kasser, *op. cit.*, pp. 316–317.
[38] G. W. MacRae, 'The Coptic-Gnostic Apocalypse of Adam', *Heythrop Journal* 6 (1965), p. 34.
[39] *Ibid.*, p. 32.
[40] S. Pétrement, 'Le Colloque de Messine', p. 368.

Indeed, unless one places the composition in the first century AD or earlier it would have been difficult for any Gnostic *not* to have been acquainted with the New Testament or at least with the basic tenets of Christianity. But there is no compelling reason to place the composition of the work that early, as we shall see, apart from Böhlig's association of the Adam *Apocalypse* with Iranian and Mandaean currents.[41] In fact, the allusions to Christianity and the New Testament are so numerous and transparent – at least to most reviewers – that they are escapable only through a conscious effort, as on the part of Böhlig and MacRae, to imagine a situation in which the writer was ignorant of the New Testament and of Christianity.

These rather obvious Christian allusions cluster especially in the Illuminator passage which I have paraphrased above, and in the following passage describing the successive generations. Wilson is understating the impression this reader gets when he says, 'the narrative, brief and summary as it is, appears too closely tailored to the figure of Jesus to be entirely independent'.[42] When one has together the following traits: (1) the working of signs and marvels, (2) the opposition of powers who will not see the Enlightener, (3) the punishment of the flesh of the Enlightener, and (4) the descent of the Holy Spirit upon the Enlightener, it would seem fairly obvious that we have here a reference to Jesus Christ.[43]

In an article published in 1964 Böhlig tried to explain the suffering of the Enlightener in terms of the prediction of the suffering of a Saviour by Zoroaster, as recorded in the writings of Theodore bar Konai, who wrote, it should be noted, at

[41] In fact, the Mandaean parallels incline Wilson to favour a late date: 'In view of this, and of the Mandean and other parallels to which Böhlig has drawn attention, I should be inclined (but very tentatively!) to disagree with him and suggest that this document represents not a pre-Christian Gnosis but a later stage.' Wilson, *Gnosis and the New Testament*, p. 139.

[42] *Ibid.*, p. 138.

[43] So the reviews by J. Daniélou, *RechSR* 54 (1966), pp. 285–293; by R. Haardt, *Wiener Zeitschrift für die Kunde des Morgenlandes* 61 (1967), pp. 153–159; by A. Orbe, *Gregorianum* 46 (1965), pp. 169–172; and by H.-M. Schenke, *OLZ* 61 (1966), cols 23–34. For Sanders to cite only the few reviews favourable to Böhlig's thesis in his discussion of the Adam *Apocalypse* without listing all the unfavourable reviews is misleading to say the least. Or was he unaware of these reviews?

the end of the eighth century AD![44] Writing in 1968, Böhlig accepted MacRae's alternative explanation in terms of the Jewish concept of the suffering Messiah as outlined by J. Jeremias.[45] But *pace* MacRae I see no reference to a *Pais* or Servant in the text, nor to the suffering of a Messiah who vicariously expiates the sins of Israel before the establishment of his rule.[46] The concept of the punishment of the flesh of the man who is the Illuminator – upon whom the Holy Spirit has descended, who does signs and marvels, but who is opposed by the powers – is not Iranian and not Jewish, but Christian.

There are also possible references to the New Testament in the following passage which describes the successive genera-tions. In the third kingdom, a child issues from the womb of a virgin and is cast out of his village with his mother. He is led to a desert and nourished there. One is reminded not only of the virgin birth, and Christ's temptation in the wilderness, but also of Revelation 12:13–14, which Böhlig himself notes, in which a mother and child are cast into the wilderness. Böhlig, however, would suggest that there might be a reference here to a myth which presumably lay behind the Revelation passage!

Böhlig prefers more distant Iranian parallels to more im-mediately available Christian parallels. Wilson asks, 'we need some further information about the Iranian parallels to which Böhlig appeals, their date and so forth'.[47] As we have already pointed out in our chapter on the Iranian evidence, almost all of the Iranian sources are post-Christian, in fact post-Parthian and even post-Sassanian. For example, when Böhlig speaks of the Phoster as Zarathustra or the Soshyant 'Saviour', he is aware that the development of an eschatological concept of the Soshyant is to be found only in the Pahlavi texts of the ninth century AD.[48] According to Zaehner, these Pahlavi texts 'almost certainly reflect the theological views of the last cen-tury of Sassanian rule (i.e. sixth–seventh century AD)'.[49] The

[44] A. Böhlig, 'Die Adamsapokalypse aus Codex V von Nag Hammadi als Zeugnis jüdisch-iranischer Gnosis', *Oriens Christianus* 48 (1964), p. 47.

[45] A. Böhlig, *Mysterion und Wahrheit*, p. 154.

[46] W. Zimmerli and J. Jeremias, *The Servant of God* (1957), pp. 77–78.

[47] R. McL. Wilson, *Gnosis and the New Testament*, p. 138.

[48] A. Böhlig, 'Die Adamsapokalypse', pp. 47–48.

[49] R. C. Zaehner, *The Dawn and Twilight of Zoroastrianism*, pp. 58–59.

Soshyant as he appears in the early *Gathas* is no eschatological figure but Zoroaster himself.[50]

Böhlig also makes references to Mithra as the background for some of the features in the *Apocalypse of Adam*.[51] And indeed the image of the child issuing from the rock in the eighth kingdom seems to be a clear reference to a well-known tradition of Mithra.[52] But does this necessarily provide us with a link with pre-Christian Iranian traditions? I think not. Apart from Asia Minor, where the cult of Mithra was strong in Cilicia, Cappadocia, Commagene, and Pontus, the spread of Mithraism to the west is a relatively late phenomenon succeeding rather than preceding the birth of Christianity.

Widengren, the greatest current advocate of Iranian influences in Gnosticism, claims that 'It is quite possible that there existed at Dura (Europos) a cult of Mithra in the form of Mithraic mysteries already at the end of the first post-Christian century (AD 80–85).' But he also says, 'the evidence is very uncertain'. He adds, 'My statement in *Handbuch der Orientalistik* . . . though hesitant in itself was too positive. I now see the difficulties quite well.'[53]

Plutarch mentions that Pompey removed some pirates from Cilicia, who were worshippers of Mithras, to Olympus in Lycia in Asia Minor in 67 BC. But apart from the visit of the Armenian king, who was a worshipper of Mithra, to Nero, there is no evidence of the penetration of Mithra to the west until the end of the first century AD. According to Vermaseren:

> 'One other point worthy of note is that no Mithraic monument can be dated earlier than the end of the first century A.D., and even the extensive investigations at Pompeii, buried beneath the ashes of Vesuvius in A.D. 79, have not so far produced a single image of the god. There is therefore a complete gap in our knowledge between 67 B.C. and A.D. 79.'[54]

[50] *Cf.* C. Colpe, *Die religionsges. Schule*, p. 164: '. . . so wie Sōšyans an ihrem Ende steht. Mit dem gnostischen Urmenschen hat das nichts zu tun. . . . Dieser Sōšyans ist ein Heros, kein inkarnierter Erlösungsgott, im Deutschen eher ein Heiland als ein Erlöser zu nennen. . . .'

[51] A. Böhlig, 'Die Adamsapokalypse', pp. 47–48.

[52] M. J. Vermaseren, *Mithras, The Secret God* (1963), p. 76.

[53] G. Widengren, 'The Mithraic Mysteries in the Greco-Roman World with Special Regard to Their Iranian Background', *Academia Nazionale dei Lincei* (1966), p. 452.

[54] M. J. Vermaseren, *op. cit.*, p. 29.

For those who may not be familiar with Mithraism, it should be pointed out that our evidence for Mithra in the west is mainly iconographic; the few inscriptions are scanty and late.[55]

In contrast to the relatively early dating of the Mithraeum at Dura advocated by Widengren, the excavation reports indicate that the Mithraeum was founded in AD 168.[56] The only dated Mithraic inscriptions from the pre-Christian period are the texts of Antiochus I of Commagene (69–34 BC) at Nemrud-Dagh in eastern Asia Minor. After that there is one possible inscription from the first century AD from Farasha in Cappadocia, one inscription from Savçilar in Phrygia dated to AD 77–78, and one inscription from Rome dated to the reign of Trajan (AD 98–117). All other dated Mithraic inscriptions and monuments belong to the second century (after AD 140), the third century and the fourth century AD.[57] It therefore seems more probable to me that the clear reference to Mithra in the Adam *Apocalypse* should be taken as an evidence for a post-Christian rather than a pre-Christian date in view of the late distribution of Mithraism in the west.

There are to be sure older Zoroastrian texts which refer to Mithra. But these older texts, such as the Mithra Yasht,[58] present a picture of Mithra which cannot serve as a background for the Redeemer myth, for the older Mithra is simply a god who watches over cattle and the sanctity of contracts.[59] Nor can the references to Mithra be readily combined with references to the Gayomart, as some have advocated, to provide an Iranian prototype for the Gnostic Redeemer.[60]

[55] The attempt of H. D. Betz, 'The Mithras Inscriptions of Santa Prisca and the New Testament', *NovTest* 10 (1968), pp. 52–80, to compare the striking second-century AD inscriptions of a Mithraeum at Rome with the New Testament is quite anachronistic.

[56] M. J. Vermaseren, *Corpus Inscriptionum et Monumentorum Religionis Mithriacae* (1956), p. 57.

[57] *Ibid.*, p. 362.

[58] *Cf.* I. Gershevitch, *The Avestan Hymn to Mithra* (1959).

[59] R. C. Zaehner, *The Dawn and Twilight of Zoroastrianism*, p. 99. *Cf.* Mary Boyce, 'On Mithra's Part in Zoroastrianism', *Bulletin of the London School of Oriental and African Studies* 32 (1969), pp. 10–34.

[60] C. Colpe, *Die religionsges. Schule*, p. 167: 'Aber so offenkundig die Analogien zwischen Gayōmart- und Mithrasmythus sind (z.B. Tötung des Urstieres, die jedoch im ersten Falle nicht von der Hand Gayōmarts, sondern durch Ohrmazd erfolgt), so deutlich ist es auch, dass Gayōmart

When we turn from the Iranian parallels to the *Apocalypse of Adam* adduced by Böhlig to the Mandaean parallels, we find again that his arguments are strained and that his conclusions go beyond the evidence. In the *Apocalypse of Adam*, Adam receives a vision of three men. Böhlig compares this to the three Uthras of the Right *Ginza* (*GR*) XI. Adam's revelation to Seth foretells an initial destruction by flood with the exception of Noah's family, and a second destruction by fire with the exception of Seth's seed. The same section of the Ginza describes three destructions: (1) by sword, (2) by fire, and (3) by flood.[61] Although the parallel is far from exact – there is no destruction by sword in the Adam *Apocalypse* and the order of the destructions by fire and flood are reversed – Böhlig maintains that the tradition in the *Apocalypse* is derived from the Mandaeans.[62] Elsewhere Böhlig recognizes that Josephus in his *Antiquities* i. 70 says, 'Adam having predicted a destruction of the universe at one time by a violent fire and at another by a mighty deluge of water . . .', and admits that the story in the *Apocalypse* may even be a distorted picture of the Old Testament story of Sodom and Gomorrah.[63] The destruction by fire will be accompanied by falling asphalt and either sulphur or pumice.[64]

The simple reference to baptism in the Adam *Apocalypse*

---

und Mithra in soteriologischer Hinsicht nicht zu vergleichen sind. Überdies ist es evident, dass auch der Mithrasmythus keine Vor- oder Nebenform desselben Erlösermythus ist, den wir in den gnostischen Systemen vor uns haben.'

[61] *GR* XI. 259ff. Citations from the *Ginza* are from Lidzbarski's translation. The Roman numeral refers to the section, and the Arabic numeral to the page of his translation.

[62] A. Böhlig, 'Die Adamsapokalypse', p. 47.

[63] A. Böhlig, *Mysterion und Wahrheit*, p. 153. *Cf.* R. McL. Wilson, *Gnosis and the New Testament*, p. 137.

[64] *Cf.* R. Kasser, 'Bibliothèque gnostique', p. 325. H Goedicke, 'An Unexpected Allusion to the Vesuvius Eruption in 79 A.D.', *American Journal of Philology* 90 (1969), pp. 340–341, even detects verbal allusions to the famous description of the eruption of Vesuvius in AD 79 as contained in the letters of the Younger Pliny to Tacitus. As Pliny died *c.* AD 117, Goedicke would date the Adam *Apocalypse* not later than the first decade of the second century. But assuming that Goedicke is correct, it would seem that the date of Pliny's death would establish the *terminus a quo* rather than the *terminus ad quem* of the *Apocalypse*, which would then date it not earlier than this.

does not justify any derivation from the Mandaeans.[65] For as Böhlig himself notes, baptism in the *Apocalypse* is spiritualized and is identified with gnosis.[66] But this is certainly not the case with baptism among the Mandaeans. With them the rite itself together with its many elaborate elements must be meticulously observed lest its potency be nullified.

We therefore conclude that Böhlig's far-reaching thesis that the *Apocalypse of Adam* by reason of Iranian and Mandaean parallels is a document of non-Christian and pre-Christian Gnosticism is simply a hypothesis which is built on too many precarious assumptions.

IV. THE PARAPHRASE OF SHEM

As a document which may yet present evidence of a non-Christian and perhaps pre-Christian Gnostic Redeemer, Robinson has called attention to the as yet unpublished *Paraphrase of Shem* (*CG* VII. 1).[67] He suggests that this tractate even more than the *Apocalypse of Adam* presents us with evidence which is unambiguous:

'Missing are the Apocalypse of Adam's reference to a redeemer from a virgin womb, to persons receiving his name on the water, and to his suffering in the flesh. Rather we have more nearly the gnostic myth as scholarship conjectured it to be presupposed in 1 Cor. ii. 6ff., when one spoke of the "pre-Christian" Gnostic redeemer myth in relation to primitive Christianity.'[68]

Frederik Wisse, who has access to the unpublished text, has argued for its non-Christian nature in a recent article.[69] The tractate has two speakers: the recipient of the revelation, Shem, and the revealer, Derdekeas. There is a sharp polemic against baptism by water. Wisse prefers to see this as a polemic not against Christian baptism, but against the bap-

---

[65] *Pace* K. Rudolph, 'Gnosis und Gnostizismus', p. 166; Rudolph has supported Böhlig's case. See his review of Böhlig and Labib in *ThLZ* 90 (1965), cols 359–362.
[66] A. Böhlig and P. Labib, *Apocalypsen aus Codex V*, p. 95; and Böhlig, 'Die Adamsapokalypse', p. 46.
[67] J. M. Robinson, 'The Coptic Gnostic Library', pp. 378ff.
[68] *Ibid.*, p. 380.
[69] F. Wisse, 'The Redeemer Figure in the Paraphrase of Shem', *NovTest* 12 (1970), pp. 130–140.

tism of some Jewish baptistic sect. A possible allusion to Jesus'
baptism in the Jordan is interpreted by Wisse as the descent
of the Gnostic Redeemer into the realm of darkness. In contrast
to the 'slim and controversial parallels with Christianity'
there are many clear allusions to the Old Testament, albeit in
a perverse sense. Wisse argues, 'if the tractate also presupposed
Christianity, however polemically, we would have expected
identifiable traces of Christian material comparable to those
from the Old Testament.' [70]

We shall, of course, have to suspend judgment until we can
see the text as it is published, especially when we remember
the difference of opinions which have been expressed as to the
alleged lack of references to Christianity in the *Apocalypse of
Adam*. Professor Andrew Helmbold, a member of the Coptic
Gnostic Library project, who has also had access to the unpublished Nag Hammadi Coptic texts, writes in response to
my query:

> '. . . I am not sold at all on the arguments of Böhlig and Wisse in
> regard to the Adam Apocalypse and Paraphrase of Shem respectively.
> . . . In fact, comparing the role of the Redeemer, Derdekeos, in Shem
> with the role of Christ, one is forced to ask if Derdekeos is a redeemer
> in any New Testament sense of the word.' [71]

[70] *Ibid.*, p. 137.
[71] Personal letter of 27 July 1971. Professor Malcolm Peel, another
member of the Coptic Gnostic Library project, in answer to my inquiry,
has written: 'I have recently read through the whole of Nag Hammadi
(that so far done and at my disposal) and cannot at the moment add anything further to your list of non-Christian tractates.' Personal letter of
17 August 1971.

CHAPTER EIGHT

THE MANDAIC EVIDENCE

I. POSITIVE EVALUATION OF THE MANDAICA AS EARLY EVIDENCE

The history of Mandaean scholarship may be divided into two phases: (1) the earlier phase from about 1900 to 1950 was dependent upon the translations of important Mandaic texts by Lidzbarski. It was characterized on the one hand by a positive evaluation by some scholars – notably Reitzenstein and Bultmann – of the Mandaica as evidence of early pre-Christian Gnosticism, and on the other hand by a negative reaction on the part of other scholars who dismissed the Mandaic materials as irrelevant to the study of the New Testament because of their late documentation. (2) A more recent phase from 1950 to the present has been stimulated by the studies of Drower, Rudolph, and Macuch, who have reaffirmed an early Palestinian origin of Mandaeism.

In our introductory chapter (section III, 'Pre-Christian Gnosticism'), we have already discussed the appropriation by Reitzenstein of the Mandaean evidence for his theories, and the decisive application of these materials by Bultmann in New Testament studies. This is not the place to go into an extensive survey of the publication of the Mandaic texts and their impact on New Testament studies, but some summary remarks are in order.[1]

---

[1] See E. M. Yamauchi, 'The Present Status of Mandaean Studies', and *GEMO*, pp. 1–10. *Cf.* also S. Schulz, 'Die Bedeutung neuer Gnosisfunde . . .', *ThR* 26 (1960), pp. 310–334; R. Macuch, 'Der gegenwärtige Stand der Mandäerforschung und ihre Aufgaben', *OLZ* 63, 1–2 (1968), cols 5–14; K. Rudolph, 'Das Christentum in der Sicht der mandäischen Religion', *Wissenschaftliche Zeitschrift der Karl-Marx-Universität* (Leipzig) 7 (1957–1958), pp. 651ff.; *Die Mandäer* I; 'Probleme einer Entwicklungsgeschichte der mandäischen Religion', in *OG* pp. 583–596; 'Problems of a History of the Development of the Mandaean Religion', *History of*

As noted earlier Bultmann in his important 1925 article,[2] drawing upon the publications by M. Lidzbarski of the *Johannesbuch* in 1905 and 1915, the *Mandäische Liturgien* in 1920, and the *Ginza* in 1925, provided a model of the pre-Christian Redeemer myth supposedly current in early Mandaean circles. Other scholars, such as W. Bauer in the second edition of his commentary on the Gospel of John,[3] and Bultmann's own students began to make extensive use of the Mandaic documents to illuminate the New Testament. In his synthetic study of the phenomenon of Gnosticism, Bultmann's student, Hans Jonas, relied primarily on Mandaic texts. He has written: 'Of inestimable value for the knowledge of Gnosticism outside the Christian orbit are the sacred books of the *Mandaeans*. . . .'[4]

Oscar Cullmann in his 1930 study of the Pseudo-Clementines revealed that he was favourably impressed by the arguments of Lidzbarski and Reitzenstein for the antiquity of the Mandaeans.[5] In an essay on the Dead Sea Scrolls published in 1957 he reiterated his faith that the Mandaeans represent an early Palestinian baptismal sect: 'We knew it before, thanks to the rediscovery of the so-called Mandean texts and their publication by M. Lidzbarski in the 1920's which acquainted us with a pre-Christian baptist movement that had spread over Palestine and Syria and must somehow have had an effect on the disciples of John the Baptist as well as on those of Jesus.'[6] In an essay published in 1968, Cullmann continues to seek support from the Mandaic texts as well as from the Dead Sea Scrolls for his view that Christianity arose 'in a *Palestinian*-Syrian Judaism of a distinctive kind, which in turn was already influenced by oriental-Hellenistic syncretism'.[7]

Religions 8 (1969), pp. 210–234, which is a translation and expansion of the article in *OG*.

[2] R. Bultmann, 'Die Bedeutung der neuerschlossenen . . . Quellen.' *Cf.* C. Colpe, *Die religionsges. Schule*, p. 57.

[3] W. Bauer, *Das Johannesevangelium* (1912; 2nd ed. 1925).

[4] H. Jonas, *The Gnostic Religion* (1958; 2nd ed. 1963), p. 39; *cf. Gnosis und spätantiker Geist* I, p. x.

[5] O. Cullmann, *Le problème . . . du roman pseudo-Clémentin*, pp. 178–180.

[6] O. Cullmann, 'The Significance of the Qumran Texts for Research into the Beginnings of Christianity', in K. Stendahl (ed.), *The Scrolls and the New Testament* (1957), pp. 19f.

[7] O. Cullmann, 'Wandlungen in der neuern Forschungsgeschichte

II. NEGATIVE EVALUATION OF THE MANDAICA AS EARLY EVIDENCE

In opposition to the enthusiastic advocates of the early date of the Mandaica there have always been scholars who argued that the late manuscripts could not justifiably be used in New Testament interpretation. Pallis argued that the Mandaeans derived their knowledge of Jewish names and ideas only at a very late date through the Qur'an.[8] Peterson was of the opinion that the sect was established in the eighth century AD.[9] The great church historian, H. Lietzmann, suggested that the Mandaeans derived the word *yardna* 'Jordan' from the use of this word for 'font' by Syrian Christians. He placed the origin of the sect in the seventh century AD.[10]

English-speaking scholars on the whole have been quite reluctant to admit an early date for the origin of the Mandaeans. F. C. Burkitt pointed out that the Mandaeans' acquaintance with the Syriac Peshitta and affinities with Marcionism and Manichaeism would point to a post-Christian date for the genesis of Mandaeism.[11] After World War II, C. H. Dodd extensively reviewed the arguments used by Lidzbarski, Reitzenstein, and Bultmann, and concluded: 'But alleged parallels drawn from this medieval body of literature have no value for the study of the Fourth Gospel unless they can be supported by earlier evidence.'[12] Dodd's verdict is accepted as sound by Neill,[13] and a similarly negative view is expressed by Casey in a *Festschrift* to Dodd.[14] In 1954 Turner could say: 'The attempt to derive the Fourth Gospel from Mandaean sources is already a curiosity of scholarship. . . .'[15]

---

des Urchristentums. Zugleich ein Beitrag zum Problem: Theologie und Geschichtswissenschaft', in *Discordia Concors* (*Edgar Bonjour Festschrift*) (1968), pp. 58ff., cited in *Trajectories*, pp. 264f.

[8] S. A. Pallis, *Mandaean Studies* (1926), pp. 116–118.

[9] E. Peterson, 'Urchristentum und Mandäismus', *ZNW* 27 (1928), pp. 55–98.

[10] H. Lietzmann, 'Ein Beitrag zur Mandäerfrage', *Sitzungsberichte der Preussischen Akademie der Wissenschaften* (1930), pp. 595–608.

[11] F. C. Burkitt, *Church and Gnosis* (1932), pp. 92–122.

[12] C. H. Dodd, *The Interpretation of the Fourth Gospel*, p. 130.

[13] S. Neill, *The Interpretation of the New Testament*, p. 178.

[14] R. P. Casey, 'Gnosis, Gnosticism and the New Testament', p. 55.

[15] H. E. W. Turner, *The Pattern of Christian Truth*, p. 113.

The major American authority on Gnosticism, R. M. Grant, was scathingly critical of Jonas's liberal use of Mandaic texts for his analysis of the Gnostic phenomenon. Grant wrote in a review of Jonas's *Gnosis und spätantiker Geist* as follows:

> 'The first chapter of the first volume deals with "the Logos of Gnosis", and relies primarily on Mandaean literature. The clarity of Jonas's picture of Mandaean gnosis is certainly not matched by the Mandaean literature itself, which is really a hodge-podge. And the choice of this starting-point means that chronology makes no difference; essentially we are dealing with the (or a) Logos of Mandaism. On this basis it is hard to see how, in Volume II, Jonas can proceed to trace historical development.'[16]

More recently, Grant in compiling a source-book of Gnostic texts concedes that some form of Mandaeism may have existed in the early Christian centuries but considers the influence of Mandaean thought on the early Gnostic teachers so problematic that he has not included any Mandaean selections.[17]

Morton Smith in a survey of Aramaic studies and the New Testament concluded rather puckishly: 'The chief contribution of Mandaean studies to New Testament criticism, therefore, is to have called forth the book of Thomas, *Le Mouvement baptiste en Palestine*, which collects the ancient evidence about baptismal sects.'[18] Sandmel holds that the Mandaean 'bubble' is unimportant for Jewish and New Testament studies.[19] Brown in his recent commentary on John writes: 'The oldest forms of Mandaean theology known to us are to be dated relatively late in the Christian era, and there is no possibility that John was influenced by this thought as we now know it. . . .'[20] MacRae in an encyclopedia article concludes: 'Though the time and place of origin of this religion are still matters of uncertainty and dispute, Mandaeism may safely be regarded as a late form of Gnostic religion, perhaps originating in the 5th century A.D.'[21]

---

[16] In *JTS*, n.s. 7 (1956), p. 309.
[17] R. M. Grant, *Gnosticism: A Sourcebook*, p. 14.
[18] M. Smith, 'Aramaic Studies and the Study of the New Testament', *Journal of Bible and Religion* 26 (1958), p. 305.
[19] S. Sandmel, *The First Christian Century in Judaism and Christianity* (1969), p. 157.
[20] R. E. Brown, *The Gospel According to John I–XII*, p. LV.
[21] G. W. MacRae in the *New Catholic Encyclopedia* VI, p. 523.

The Scottish scholar, R. McL. Wilson, in a survey of the problem of Gnosticism published in 1958, wrote that 'our evidence does not seem to permit of our placing the Mandeans before 400 A.D. . . .'[22] But in a work published in 1968 he is open to the possibility of a first-century AD origin of Mandaeism but warns against the facile assumption that what we find in the extant texts was in existence from the very outset.[23]

III. RECENT RE-EVALUATIONS

As the change in Wilson's position indicates, recent Mandaean studies have opened up the possibility that the Mandaeans may have originated in an earlier period than some have been willing to concede. The publications of Mandaic magical texts in the 1930s and 1940s by E. S. Drower and Cyrus H. Gordon had little direct impact upon New Testament studies.[24] It was the publication by Lady Drower in 1953 of the *Haran Gawaita* – a text purportedly narrating the exodus of the Mandaeans from Palestine to Mesopotamia – which re-awakened interest in the claims for the early Palestinian origin of the Mandaeans.[25] Macuch first called attention to the possible implications of this document in an article published in 1957.[26] Further interest was aroused when K. Rudolph expanded his 1956 Leipzig dissertation into a magisterial two-volume work on the Mandaeans published in 1960–1961.[27]

The common conviction of the three leading Mandaic scholars – Drower, Macuch, and Rudolph – that the Mandaeans had their origin in pre-Christian Palestine is having an increasing influence upon Gnostic and New Testament studies. Quispel, for example, writes: 'And after the publications of Lady Drower, Macuch and Rudolph we may assume

---

[22] R. McL. Wilson, *The Gnostic Problem*, pp. 66f.
[23] Wilson, *Gnosis and the New Testament*, p. 14.
[24] See E. M. Yamauchi, *Mandaic Incantation Texts* (1967); and 'A Mandaic Magic Bowl from the Yale Babylonian Collection', *Berytus* 17 (1967), pp. 49ff.
[25] E. S. Drower, *The Haran Gawaita*.
[26] R. Macuch, 'Alter und Heimat des Mandäismus nach neuerschlossenen Quellen', *ThLZ* 82 (1957), cols 401–408.
[27] K. Rudolph, *Die Mandäer* I and II.

that the Mandaeans are of Palestinian, prechristian origin.'[28]
Quispel has also declared that even if Mandaeism turns out to
be neither so old nor of Palestinian origin, the obligatory
reading of Mandaean writings could serve New Testament
students as a good preparation for the right understanding of
the Fourth Gospel.[29] Elsewhere Quispel expresses himself
more cautiously and notes: 'The relationship between Proto-
Mandaeism and Gnosticism of the first and second century is
still not clear.'[30]

Schenke places the origin of the Mandaeans in the Jordan
Valley in the first Christian century. He conceives of Mandaeism as having evolved through three stages: (1) Originally
the Mandaeans were a heretical Jewish baptismal sect, one
among many. (2) The Mandaeans then accepted a Gnostic
Weltanschauung. (3) This Gnosis was finally institutionalized.[31]
Arai counts the Urmandäer of the Jordan together with the
Simonians of Samaria as the oldest Gnostics.[32] On the basis of
recent studies, Kümmel concludes:

'It is confirmed that John could not have been influenced by the
Mandaean texts which have been preserved, indeed, that a direct
connection of John with Mandaean or primitive Mandaean circles is out
of the question. Yet the similarity of the Johannine and the Mandaean
conceptions, repeatedly observed (Rudolph, Widengren), points to the
conclusion that the Mandean texts are late and deformed witnesses
for a Jewish Gnosticism which took form on the edge of Judaism, and
which is to be accepted as the spiritual background of John.'[33]

With less caution James Robinson has hailed the Mandaean
contributions as follows: 'Meanwhile Lady Drower has published Mandaean texts in hitherto unequaled quantities, and
research in this field, though less well known than Qumran
studies, has progressed steadily, with the result that the position of Lidzbarski presupposed by Bultmann has been steadily
strengthened.'[34] Schmithals, who is heavily dependent upon

---

[28] In a review of S. Sandmel, *The First Christian Century*, in *BiOr* 27.
1–2 (1970), p. 69.
[29] G. Quispel, 'Gnosticism and the New Testament', p. 266.
[30] Quispel, 'Gnosis', p. 30.
[31] H.-M. Schenke, 'Die Gnosis', pp. 396ff.
[32] S. Arai, 'Zur Definition der Gnosis', in *OG*, p. 186.
[33] Feine–Behm–Kümmel, p. 159.
[34] *Trajectories*, p. 263.

the Mandaean texts for his reconstructions, writes: 'We remember that the Mandaeans at the outset were at home in the Palestinian setting and, in fact, in the primitive Christian time.'[35] In a footnote he adds: 'The early dating of the beginnings of the Mandaean literature in the pre-Christian and early Christian period is less disputed today than ever.'[36]

IV. THE ROLE OF JOHN THE BAPTIST

When the Mandaeans first became known to the Europeans in the seventeenth century, Ignatius a Jesu, a Catholic missionary, called them 'Christiani S. Joannis Baptistae' because of their veneration for John the Baptist. This is in marked contrast to their attitude to Jesus, whom they denounce as a false prophet.

According to Reitzenstein the primitive Christian conception of baptism borrowed from John was in its basic outlines identical with that found in the Mandaean liturgies, where a rite mediating forgiveness and elevation into heaven was transformed into an initiatory rite.[37] Bultmann in his 1925 article suggested as 'ausserordentlich wahrscheinlich' that the Mandaeans originated as a baptismal sect, founded by John the Baptist.[38] Similar suggestions have been repeated. Max Pulver wrote in 1943: 'Among the Mandaeans baptism is performed in the river of light, the Jordan. From this Mandaean baptism possibly is descended the baptism of John, which is in turn connected with that of the Christians.'[39]

The identification of the baptism of the Mandaeans, of John the Baptist, and of the Essenes of Qumran has been most recently advocated by Huth. He asserts that the Dead Sea Scrolls provide us with a solution to the Mandaean problem which confirms Lidzbarski's hypothesis of a Palestinian

[35] W. Schmithals, *The Office of Apostle*, p. 185.

[36] *Ibid.*, p. 185, n. 385.

[37] R. Reitzenstein, *Die Vorgeschichte der christlichen Taufe* (1929; repr. 1967).

[38] R. Bultmann, 'Die Bedeutung der neuerschlossenen . . . Quellen', pp. 142–143.

[39] M. Pulver, 'The Experience of Light in the Gospel of St. John, in the "Corpus hermeticum", in Gnosticism, and in the Eastern Church', originally published in 1943, reprinted in *Spiritual Disciplines* (*Papers from the Eranos Yearbooks*) (1960), p. 242.

origin of the Mandaeans. He further argues as follows: (1) John the Baptist was an Essene. (2) Jesus was a disciple of the Baptist. (3) Jesus later separated himself from John.[40] Huth follows Widengren in maintaining that the Mandaean traditions of John the Baptist belong to the oldest strata.[41]

Most recent studies, however, relegate John the Baptist to a late stage of the Mandaean traditions. Dodd, who stressed the difference between the single baptism of the Baptist and the repeated lustrations of the Mandaeans, wrote: 'In view of these considerations, the connection between John and the Mandaeans begins to wear thin.'[42] He also notes the fact that John is not only known as Yohanan among the Mandaeans, but also under the Arabic form Yahya by which John is known in the Qur'an. According to Dodd:

'Although Lidzbarski seeks to minimize the significance of this fact, the natural inference is that many of the allusions to John, particularly in the Book of John, belong to the Islamic period. This lends colour to the view that the prominence of John the Baptist is a late development.'[43]

Rudolph also notes that John does not appear in the baptismal ritual of the Mandaeans. He would consider all the traditions concerning John in Mandaean sources as secondary, without any historical authenticity. John is not a redeemer figure, nor does he play any decisive role in the constitution of Mandaean religion.[44] Segelberg's conclusions are similar:

'Probably the Johannine traditions do not belong to the most ancient strata of the Mandaean literature. Except in the Book of John they appear mainly in the Haran Gawaita. . . . In the liturgies, where Rudolph . . . regards them as entirely unknown, they nevertheless appear, both in Abahatan and in CP (The Canonical Prayerbook), 105, which is known under the name *Asiet Malkie*. None of these texts seem to belong to the most ancient liturgical texts, at least not in their present form.'[45]

[40] O. Huth, 'Das Mandäerproblem', pp. 24, 35.
[41] *Ibid.*, p. 38, citing G. Widengren, 'Die Mandäer', in B. Spuler (ed.), *Handbuch der Orientalistik* VIII. 2 (1961), p. 91.
[42] C. H. Dodd, *The Interpretation of the Fourth Gospel*, p. 124.
[43] *Ibid.*
[44] K. Rudolph, *Die Mandäer* I, pp. 66–80.
[45] E. Segelberg, 'Old and New Testament Figures in Mandaean Version', pp. 236–237.

The consequences for New Testament studies of this evaluation were perceived by Schweizer, who realized that analysis
showed that the Baptist was only lately introduced into the
Mandaean traditions: 'The stories about him are pure legends,
and not even old legends at that.'[46] More recently Meeks has
dismissed the figure of John as follows: 'The emphasis on
John the Baptist as "our prophet" is a secondary development
in the face of Islamic pressure; "Iaia" or "Iuhana" is never a
significant revealer and not one of the apostles sent from the
light world in the earlier texts.'[47]

V. ARGUMENTS FROM THE COLOPHONS AND FROM EPIGRAPHY

Although an increasing number of New Testament scholars
are citing the works of Rudolph and of Macuch to support
an early date for the origins of the Mandaeans, there have
been few critical examinations of their arguments. We should
like therefore to subject their arguments to a detailed examination in the following pages.

The important study of T. Säve-Söderbergh, by demonstrating that some of the *Psalms of Thomas* – the disciple of Mani –
are adaptations of Mandaean materials, has shown that some,
at least, of the Mandaean texts must have originated by the
third century AD.[48] An important Middle Persian inscription
of a zealous Zoroastrian named Kartir, dated to *c*. AD 275
early in the Sassanid period, and found at Naqsh-i-Rustam
may possibly point to the same conclusion.[49] Among the non-
Zoroastrian groups whom Kartir persecuted are listed the
kristiyānē and the *nāṣorāyē*. The former group are clearly the
Christians, but who are the latter? Now the name *mandaiia*,
from which we derive the name 'Mandaean', is the name given
to the laity of the community. Their initiated priests are called
naṣuraiia or 'Naṣoraeans'. The identification of Kartir's group
with the Mandaeans is therefore favoured by Rudolph,[50] by

---

[46] E. Schweizer, *Ego Eimi*, p. 51.
[47] W. Meeks, *The Prophet-King*, p. 284.
[48] T. Säve-Söderbergh, *Studies in the Coptic Manichaean Psalm Book.*
[49] M. Sprengling, *Third Century Iran: Sapor and Kartir* (1953).
[50] K. Rudolph, *Die Mandäer* I, p. 115.

Widengren,[51] and with some hesitation by Frye.[52] On the other hand, Quispel suggests that Kartir's 'Nazorees' (sic) may include both the Jewish Christians in the Persian Empire and the indigenous Christians who use Aramaic as opposed to the Greek-speaking Gentile Christians.[53]

The extant Mandaic manuscripts are admittedly quite late. The oldest dated manuscript comes from the sixteenth century.[54] Most of the other manuscripts come from the eighteenth and nineteenth centuries.[55] If we accept, as Macuch does, the colophon in the first part of the Canonical Prayerbook,[56] which lists the copyists and their dates, we may arrive at a date in the second half of the third century AD for the original composition.[57]

In addition to the manuscripts, which are late copies, there are some early and original Mandaic magic bowl texts and lead strips. The bowls are dated quite certainly about AD 600, since they are very similar to Aramaic bowls, some of which were found in a datable context at Nippur.[58]

Until recently the only lead strip that had been deciphered was one published by Lidzbarski in 1909.[59] This was dated by him to AD 400, and was therefore considered the oldest Man-

---

[51] G. Widengren, *Mani and Manichaeism*, p. 16.

[52] R. N. Frye, *The Heritage of Persia* (1963), p. 210.

[53] G. Quispel, 'The Discussion of Judaic Christianity', p. 88.

[54] R. Macuch, *Handbook of Classical and Modern Mandaic* (1965), p. LVI.

[55] Lady Drower donated her extensive collection of manuscripts to the Bodleian Library in Oxford. Many of these are as yet unpublished. Thanks to a grant from the American Philosophical Society, the writer was able to spend part of the summer of 1970 in beginning an examination of some of these manuscripts.

[56] E. S. Drower, *The Canonical Prayerbook*, p. 71.

[57] R. Macuch, 'Anfänge der Mandäer', in F. Altheim and R. Stiehl (eds), *Die Araber in der Alten Welt* II (1965), pp. 160–162.

[58] J. Montgomery, *Aramaic Incantation Texts from Nippur* (1913); cf. E. M. Yamauchi, 'Aramaic Magic Bowls', *JAOS* 85 (1965), pp. 511–523. Cf. J. Teixidor, 'The Syriac Incantation Bowls in the Iraq Museum', *Sumer* 18 (1962), pp. 51–62. See also Yamauchi, *Mandaic Incantation Texts*, and 'A Mandaic Magic Bowl'.

[59] M. Lidzbarski, 'Ein mandäisches Amulett', in *Florilegium ou recueil de travaux d'érudition dédiés à M. Melchior de Vogüé* (1909), pp. 349–373. See Yamauchi, *Mandaic Incantation Texts*, pp. 234–255, for the text (transliterated into Hebrew characters) and translation of this important document.

daic text. Then in 1967 Macuch published a lead roll,[60] and then three others in 1968.[61] The first lead roll Macuch would date to the middle of the third century AD. The occurrence of an angel named Estaqlos in this lead roll and in the section of the Canonical Prayer-book assigned to this early date forms the basis of his dating.[62] He dates the second and third rolls to the end of the pre-Islamic period, and the fourth roll to the Islamic period. He would also predate Lidzbarski's roll to the third or even to the second century AD.[63] Elsewhere he emphasizes the difficulty of ascertaining an exact date for such rolls.[64]

Other scholars question Macuch's early dates for these texts. Rudolph considers the lowering of the dates to the second or third century 'not yet provable'.[65] Speaking of Macuch's dating of his first lead roll to the third century, Naveh writes: 'Since this text, like some other incantation texts, has "cursive" forms which were developed from the Mandaic bookhand, such an early date cannot be based on palaeographical evidence.'[66]

Although they are not in every respect exactly like the Mandaic script, the inscriptions on certain coins from the southern Mesopotamian area of Characene,[67] and Elymaean inscriptions from south-western Iran have been adduced as objective evidence for the early presence of Mandaeans in these regions. The coins from Characene date from the third and possibly the second century AD. There are four coins in one series with the same two-word inscription – *Ibignai mlka*.

[60] R. Macuch, 'Altmandäische Bleirollen I', in F. Altheim and R. Stiehl (eds), *Die Araber in der Alten Welt* IV (1967), pp. 91–203, plates on pp. 626–631.

[61] R. Macuch, 'Altmandäische Bleirollen II', in F. Altheim and R. Stiehl (eds), *Die Araber in der Alten Welt* V (1968), pp. 34–72, plates on pp. 454–468. I am indebted to Professor Macuch for sending me copies of these two important publications.

[62] Macuch, 'Altmandäische Bleirollen I', pp. 96–97, 189.

[63] Macuch, 'Anfänge der Mandäer', pp. 138–139.

[64] Macuch, *Handbook*, p. LVI.

[65] K. Rudolph, 'Problems of . . . the Mandaean Religion', p. 225.

[66] J. Naveh, 'The Origin of the Mandaic Script', *Bulletin of the American Schools of Oriental Research*, no. 198 (1970), p. 33.

[67] J. Hansman, 'Charax and the Karkeh', *Iranica Antiqua* 7 (1967), pp. 21–58, after a restudy of the Hellenistic names of rivers in the area, locates ancient Charax at a mound called Jabal Khayābir, some 10 miles south of Qurna on the east bank of the Shatt al-Arab.

Lidzbarski dated the reign of King Ibignai between 150 and 224 AD, more probably towards the end of this period.[68] A coin bearing the name of the famous *Mani*, founder of Manichaeism, is dated to the end of the third century. Altheim, on the basis of Ishodad's Syriac commentary on Genesis, has suggested that the Characene–Mesene script may have been created between the accession of Ardashir I in AD 208 and the defeat of the Arsacid Artabanus in AD 224. Though only twelve of a possible sixteen of the Characene letters can be indisputably identified, there is still a striking resemblance to the Mandaic script.

The second-century AD Elymaean inscriptions, although known to earlier scholars, have been but recently deciphered. There is one coin legend.[69] Rock inscriptions from Tang-i Sarvak were first published by Henning in 1952.[70] Their importance for the Mandaeans was noted by Macuch in his article published in 1957.[71] In 1964 five more inscriptions from Tang-i Butān in the Shīmbār area were published by Bivar and Shaked.[72] The two sets of inscriptions give us a full twenty-three-letter alphabet to compare with the Mandaic alphabet. There are in addition some still undeciphered dipinti in Tang-i Chilau.

Also to be considered is the script of the Nabataeans, whose capital was at Petra, and the Palmyrene Syriac script.[73] Earlier

[68] M. Lidzbarski, 'Die Münzen der Characene mit mandäischen Legenden', *Zeitschrift für Numismatik* 33 (1922), p. 87.

[69] A. de la Fuye, 'Les monnaies de l'Elymaïde', *Revue numismatique*, 4th ser. 22 (1919), pp. 45–84. Recently about 100 Elymaean coins were found at Masjid-i-Solaiman. Professor Frye informs me that Robert Goble of Vienna has been entrusted with the publication of these coins.

[70] W. B. Henning, 'The Monuments and Inscriptions of Tang-i Sarvak', *Asia Major* n.s. 2 (1952), pp. 151–178.

[71] R. Macuch, 'Alter und Heimat', cols 401–408.

[72] A. D. Bivar and S. Shaked, 'The Inscriptions at Shīmbār', *Bulletin of the School of Oriental and African Studies* 27 (1964), pp. 265–290.

[73] For charts illustrating the Nabataean and Palmyrene scripts, see F. M. Cross, Jr, 'The Development of the Jewish Scripts', in G. E. Wright (ed.), *The Bible and the Ancient Near East* (1961), pp. 163–164. For a chart illustrating the varieties of Mandaic scripts, see Yamauchi, *Mandaic Incantation Texts*, p. 68. For charts of the Elymaic script, see W. B. Henning, *op. cit.*, p. 168, and Bivar and Shaked, p. 270. There are comparative charts of the several scripts in Naveh, p. 35, and in P. W. Coxon, 'Script Analysis and Mandaean Origins', *Journal of Semitic Studies* 15 (1970), p. 21.

scholars, including Lidzbarski and Nöldeke, were especially impressed with some of the Mandaic parallels with the Nabataean script. Kraeling, for example, wrote in 1929:

> 'The Mandaic codices, for example, show the use of a small circle, like that of the Syriac *Waw* to indicate the letter *Aleph*. The only analogy is that of the Nabatean and Palmyrene inscriptions, where *Aleph* is represented by a line ending in a small circle. The Mandaic codices lack the initial downward stroke, the line, but the lead amulet, published by Lidzbarski as the earliest Mandaic monument, still shows that line connected with the circle.' [74]

This resemblance was furthermore taken as an evidence of the western origins of the Mandaeans as, *e.g.*, by Schweizer, who claimed: 'The Mandaic script is originally western Aramaic. The proof of this is above all the *aleph*, the oldest Mandaic form of which is so singular and so similar to the Nabataean, that a genuine relationship can hardly be denied.' [75] In a recent publication, McCullough maintains: 'Actually the Aramaic script used by the Mandaeans . . . seems to be a development of that used in the Nabataean and Palmyrene inscriptions.' [76]

It is above all Macuch who has in recent years stressed the resemblances of the Mandaic script to the Nabataean and to the new Elymaic script, and the possible implications of these resemblances for the early presence of Mandaeans in the east. He has argued that the Mandaic script was an intermediary stage between the Nabataean and Elymaic, standing more closely to the former than to the latter. The Mandaeans must have brought this script with them from the west to the east, where the Elymaeans then adopted it in the second century AD. If this were the case, then the Mandaeans would have been in the area of southern Mesopotamia and south-western Iran by the second century AD. [77]

Other scholars have questioned both Macuch's conclusions

---

[74] C. H. Kraeling, 'The Origin and Anitquity of the Mandaeans', *JAOS* 49 (1929), p. 211.

[75] E. Schweizer, *Ego Eimi*, p. 47.

[76] W. McCullough, *Jewish and Mandaean Incantation Bowls in the Royal Ontario Museum* (1967), p. xvi.

[77] R. Macuch, 'Alter und Heimat', cols 401–408; 'Anfänge der Mandäer', pp. 139–158; R. Macuch, 'Zur Frühgeschichte der Mandäer', *ThLZ* 90 (1965), cols 650–660.

and also the comparisons on which he has based these conclusions. Since we have evidence of Nabataean traders in
Characene from the first century BC,[78] and of Palmyrene
traders there from the first century AD,[79] there is the possibility
that the Mandaeans may have adopted their script in the
east. Rudolph doubts whether the proto-Mandaic Elymaean
script is any certain evidence for the presence of the Mandaean
sect:

> 'Does the Mandaean writing as we find it in the aforementioned non-
> Mandaean inscriptions presuppose the existence of the sect? Macuch
> answered this question with a decisive "yes" as opposed to the answer
> given by W. B. Henning and me, but he has not yet completely con-
> vinced me since the simplest answer is not always the most correct.
> Could not the Mandaean authors have developed their own writing out
> of these south Babylonian Aramaic characters and in association with
> Nabataean writing known to them? Macuch himself calls the Elymaean
> form of letters "clear prototypes of Mandaean writing." However, let
> us leave this problem to the specialists.'[80]

Two epigraphic specialists who have examined Macuch's
arguments in detail independently of each other – Coxon and
Naveh – have both disagreed with the analyses which form
the basis of Macuch's conclusions. In the first place, Naveh
claims that 'There is no connection at all between the Nabataean and the Mandaic scripts'.[81] The Mandaic circular
aleph is rather to be derived from a simplification of the Elymaic heart-shaped *aleph*. The Nabataean looped *aleph* represents an altogether separate development. Coxon suggests
either a reduction of the Elymaic *aleph* or a common ancestry
for the Mandaic and Nabataean *aleph*.

In the second place, both Naveh and Coxon agree that the
Mandaic script is derived from the Elymaic, rather than the
other way around as advocated by Macuch. According to
Coxon, 'the corpus of the comparative evidence points to the

---

[78] S. A. Nodelman, 'A Preliminary History of Characene', *Berytus* 13
(1960), p. 93.

[79] *Ibid.*, p. 101.

[80] K. Rudolph, 'Problems of . . . the Mandaean Religion', p. 225.
Coxon, p. 30, also doubts that the script is a necessary proof of the existence
of the sect: 'The existence of a script which may be the closest thing we
possess to that of Mandaic does not prove the concomitant presence of the
Mandaean sect in southern Mesopotamia in the second century A.D.'

[81] J. Naveh, *op. cit.*, p. 33.

primacy of the Elymaean over against the Mandaean forms of the letters and that the latter seem to be stylized reductions of the older Elymaean orthography'.[82] As against Macuch's derivation of the use of ligatures in Mandaic script from the Nabataeans, Naveh suggests that the Mandaeans developed this from the semi-ligatured Elymaic script. 'As the Elymaic cursive script of the second century A.D. was not ligatured while the earliest Mandaic bookhand was, we must take into account quite a long span of time for this development', *i.e.*, a long time after the second century. Naveh therefore concludes: 'At any rate palaeographic criteria support neither the theory of a western origin of the Mandaeans nor the existence of the sect in Khuzistan in the second century A.D.'[83]

In a recent counter-rebuttal Professor Macuch makes the following points:

1. It is still his conviction that the Elymaean inscriptions 'are absolutely dependent on the script and language known to us as Mandaic and not the other way round, even if the most ancient documents of the Mandaic script and language can only be dated a century later'.[83a]

2. As against Naveh, Macuch still maintains that the Mandaic script has genuine Nabataean associations, *e.g.* in the *Alef*.

3. He notes that Coxon's treatment is quite deficient in his awareness of the various forms of the Elymaean and Mandaic letters.

4. He denies Naveh's major contention that the ligatured Mandaic letters developed from the semi-ligatured Elymaean letters, by arguing that the latter is an imitation of the former – but only on stone, which would explain the incompleteness of the ligatures.

5. Macuch's epigraphical analysis is reinforced by his convictions regarding the early Mandaean exodus from Palestine.

---

[82] P. W. Coxon, *op. cit.*, p. 29.

[83] Naveh, p. 37.

[83a] R. Macuch, 'The Origins of the Mandaeans and Their Script', *Journal of Semitic Studies* 16 (1971), pp. 174–192. (I am indebted to Professor Macuch for sending me a copy of this article.) He argues that the relative particle *d̠*- and the conjunction *kd̠* in the Elymaic inscriptions have been borrowed from Mandaic as they are not known in any other Aramaic dialect.

'Could these genuinely Palestinian elements have been preserved for centuries,' he asks, 'without having ever been written down?'

6. He concludes:

> 'To sum up, then, (1) my postulate of a Mandaean script in the second century A.D. is justified and substantiated, and (2) there is no substantial difference between the Elymaean, Characenian and Mandaean scripts, even if we consider the last one in its fully developed modern form. Coxon's and Naveh's objections consist of trivialities which are to be explained by different writing materials rather than by the unnecessary supposition of substantial differences between the two scripts.' [83b]

VI. THE HARAN GAWAITA

We have had occasion to mention the *Haran Gawaita*, the important text published by Lady Drower in 1953. It is the one Mandaean document which professes to give a history of the sect. It has been hailed by Schnackenburg as a text which confirms the thesis of an exodus of the Mandaeans from Palestine 'mit Sicherheit'. [84] But a closer examination of the text itself may temper one's enthusiasm for its significance.

The text has survived in two manuscripts dated to the early eighteenth century AD. The colophons reach back into the early Islamic period. The text has been poorly transmitted and is difficult to translate. After a prologue by the copyist, the manuscript begins:

> '. . . and Haran Gawaita receiveth him and that city in which there were Naṣoraeans, because there was no road for the Jewish rulers. Over them was King Ardban. And sixty thousand Naṣoraeans abandoned the

---

[83b] *Ibid.*, p. 190. Although Professor Macuch has been able to point out some misunderstandings and deficiencies in Naveh's and especially in Coxon's article, the following question remains in my mind: Can the differences between the scripts be explained simply on the basis of different writing materials? Both Naveh and Coxon in their charts illustrate lapidary (monumental) and cursive forms of Nabataean, for example, and the differences between these forms is slight compared to the difference between Elymaic and Mandaic. Mandaic forms on lead and on terracotta are not that different either. Comparative epigraphy is based on what Professor Macuch dismisses as 'trivialities'.

[84] R. Schnackenburg, 'Der frühe Gnostizismus', *Kontexte* 3 (1966), p. 115.

Sign of the Seven and entered the Median hills, a place where we were free from domination by all other races.'[85]

Mary, a daughter of Moses, conceives and gives birth to the false Messiah. He dwells on Mount Sinai with his brother and gathers to himself a people called Christians. Yahia-Yuhana (John the Baptist) is then born. He is instructed in secret gnosis and heals the sick miraculously.[86] Sixty years after the death of John, the Jews persecute the Nasoraeans and Hibil-Ziwa destroys Jerusalem as a judgment. At the same time he punishes the Jews in Babylonia, where 400 of their rulers had reigned for 800 years.[87] After the descendants of King Artabanus (the Parthians), a Hardabaean (Sassanian) dynasty rules for 360 years, and then the Son of Slaughter, the Arab (Muhammad), arises and conquers the land.[88] After the latter has completed his allotted 4,000 years, the false Messiah will come again and perform miracles.[89] He will reign for 6,000 years.[90] After other ages the final epoch of Hibil-Ziwa will come at the end.

We may first ask concerning the location of Haran Gawaita or 'Inner Haran'. The text itself identifies it with the Median mountains.[91] The one reference to Haran in the *Ginza* XVIII. 409 is to cedars from Haran; Lidzbarski, however, emended this to Haman, *i.e.* Amanus in Lebanon. Macuch favours the identification with Harran in north-western Mesopotamia and cites the Sabians of Harran from the Islamic period, without identifying the Mandaeans with the latter, as does Drower.[92]

We may then ask about the identification of King Artabanus. Now there were five Parthian kings named Artabanus: Artabanus I, *c.* 211–191 BC; Artabanus II, *c.* 128–123 BC; Artabanus III, *c.* AD 12–38; Artabanus IV, *c.* AD 80–81; and Artabanus V, *c.* AD 213–224.[93] Bammel believes that the king in question is Artabanus IV.[94] Rudolph, who is quite sceptical of the

---

[85] E. S. Drower, *The Haran Gawaita*, p. 3.
[86] *Ibid.*, pp. 6–7.   [87] *Ibid.*, p. 9.   [88] *Ibid.*, p. 15.
[89] *Ibid.*, p. 19.   [90] *Ibid.*, p. 20.   [91] *Ibid.*, p. 10.
[92] *Cf.* E. S. Drower, appendix to *The Secret Adam*; D. Chwolsohn, *Die Ssabier und der Ssabismus* (1856); J. B. Segal, 'The Sabian Mysteries', in E. Bacon (ed.), *Vanished Civilizations* (1963), pp. 201–220.
[93] R. Frye, *The Heritage of Persia*, p. 282.
[94] E. Bammel, 'Zur Frühgeschichte der Mandäer', *Orientalia* 32 (1963), p. 225, n. 2.

historical worth of the document,[95] thinks that Artabanus V is intended.[96] Macuch, who takes the document seriously and who for other reasons believes in the existence of pre-Christian Naṣoraeans (Mandaeans), argues for Artabanus III. In this case the Mandaean exodus would have taken place shortly after the crucifixion of Jesus or even before it.[97] Drower would agree with Macuch.[98]

The *Haran Gawaita*, however, is a document that is thoroughly permeated with fantastic legends. Macuch himself warns us that the account may be 95 per cent legend.[99] In order to extract history from such a work, he maintains that we must work as a detective or psychoanalyst.[100] And if one should object that the work's tradition about Jerusalem is confused (it is placed in Babylonia!), he reminds us, 'All Mandaean traditions are confused but nonetheless for one who is able to read them, they are clear.'[101]

Many of my own strictures and reservations regarding the *Haran Gawaita* and its interpretation by Macuch have also been expressed by Rudolph:

'Macuch admits the unclear, fantastic, legendary, and highly contradictory character of the statements about Jerusalem in this document with its many lacunae, speaks also of the "fictitious report

[95] K. Rudolph, *Die Mandäer* I, p. 46; he objects that the text is a secondary working of an older tradition, whose redactor had no clear concept of the oldest Mandaean history.
[96] *Ibid.*, p. 55. Elsewhere Rudolph holds that an exodus of the Mandaean community to Harran in the first century would be too early 'for the undeniable contacts with the Syrian odes of Solomon. . . .' 'Problems of . . . the Mandaean Religion', p. 224.
[97] R. Macuch, 'Alter und Heimat', and 'Anfänge der Mandäer' are based on an exposition of this text. In my earlier monograph, *GEMO*, p. 69, n. 340, I had unjustly credited Macuch with taking seriously the figure of 60,000 exiles. This is an error on my part. It may be noted that the text itself does not say that the 60,000 left Palestine, but that they 'abandoned the Sign of the Seven', *i.e.* the area of the Planets' influence. This may refer to Harran, where astrological influence was quite strong.
[98] E. S. Drower, *The Secret Adam*, p. xi.
[99] R. Macuch, 'Anfänge der Mandäer', p. 117.
[100] *Ibid.*, p. 122.
[101] *Ibid.*, p. 127. After having attempted a historical rehabilitation of the Mandaean exodus from the *Haran Gawaita*, Macuch concedes that a pre-Christian origin for the Mandaeans does not for him rest upon such a legendary account but rather on the harmony of the oldest Mandaic hymns with New Testament passages. See below, chapter 11, sect. III, 'The New Testament Itself as Evidence'.

about the Palestinian events of the Mandaean exodus", and maintains further that the description of the history of Jesus, John the Baptist, and the Jews is "even more absurd and foolish than that which is exhibited to us by earlier known Mandaean writings." Do the other statements at the beginning of the document deserve more confidence? In any case, Macuch draws far-reaching conclusions precisely from these lines which are likewise passed on in fragmentary fashion.'[102]

VII. THE ALLEGED JEWISH ORIGINS OF MANDAEISM

Although I would agree with Rudolph's criticism of Macuch's reconstructions, I cannot agree with Rudolph's own hypothesis of an early Jewish origin of the Mandaeans. He holds that Mandaeism is derived from 'a heretical Jewish Gnosticism uninfluenced by Christianity'.[103] Drower,[104] Macuch,[105] and Schenke[106] also favour a derivation of Mandaeism from some form of Judaism, but it is Rudolph who has set forth the most extensive arguments for this hypothesis. His conviction rests basically on the fact that in the Mandaic texts we find: (1) allusions to the Old Testament; (2) parallels to the ethics of Judaism; and (3) a high regard for marriage as in Judaism.

Speaking about the account of the creation of Adam in the Mandaic texts, Rudolph says, 'The closeness to the Old Testament text must one especially observe here.'[107] It is my impression, however, that the alleged references to the Genesis account are so distorted that one cannot rule out the possibility of a second-hand knowledge of the Old Testament. This conviction is further strengthened when one compares the Coptic *Apocryphon of John*, which even contains quotations from Genesis.[108] This raises the suspicion that in the case of

---

[102] K. Rudolph, 'Problems of . . . the Mandaean Religion', p. 223.

[103] K. Rudolph, 'War der Verfasser der Oden Salomos ein "Qumran-Christ"?' p. 553; cf. *OG*, p. 589. In the following pages I can only summarize the more extensive arguments which I have set forth in the monograph, *Gnostic Ethics and Mandaean Origins*, published by Harvard University Press in 1971, pp. 53ff.

[104] E. S. Drower, *The Secret Adam*, p. xi.

[105] R. Macuch, 'Anfänge der Mandäer', p. 98.

[106] H.-M. Schenke, 'Das Problem der Beziehung zwischen Judentum und Gnosis', *Kairos* 7 (1965), p. 130.

[107] K. Rudolph, 'Ein Grundtyp gnostischer Urmensch-Adam-Spekulation', *ZRGG* 9 (1957), p. 6.

[108] S. Giversen, 'The Apocryphon of John and Genesis', *StTh* 17 (1963), pp. 60–76.

the parallels between the Mandaic texts and the *Apocryphon of John*, pointed out by Rudolph,[109] the Mandaic account is secondary.

The names of three prominent Uthras (spirits of life) – Hibil, Anosh, and Shitil – are based on the three biblical figures, Abel, Enoch, and Seth. The relationship of Adam and Eve to their son Abel is sometimes reversed in the Mandaean traditions. In *GR* V Hibil Yawar claims that he has created Hawwa (Eve) for Adam. It is curious that Cain seems to be entirely unknown to the Mandaeans. In the Mandaean tradition Hibil is especially prominent as a saviour.

Noah and his sons, who are called Shum, Iam, and Iapit, are known as the survivors of the flood. Only Shum, who is regarded as the renewer of the world, has any prominence; his brothers are not important. As Segelberg has observed:

> 'The Genesis-genealogy and the function of its important persons, not quite accurately known by the Mandaeans, has become entirely transformed in the final Mandaean stage. Originally regarded as an historical description it has become a celestial reality. They have become living, celestial beings, spirits, carrying out essential functions in the drama of salvation.'[110]

It should be noted that the Mandaeans' knowledge of the Old Testament was more extensive – if not necessarily more intensive – than that of many Gnostics whose knowledge seems not to have exceeded the prediluvian section of Genesis. The Mandaeans know Abraham and Moses as prophets of the evil Ruha ('Spirit'). David is known simply as the father of Solomon. The latter is known chiefly for his magical powers over demons. The prophets are conspicuous by their absence.

As to more specific Old Testament allusions, a passage in *GR* V. 180:20–21 has been compared to Isaiah 5:12 (but this seems to be a typical gnomic statement). A passage in the Canonical Prayer-book has been influenced by Psalm 22:1. Other allusions may be detected, but there is only one long, direct citation (freely rendered) of an Old Testament passage.[111] The same passage is found in both the *Ginza* and the

[109] K. Rudolph, 'Ein Grundtyp', pp. 1–20.
[110] E. Segelberg, 'Old and New Testament Figures', p. 238.
[111] Noted by M. Lidzbarski, *Das Johannesbuch*, pp. xxif.

Qolasta and is parallel to Psalm 114.[112] Burkitt attempted to prove that this was borrowed from the Syriac Peshitta.[113] Widengren prefers to trace this to an Aramaic Targum.[114] Rudolph admits that it is quite remarkable that there is hardly any citation of the Old Testament, and comments: 'An explanation of this phenomenon is not easy. Was there a heretical sect of Judaism without biblical literature?'[115]

Rudolph speaks of the strong Jewish contacts in the Mandaic magical bowl texts. He overstates his case here. The Jewish contribution to the Mandaic bowl texts is quite restricted and possibly second-hand. We have the following Jewish elements: (1) the names of angels built on a Hebrew model, (2) the words Amen and Selah, and (3) one occurrence of the Jewish *geṭ* or divorce formula.[116] What is notable – although this may prove to be an argument from silence – is that unlike the similar Aramaic bowls with their numerous Old Testament citations,[117] the Mandaic bowls published thus far contain not a single Old Testament quotation.

As far as the parallels in ethics are concerned, Rudolph claims as one of the Jewish elements the giving of alms.[118] But this is not necessarily Jewish; it is one of the pillars of Islam. He further cites the negative expression of the Golden Rule, *i.e.* the Silver Rule in *GR* I. 22 as a Jewish element.[119] But this ethical maxim is quite widespread.[120] The restriction against eating the blood of animals in *GR* I. 20 is also shared by Arabs.[121] All of these elements may have come from the Jews, but they may just as well have not.

Rudolph considers the Mandaeans' high regard for marriage

---

[112] *GR* V. 178–179; E. S. Drower, *The Canonical Prayerbook*, p. 73.
[113] F. Burkitt, 'Notes and Studies', *JTS* 29 (1928), pp. 235–237.
[114] G. Widengren, 'Die Mandäer', p. 90.
[115] K. Rudolph, *Die Mandäer* I, pp. 92–93.
[116] E. M. Yamauchi, *Mandaic Incantation Texts*, p. 231; *cf.* pp. 45–47. *Cf.* B. A. Levine, 'The Language of the Magical Bowls', in J. Neusner, *A History of the Jews in Babylonia* V (1970), pp. 343–375; J. Neusner and J. Z. Smith, 'Archaeology and Babylonian Jewry', in J. A. Sanders (ed.), *Near Eastern Archaeology in the Twentieth Century* (1970), pp. 331–347.
[117] Yamauchi, 'Aramaic Magic Bowls', pp. 511ff.
[118] K. Rudolph, *Die Mandäer* I, p. 85.
[119] *Ibid.*, p. 86, n. 2.
[120] *Cf.* A. Dihle, *Die goldene Regel* (1962), ch. 6.
[121] J. Wellhausen, *Reste arabischen Heidentums* (1887), p. 217. On other alleged ritual parallels, see S. A. Pallis, *Mandaean Studies*, pp. 143ff.

and for procreation as a clear proof of their Jewish background.[122] But this same concern for children can be seen in Mesopotamian, Iranian, and Arabic sources. The concern for the protection of pregnant women and little children against the lilith seen in the magic bowls and the lead rolls may be seen as a continuation of the Mesopotamian spells against the Labartu.[123] Though some of the sexual taboos parallel Jewish ordinances, the extreme concern of the Mandaeans for ritual purity goes far beyond anything in Judaism.[124] A woman who died while menstruating was condemned to a period of punishment in a purgatory.[125]

Against these possibly ambiguous Jewish traits in Mandaeism we must consider the unambiguous anti-Jewish elements. The Old Testament is used, but it is used in a deliberately perverse way. *Adunai* is the chief of evil spirits. The word *Qadush* ('holy' in Hebrew) is used for that which is unholy.[126] *Ruha* ('Spirit' in Hebrew) is an evil, female demon. Segelberg notes the following transformations: 'Striking is also the change of the root jahaduta, jahuduta, Judaism, to jahuṭaiia from the root jahṭa, abortion and to the root hṭa, to sin. Thus "jahuṭaiia, iahṭia unipṣia" – the Jews, abortion and excrements (*GR* 231:5).'[127]

The Mandaeans do not circumcise; they resent those who do.[128] They do not spiritualize circumcision as some of the Coptic Gnostic texts.[129] There is a studied denigration of the Sabbath and a corresponding exaltation of Sunday.[130] When Rudolph suggests that 'The later Sunday holiday probably proceeded from an original honoring of the Sabbath',[131] he

---

[122] K. Rudolph, *Die Mandäer* I, p. 85; *cf. OG*, p. 592.

[123] F. Thureau-Dangin, 'Rituel et Amulettes contre Labartu', *Revue d'assyriologie et d'archéologie orientale* 18 (1921), pp. 162–198.

[124] See my extended discussion of Mandaean ethics in *GEMO*, ch. 5.

[125] E. S. Drower, *Diwan Abatur or Progress through the Purgatories* (1950), p. 26.

[126] E. S. Drower, 'Mandaean Polemic', *Bulletin of the School of Oriental and African Studies* 25 (1962), p. 439.

[127] E. Segelberg, 'Old and New Testament Figures', p. 236.

[128] E. S. Drower, *Diwan Abatur*, p. 17. *Cf.* W. Thesiger, *The Marsh Arabs* (1964), p. 126.

[129] *Cf. Gospel of Thomas* 90:18–23.

[130] E. S. Drower, *The Canonical Prayerbook*, pp. 98, 110, 116.

[131] K. Rudolph, *Die Mandäer* I, p. 87.

does not supply the missing links for this alleged devolution of Judaism into an anti-Jewish polemic.[132]

The most distinctive element of Judaism – its monotheism – is nowhere to be seen. There is, to be sure, a 'monistic' version of the cosmogony in which a good demiurge is responsible for creation.[133] The dualistic version of the cosmogony attributes the creation to the evil demiurge Ptahil, who sins and repents.[134] The dualistic version was held to be the later version, but Rudolph has now demonstrated the reverse.[135] Now it is clear that the dualism involved is not merely an ethical but an ontological dualism.[136] It would seem to me to be quite contradictory to hold on the one hand that the Mandaeans originated from Judaism, and to maintain on the other hand that the earliest Mandaean accounts of cosmogony are dualistic.

Indeed, if we accept Rudolph's assumption of a Jewish origin for the Mandaeans we have the rather odd result that our alleged Jewish proto-Mandaeans have by some unexplained centrifugal tendency shed the most distinctive Jewish elements (monotheism, circumcision, the Sabbath), and have become virulently anti-Jewish in the process, while at the same time through an unexplained centripetal force retained other alleged Jewish elements.

We must therefore ask if a Jewish origin is necessary to explain these latter elements. I would prefer to see in the Jewish elements in Mandaeism, in particular their references to the Old Testament, as indications not of their consanguinity but only of their contiguity with the Jews. This would explain the Mandaeans' rejection of circumcision and the Sabbath, their antagonism to the Jews, and their garbled and truncated knowledge of the Old Testament. Such a relationship and development can be illustrated from the analogy of a well-known religion – Islam.

We can find in the Qur'an and the Hadith many of the same elements which have been used by Rudolph to prove a

---

[132] *Cf.* Drower, *The Canonical Prayerbook*, p. 149.
[133] K. Rudolph, *Theogonie, Kosmogonie und Anthropogonie in den mandäischen Schriften* (1965), pp. 196ff., 306ff.
[134] Rudolph, *OG*, p. 590.
[135] *Cf.* R. Macuch, 'Der gegenwärtige Stand', col. 7.
[136] Rudolph, *Theogonie*, p. 83.

genetic relationship between the Mandaeans and the Jews:
(1) allusions to the Old Testament, (2) parallels in ethics,
(3) a positive emphasis upon marriage and procreation.[137] All
of these Jewish elements, however, are the result not of consanguinity but merely of contiguity. I believe that this is also the
case with the Mandaeans.

VIII. A PROPOSED RECONSTRUCTION

Having rejected the theories of Macuch and of Rudolph concerning the origin of the Mandaeans, we may well be asked
what we propose as a substitute. We have argued for a proposed reconstruction in another monograph,[138] and can make
only a few suggestions here.

It should be noted first of all that the Mandaeans are a
unique Gnostic sect. They are the only Gnostic group to have
survived. Their ethics, which emphasize sexual and ritual
purity, are quite unlike those of other Gnostic groups. Their
ethics in fact cannot be derived from their Gnostic cosmology,
but must be more primeval than the latter. The fundamental
cleft between the Gnostic theology of the Mandaeans and their
non-Gnostic ethics can best be explained as the result of an
assimilation of Gnostic ideas from the west into an eastern
mythology, accompanied by a reinterpretation of an indigenous Mesopotamian cult – all of which did not transform
the original eastern ethics and mores.

If such a fusion resulted in the creation of the Mandaean
religion, it could have been accomplished without the exodus
of a sizeable Mandaean community from Palestine. The introduction of Gnostic theology could well have been accomplished
by the catalyst of a relatively few individuals. Moreover, since
it is this fusion which has given the Mandaean religion its
character and since such a fusion could take place only in
Mesopotamia, it is misleading to speak of a 'western' origin of
Mandaeism or even of Mandaeism in Palestine. I would
prefer to speak of a western proto-Mandaean component and
an eastern proto-Mandaean component.

[137] *Cf.* S. D. Goitein, 'The Jewish Tradition in Islam', ch. 4 in his
book, *Jews and Arabs* (1964).

[138] *GEMO*, which has appeared in the Harvard Theological Studies series.

As to the western component, I can conceive of a group with the following characteristics: (1) They would be non-Jews who were superficially acquainted with the Old Testament.[139] (2) They would be antagonistic to the Jews. (3) They would speak an Aramaic dialect and perhaps be familiar with the Nabataean script. (4) They would probably be dwellers in Transjordan, who worshipped the god of the Hauran range east of Galilee.[140] (5) Whether they knew John the Baptist or not is quite problematic. It would be almost certain that they had no first-hand knowledge of Christ or Christianity.[141]

The retaliatory attack of the Jews upon the Gentiles in the areas east and south-east of the Sea of Galilee upon the eve of the war with Rome in AD 66 may have been the occasion to force these people north to the region of Antioch.[142] There, about the turn of the century, they may have accepted the Gnostic teachings of Menander, having been attracted by his teaching that they could achieve immortality through baptism. Their own regard for baptism may have been similar to the

[139] There were many non-Jews in Palestine, especially in Transjordan. *Cf.* J. Daniélou in a review of Rudolph, *Die Mandäer* I, in *RechSR* 48 (1960), p. 614: 'It is as if the Mandaeans especially interested themselves in the Jewish tradition . . . which is anterior to Abraham, that is to say to Judaism. I would ask myself if this has any relationship to the populations east of the Jordan, the Moabites and Edomites, who then formed the Nabataean kingdom and who recognized as their ancestors the non-Jewish personages of the Old Testament, just as did much later, in the same region, the Christians who venerated Job, Lot or Noah.'

[140] The name *Hauran* and its variant *Hauraran* appear in the Mandaic texts both as a place name and as a personified heavenly power. M. Lidzbarski, *Mandäische Liturgien*, p. xix, guessed that this reflected a worship of the god of Mount Hauran. *Cf.* E. S. Drower, *The Haran Gawaita*, pp. v-vi; R. Macuch, 'Anfänge der Mandäer', p. 147. That this is an ancient belief is attested by its appearance in Macuch's first lead roll, Ia. 5–6, 'Altmandäische Bleirollen I', pp. 116–117: 'through the power of the mighty Haurārān'.

[141] Jesus is always the false Messiah. According to Segelberg, 'Old and New Testament Figures', p. 237: 'In fact it is impossible to find one single positive pronouncement about Jesus in the whole Mandaean literature.' The polemic against Christianity which does appear is directed against the later Christian monasticism whose celibacy was compared to infanticide. According to Drower, 'Mandaean Polemic', pp. 441–442: 'In the earlier Mandaean books and in priestly commentaries there is little polemic, indeed usually none whatever, against Christianity, and the main tide of venom flows against the Jews.'

[142] Josephus, *Antiquities* ii. 458–459.

magical concept of Elchasai,[143] who also seems to have come from the Transjordan.

Seeking a region where they could be free 'from domination by all other races', and moving eastward, they may have stopped at Harran, and then gone on to the region of Adiabene (the so-called 'Median Hills'). But becoming dissatisfied with the growing Christian influence at Edessa and at Arbela, and the strong Jewish influence at Nisibis, they may have finally found the refuge they desired in the marshes of southern Mesopotamia, converting in the process an indigenous Aramaean population. The Mesopotamian tradition held out no hope for life after death. Immortality through gnosis would be the good news that these newcomers from the west would have to offer. It was this fruitful union of the vitality of Gnosticism and the tenacity of Mesopotamian cult and magic that resulted in the birth of a hardy new religion, perhaps by the end of the second century AD.[144]

[143] On Elchasai, see *GEMO*, pp. 62ff.; *NTA* II, pp. 745–750.

[144] *Cf.* H.-M. Schenke, 'Die Gnosis', p. 401. According to Wilson, *Gnosis and the New Testament*, p. 14:

'It is not difficult to imagine a group like that represented by the Dead Sea Scrolls migrating in the course of the first century, adopting some elements of the teaching of Marcion or of Gnosticism in the second, or of Manicheism in the third, reacting violently against persecution by more "orthodox" neighbours at another stage, and finally emerging after several centuries with a collection of treasured documents which to some extent reflected their chequered history, but were no longer fully understood by the wisest of their number.'

Cf. C. Colpe, 'Mandäer', *RGG*³ IV, col. 711: 'The Gnostic Soul-, Primal Man- and Redeemer-Myth in any case does not cohere together with their cult from the beginning, but has been adopted at a later date and transformed.' In a study based upon a comparison of the Manichaean *Psalms of Thomas*, 'Die Thomaspsalmen als chronologischer Fixpunkt . . .', p. 84, Colpe suggested the following stages:

'Die erste Etappe ist die Gnostisierung palästinisch-westaramäischer Überlieferungen, die am Ende des 2. bis Anfang des 3. Jh. einem bestimmten Status frühgnostischer Religiosität nahegekommen sein muss. Die zweite Etappe ist dieser Status selbst, in dem wahrscheinlich ein wichtiges iranisches Element hinzugekommen ist; er wird durch die Schicht repräsentiert, die Thomaspsalmen und mandäischen Schriften gemeinsam ist. Die dritte Etappe ist die über diese Schicht hinausgehende frühmanichäische Mythenbildung innerhalb der Thomaspsalmen. Die vierte Etappe ist das ausgebildete, gegenüber der Gnosis der Thomaspsalmen ingesamt weiterentwickelte manichäische System. Die fünfte Etappe ist die volle mandäische Gnosis, die unter anderem auch die vier genannten Etappen in verschiedener Weise voraussetzt.'

THE JEWISH EVIDENCE

I. THE USE OF THE OLD TESTAMENT

One of the marked developments in the history of recent research into the origins of Gnosticism is the increasing emphasis on the possibility of a Jewish origin of Gnosticism. This emphasis was seen in many papers read at the conference on Gnostic Origins at Messina in 1966.

What has impressed many investigators is the clear use of the Old Testament, especially as found in some of the newly published Coptic texts from Nag Hammadi. As in the case of the Mandaeans, however, it is necessary to take a closer look at the particular portions of the Old Testament which were used by the Gnostics and the manner in which they were used before jumping to the conclusion that Old Testament citations are necessarily a proof of Jewish origins.

Even before the publication of the Nag Hammadi finds, it was already clear from patristic accounts that the early Gnostics were fond of the account of creation in Genesis 1–2. According to Irenaeus, *Adversus Haereses* I. xxiv. 1–2, Saturninus, who lived at Antioch in the early second century AD, taught:

> 'Man is the creation of these angels. . . . They exhorted themselves and said, "Let us make a man after the image and after the likeness" (Gen. 1:26, deleting "our"). When he had been made, and what was formed (Gen. 2:7) could not stand erect because of the angels' weakness but wriggled like a worm, the Power above took pity on him because he was made in its likeness, and it sent a spark of life which raised the man and made him upright and made him live. . . . The God of the Jews is one of the angels; and because all the Archons willed to destroy their Father, Christ came to destroy the God of the Jews and to save those who believed him. . . . Some prophecies were spoken by those angels who made the world, others by Satan.'[1]

[1] Cited in R. M. Grant, *Gnosticism: A Sourcebook*, pp. 31–32.

The *Apocryphon of John* from Nag Hammadi contains not only allusions and free renderings but even quotations from Genesis 1–7.[2] Quispel finds that the *Gospel of Thomas*, which he believes to be Encratite rather than Gnostic, contains a number of citations and allusions from both the Hebrew and the Septuagint not only to Genesis but also to Isaiah, the Psalms, *etc.*[3]

We may ask if the use of the Old Testament and other Jewish elements by the earliest Gnostics presupposes an ultimate derivation from the Jews themselves. MacRae, for one, believes that this must have been the case. Notwithstanding the fact that Gnosticism is a revolt against Judaism, 'Yet it must be conceived as a revolt *within* Judaism.'[4] He argues: 'Moreover, the familiarity which Gnostic sources show toward details of Jewish thought is hardly one that we could expect non-Jews to have.'[5] Daniélou likewise explains the ultimate origins of pagan Gnosticism as a development of Jewish Gnostic exegesis of Genesis. In Jewish Gnosticism, however, gnosis meant the knowledge of eschatological secrets. Later gnosis became mystical and led to the development of pagan Gnosticism in which gnosis was 'to be regarded as actual salvation, and not merely as the knowledge of the saving event'.[6]

It should again be observed, however, that for the most part the Gnostics' knowledge of the Old Testament seems very truncated and limited generally to the opening chapters of Genesis. There is to be sure some mention of Abraham and of Moses, *etc.* But there is no interest in the fortunes of Abraham's descendants or in the law given to Moses as the law in any traditional sense.[7] As Betz points out, the Gnostics were only interested in the God of the beginning and of the end; they were not interested in the 'Gott der Mitte' who revealed himself in Israel's history.[8] Laeuchli notes that 'Even though

[2] S. Giversen, 'The Apocryphon of John and Genesis'.

[3] G. Quispel, 'Das Thomasevangelium und das Alte Testament'.

[4] G. W. MacRae, 'The Jewish Background of the Gnostic Sophia Myth', *NovTest* 12 (1970), p. 97.

[5] *Ibid.*, p. 98.

[6] J. Daniélou, *The Theology of Jewish Christianity*, p. 366.

[7] A. Böhlig in *OG*, pp. 127–129.

[8] O. Betz, 'Was am Anfang geschah: Das jüdische Erbe in den neuge-

Gnostic texts still use Old Testament vocabulary, this vocabulary is no longer understood.'[9] This leads to the 'loss of the
Creator', which in turn opens Gnosticism up to extravagant
syncretism.

Then, too, most of the Old Testament materials are used in
quite a perverse way. In the first place, the God of the Old
Testament is frequently degraded into an inferior, obtuse
demiurge. The perversion is especially seen in the transformation of Old Testament figures who originally represented evil
into Gnostic heroes. The serpent is revered as the first bringer
of 'knowledge'. Sodom and Gomorrah are transformed into
the cities of the good seed.[10]

The limited use of the Old Testament by the Gnostics has
led W. van Unnik to suggest that this may have been due to the
fact that this knowledge was only oral knowledge or the
knowledge of Gentile proselytes.[11] I have suggested that in the
case of the proto-Mandaeans the knowledge of the Old Testament may be that of the pagan neighbours of the Jews in
Transjordan.[12]

II. THE APOCRYPHA AND THE JEWISH
WISDOM TRADITION

As indicated earlier (chapter 5, III), A. Adam has argued that
the *Wisdom of Solomon* 18:14–16 is based upon the *Vorlage* of
the Manichaean *Psalm of Thomas* I. He dates the latter to the
second century BC and the former to the first century BC.[13]
Rudolph has suggested that the negative evaluation of the
physical body found in the *Wisdom of Solomon* 3:13–4:2 and
9:15 betrays a sceptical wisdom tradition which may have

---

fundenen koptischen-gnostischen Schriften', in O. Betz *et al.* (eds), *Abraham
unser Vater: Juden und Christen im Gespräch über die Bibel* (1963), p. 43. *Cf.*
H.-C. Puech, 'Gnosis and Time', in *Man and Time* (1957), pp. 38–84;
E. M. Yamauchi, 'The Gnostics and History', *Journal of the Evangelical
Theological Society* 14 (1971), pp. 29–40.

[9] S. Laeuchli, *The Language of Faith*, p. 84.

[10] H. Jonas in *OG*, pp. 101, 155; A. Böhlig in *OG*, p. 128.

[11] W. C. van Unnik, 'Die jüdische Komponente in der Entstehung der
Gnosis', *VigChr* 15 (1961), pp. 78–81.

[12] See above, chapter 8, VI. *Cf. GEMO*, pp. 66ff., 86ff.

[13] B. Metzger, *An Introduction to the Apocrypha* (1957), p. 67, places the
composition of *Wisdom* 'between about 100 B.C. and A.D. 40'.

served as the best soil upon which Gnosticism could find root and bloom.[14] But the former *Wisdom* passage is not a diatribe against the procreation of children as such, which is typical of Gnosticism, but a warning against the multiplication of the wicked children of parents who reject wisdom, which is quite another matter.

Daniélou finds in such second-century BC pseudepigraphical works such as *1 Enoch*, *Jubilees*, etc. attestation of the descent and ascent motif which he thinks served as the prototype of the Gnostic myth. He writes: 'We are then led to the conclusion that the Gnostic traditions are the continuation in Christianity of a Jewish esotericism, which concerned the domain of the celestial world.'[15]

Much interest has recently focused upon the hypostatization of Wisdom in Jewish sources as the prototype of either the heavenly Redeemer or of the Gnostic Sophia. Schmithals and Sanders take the hypostatized Wisdom of Jewish literature as the prototype of a heavenly Redeemer figure.[16] Wilckens in particular has developed Bousset's suggestion that the Sophia tradition may be traced back to an ancient oriental myth of the freeing of a goddess by a god.[17] This is suggested as the background to the Simonian legend about the freeing of Helen. Wilckens himself concludes that the figure of the Babylonian Ishtar lay at the root both of the personification of Wisdom in Judaism and of the Gnostic Sophia.[18] These originally in-

---

[14] K. Rudolph, 'Randerscheinungen', pp. 109ff., 118ff.

[15] J. Daniélou, 'Judéo-christianisme et gnose', p. 156.

[16] J. T. Sanders, *The New Testament Christological Hymn*, p. 96. W. Schmithals, *The Office of Apostle*, p. 126. Cf. Schmithals's preface to Bultmann's *The Gospel of John*, p. 8: 'The influence of pre-Christian Gnosticism can also be discerned . . . particularly in speculation of late Judaism, e.g. the wisdom myth. . . .'

[17] U. Wilckens, *Weisheit und Torheit*, p. 194.

[18] The suggestion that the Ishtar-Tammuz myth may have served as the background of the fall of Sophia (cf. Bianchi in *OG*, pp. 726–727) rests on a fundamental modern misconception of the myth of 'The Descent of Ishtar'. As S. N. Kramer, *The Sumerians* (1963), pp. 155ff., has pointed out, Ishtar did not descend to the Netherworld to rescue a dead Tammuz, but rather to seize dominion from her sister Ereshkigal. Cf. E. M. Yamauchi, 'The Descent of Ishtar', in C. Pfeiffer (ed.), *The Biblical World: A Dictionary of Biblical Archaeology* (1966), pp. 196–200; also 'Tammuz and the Bible', *JBL* 84 (1965), pp. 283–290. Cf. my criticisms of Oppenheim's soteriological interpretation of the myth in 'Additional Notes on Tammuz', *Journal of Semitic Studies* 11 (1966), pp. 10–15.

dependent traditions then came together in the Jewish Diaspora during the Hellenistic period.[19]

Betz, who favours some derivation of the Sophia of Gnosticism from Jewish speculations about Wisdom, recognizes the difficulty that in Judaism proper Wisdom was conceived of as a positive power and not as an evil or at best a misguided demiurge.[20] As another advocate of this position admits, there is still an inexplicable gap between the Jewish descent of Sophia and the Gnostic fall of Sophia. MacRae writes: 'No single form of Jewish tradition can account for the pre-cosmic fall, nor indeed can any single line of non-Jewish thought account for it.'[21]

III. PHILO OF ALEXANDRIA

Zandee has drawn attention to the Wisdom speculation as it was further developed by Philo Judaeus of Alexandria (BC 20 – AD 40) as a possible root of pre-Christian Jewish Gnosticism or of proto-Gnosticism.[22] Bultmann believes that Gnosticism can be found in the writings of Philo.[23] Jonas has used Philo's writings, particularly his concepts of virtue and of the knowledge of God, as examples of Gnostic mystical philosophy.[24]

Cerfaux considered the theological atmosphere of Philo to be already that of Alexandrian Gnosticism, and cited Philo's allegorical method of exegesis, his opposition between God and matter, his tendency to asceticism, and his development of the theory of the Logos and Powers as indications of this. Cerfaux speculated that already in the first century BC in Alexandria there may have been a pagan Gnostic movement with roots stemming back to the Egyptian theosophy of the Hellenistic period.[25]

[19] U. Wilckens, op. cit., pp. 195, 197.
[20] O. Betz, 'Was am Anfang geschah', p. 40.
[21] G. W. MacRae, 'The Jewish Background', p. 98.
[22] J. Zandee, 'Die Person der Sophia in der Vierten Schrift des Codex Jung', in OG, p. 212. Cf. Betz, 'Was am Anfang geschah', p. 39.
[23] R. Bultmann, Primitive Christianity, p. 163. Cf. Schmithals's preface to Bultmann's The Gospel of John, p. 8: 'The influence of pre-Christian Gnosticism can also be discerned in Philo of Alexandria. . . .'
[24] H. Jonas, Gnosis und spätantiker Geist II: Von der Mythologie zur mystischen Philosophie (1954), pp. 70–121; OG, pp. 374–375.
[25] L. Cerfaux, 'Gnose préchrétienne', cols. 686–690.

On the other hand, Wilson points out that 'there are Jewish elements in Gnosticism which are not to be found in the voluminous pages of Philo, although Alexandria was later to become one of the chief centres of Gnosticism'.[26] M. Simon, after admitting that there are elements in Philo which may seem 'Gnostic', none the less concludes that Philo cannot be considered a Gnostic inasmuch as he is dominated by biblical categories: 'He would not admit in particular the existence of an evil principle capable of counter-balancing the action of God in the cosmos, or even of assuming the creative function.'[27] Bianchi also remarks that the dualistic anthropology found in Philo is not the theological dualism of Gnosticism.[28] Colpe summarizes the differences between Philo and Gnosticism as follows:

> 'It cannot yet be assumed that the Gnostic Redeemer doctrine is as explicit in pre-Christian times as it is claimed to be. Even Philo's speculations do not constitute evidence for such a claim. . . . In spite of Philo's distinction between the immortal soul and the mortal body, nevertheless man's lower part is not to be taken as exiled in a demonized world into which this part is supposed to have fallen in its pre-existence and from which this lower part must be freed by its upper part which comes down to the lower as an alien being. Herein lies a basic distinction to Redemption in Gnosis. In Gnosis it is not the Philonic, basically Stoic-harmonistic values which are pre-supposed. Rather, here Gnosis presupposes only the important concepts of the Philonic world picture.'[29]

IV. THE MINIM IN RABBINICAL SOURCES

One of the earliest attempts to prove a Jewish, pre-Christian origin for Gnosticism was the work by M. Friedländer, published in 1898.[30] The author argued that when Philo attacked a class of Jews who understood the Mosaic laws in a philosophical sense – disregarding all the religious ceremonies, such as the Sabbath, the feast days, circumcision, etc. – Philo was referring to early Jewish Gnostics. Furthermore, these were also to be identified with the heretics known in the rabbinical texts as *Minim*. It is not at all certain that all the references to

---

[26] R. McL. Wilson, *Gnosis and the New Testament*, p. 26.
[27] M. Simon, 'Éléments gnostiques chez Philon', in *OG*, p. 374.
[28] *OG*, p. 20, n. 3.
[29] C. Colpe, 'New Testament and Gnostic Christology', p. 235.
[30] M. Friedländer, *Der vorchristliche jüdische Gnosticismus* (1898).

the *Minim* are to antinomian Jewish Gnostics as Friedländer held.[31] Many scholars have taken the *Minim* as simply Jewish Christians. The fact, however, that some of them seem to reject the unity of God inasmuch as they spoke of two powers has inclined some scholars to agree that these *Minim* may have either provided the occasion for the development of Jewish Gnosticism,[32] or were indeed Jewish Gnostics.[33]

Jonas, who opposes the Jewish derivation of Gnosticism, none the less admits that there were Jewish Gnostics. He cites the famous rabbinical saying, 'he who speculates on four things would better not have been born: what is above and what is below, what was before and what comes after. . . . And he who does not spare the honour of his Creator, for him it were better he were not born.'[34] But he does not think that this proves that Gnosticism came from heretics within Judaism. Schubert in criticizing Quispel's exposition of Jewish anthropological speculations as the background of the Gnostic Anthropos myth writes:

> 'In this, however, he is relying heavily on rabbinical citations that are more recent than the Gnostic teachings that are supposed to depend on them. In these cases it is a matter of rabbinical Haggadah being influenced by Gnostic materials rather than of Gnostic concepts being influenced by Jewish motifs.'[35]

In other words, rabbinical references to Jewish Gnostics, as they are late, may teach us that there were Jewish Gnostics, but they do not teach us about a Jewish origin of pre-Christian Gnosticism.

V. SCHOLEM'S MERKABAH MYSTICISM

Gershom Scholem has called attention to certain mystical speculations of some rabbis which is called Merkabah ('chariot', *cf.* Ezk. 1) Mysticism. These rabbis belonged to a

---

[31] *Cf.* review of Friedländer by E. Schürer in *ThLZ* 23. 6 (1899), cols 167–170.

[32] R. M. Grant in *OG*, p. 153.

[33] K. Rudolph, 'Randerscheinungen', p. 116. See R. Marcus, 'Pharisees, Essenes and Gnostics', *JBL* 73 (1954), pp. 159ff., who in agreement with Louis Ginzberg considers the Tannaitic references to the *Minim* as references to Jewish Gnostics.

[34] *OG*, p. 105.

[35] K. Schubert, 'Gnosticism, Jewish', in the *New Catholic Encyclopedia*, VI, p. 529.

'gnosticizing' circle of Pharisaic Judaism. Many of them were the pupils of Johanan ben Zakkai, who flourished at the end of the first century AD after the destruction of the temple in AD 70, or the pupils of Akiba, who supported the Second Jewish Revolt in AD 132–135. The texts come from the tractates of the Tannaitic or early Amoraic period (*i.e.* first-third centuries AD).[36]

Like other Pharisees, these teachers were still pure mono-theists and still revered the Mosaic law. Their only difference concerned esoteric speculations about the celestial domains which were not to be revealed without caution.[37] In a document called the *Greater Hekhaloth* the journeys of the mystics through the seven palaces in the seven heavens are described. As in pagan Gnosticism the ascent is hindered by the hostile rulers of the seven planetary spheres. These rulers may be overcome only by the possession of seals with secret names. Unlike the Gnostic, however, the mystic is not reabsorbed into the deity. 'The mystic who in his ecstasy has passed through all the gates, braved all the dangers, now stands before the throne; he sees and hears – but that is all.'[38]

It may be asked on what basis does Scholem call this esoteric Jewish mysticism Gnosticism. Scholem would argue that the ascent of the adept is a direct parallel to the ascent of the soul in Gnosticism, and that in both cases magical preparations are necessary. In a conference at Dartmouth in 1965 Professor Scholem is reported as saying that it does not matter whether you use the term 'Jewish Gnosticism', 'Jewish Esotericism', or 'Merkabah Mysticism'.

Other scholars, however, have objected to Scholem's loose and sometimes contradictory usage of terms.[39] Drijvers, for example, comments:

'It is true there was an esoteric development in Judaism also, which G. Scholem calls "Jewish Gnosticism", but it was accepted by Pharisees and rabbis, and remains within the bounds of established Judaism, even

---

[36] G. Scholem, *Jewish Gnosticism, Merkabah Mysticism, and Talmudic Tradition* (1960); *Major Trends in Jewish Mysticism* (1961).
[37] J. Daniélou, 'Judéo-christianisme et gnose', p. 145; Schubert, 'Jüdischer Hellenismus', p. 459.
[38] G. Scholem, *Major Trends*, p. 56.
[39] *E.g.* on p. 65, *ibid.*, Scholem writes: 'A dualism of the Gnostic kind would of course have been unthinkable for Jews . . .', but on p. 50 he speaks of a 'Judaized and monotheistic Gnosticism'.

if it may go off the rails in incidental cases. Scholem's terminology, however, has led to all kinds of misunderstandings and his work is sometimes read, understood and digested in quite different ways.'[40]

Jonas especially remonstrates at 'the semantic disservice which Scholem did to clarity when he called his Palestinian Hekhaloth mysticism a "Gnosis"'.[41] Jonas himself does not consider the mystical writings cited by Scholem to be Gnostic in the proper sense of the word:

'Are there *Hebrew* writings of that period which are Gnostic in the sense here specified? Now if Scholem's book (*Jewish Gnosticism, Merkabah Mysticism, and Talmudic Tradition*), which I read very differently from the way Quispel seems to read it, has demonstrated one thing to me, it is that there are not. And here I trust my friend Scholem: if he, with his avid appetite for the unorthodox and aberrant, his exquisite nose for the scent of it, and his unique knowledge of the field, has failed to bring up from this hunting trip even one example of that kind of "unorthodoxy", I am satisfied that it wasn't there.'[42]

VI. THE DEAD SEA SCROLLS

The Dead Sea Scrolls have been hailed by some of the proponents of pre-Christian Gnosticism as providing evidence to confirm their thesis. Widengren, for example, states that the discovery of the Scrolls has fully confirmed Reitzenstein's view that the Mandaeans originated as a pre-Christian movement.[43] Bultmann has claimed that '. . . a gnosticizing pre-Christian Judaism' which could hitherto be inferred only from later sources is now attested by the newly discovered Dead Sea Scrolls.[44]

In an article dedicated to Bultmann, Rudolph commends

[40] H. J. W. Drijvers, 'The Origins of Gnosticism', p. 347. Rudolph, 'Randerscheinungen', p. 114, considers Scholem's terminology not a very happy choice. Schubert, *OG*, p. 213: 'Scholems Gnosis-begriff ist vielleicht etwas zu weit.'

[41] H. Jonas in J. P. Hyatt (ed.), *The Bible in Modern Scholarship*, p. 291.

[42] *Ibid.*, p. 290.

[43] Review of C. Colpe, *Die religionsges. Schule*, by G. Widengren in *OLZ* 58. 11–12 (1963), col. 533: 'Diese Sicht hat sich trotz heftigen Widerstandes während der zwanziger und dreissiger Jahre vor allem dank der Entdeckung der Qumran-Texte siegreich behauptet und kann jetzt als die allgemein vorherrschende betrachtet werden.'

[44] R. Bultmann, *Theologie des Neuen Testaments* (1953), p. 361, n. 1. *Cf.* W. Meeks, *The Prophet-King*, p. 12, n. 1, who notes: 'Bultmann himself, with dubious justification, has hailed the Qumran texts as proof of the early penetration of gnostic influence into Jewish-Palestine (*Theology*, II, 13, n.; *cf. Ev. Joh.*, Ergänzungsheft, p. 11).'

the keen insight of Bultmann who had suggested that new
materials on the Essenes would help solve the problem of
Jewish Gnosticism.[45] Rudolph himself feels that the ethical
dualism of Qumran already has cosmological features which
place it in the proximity of a 'gnostisierender Kreise', and
cites an article by K. Schubert in which the latter finds in the
Manual of Discipline (iii. 13–iv. 28) the earliest proof of a
Jewish Gnosticism.[46]

Schmithals in his preface to the English translation of Bultmann's commentary expresses the conviction that the influence
of pre-Christian Gnosticism can be found in the Qumran
writings.[47] Schmithals himself in arguing that the Galatian
heresy was a Gnostic one suggests that the reference in
Galatians to the observation of holy days may not necessarily
be an indication of Jewish orthodoxy but may be a sign of
Essene practices which lead back to a 'gnostisierende Beein-
flussung'.[48] He also asserts that the relations between late
Jewish texts such as the Dead Sea Scrolls and Gnosticism are
undeniable, though one should not expect a 'pure' pre-Christian Gnosticism in them.[49]

Smith points out that Bultmann in 1925 in his famous
article on the Mandaeans had suggested a Semitic and even
Palestinian origin of the Johannine materials.[50] But even
Robinson, who also supports Bultmann on this point, concedes
that 'The absence of the gnostic redeemer myth at Qumran
did seem to diverge from what Bultmann had anticipated
concerning Jordanian baptismal sects. . . .'[51]

Indeed, Albright has argued that the resemblances of John
to the Dead Sea Scrolls have shown Bultmann to be mistaken:

'All the concrete arguments for a late date for the Johannine literature
have now been dissipated, and Bultmann's attempts to discern an earlier

[45] K. Rudolph, 'War der Verfasser der Oden Salomos ein "Qumran-
Christ"?', p. 555.
[46] K. Rudolph, 'Stand und Aufgaben', p. 92; K. Schubert's article
which is cited is 'Der Sektenkanon von En-Feschcha und die Anfänge der
jüdischen Gnosis', *ThLZ* 78 (1953), cols 495–506.
[47] R. Bultmann, *The Gospel of John*, p. 8.
[48] W. Schmithals, *Paulus und die Gnostiker*, pp. 30, 32, n. 93.
[49] *Ibid.*, p. 45.
[50] D. M. Smith, 'The Sources of the Gospel of John: An Assessment of
the Present State of the Problem', *NTS* 10 (1963–1964), p. 351.
[51] *Trajectories*, p. 234, n. 4.

and later form of the Gospel have proved to be entirely misleading, as both of his supposed redactions have similar Jewish background.'[52]

In a similar fashion Brown has concluded:

> 'Another fact that casts doubt on Bultmann's theory is that the thought of the Qumran community does not resemble Bultmann's reconstruction of what a Palestinian baptizing sect in the 1st century was thinking about. And yet this community has undeniably close geographical and theological affinities with John the Baptist, and so might have been expected to be somewhat similar to the Gnostic sectarians of John the Baptist posited by Bultmann.'[53]

Those who think that Bultmann was correct in his intuition conceive of Qumran as a proto-Gnostic stage on the way to full-fledged Gnosticism. According to Rudolph the Qumran community represents a heretical Judaism already influenced by Gnostic trends: its dualism is one that is already on the way to Gnostic dualism.[54] In an article published in 1950, K. G. Kuhn hailed the Qumran materials as a 'Vorform' of Gnostic thought centuries before other Gnostic texts.[55] Robinson has also suggested that Qumran has indicated 'steps toward Gnosticism'.[56] Similarly, Reicke considers the Scrolls to represent 'a stage on the way to Jewish gnostic speculations'.[57]

But the question must still be raised as to whether or not we can consider the Qumran writings Gnostic or a predecessor to Gnosticism. Do they represent a proto-Gnostic stage, an incipient Gnosticism, which blossomed into later Gnosticism? Or do they simply contain elements which are akin to certain Gnostic features – pre-Gnostic elements which may have been used by later Gnostics? The answer to these questions depends in part on how loosely one is prepared to define Gnosticism. As Wilcox points out:

> 'Was the sect at Qumran a Gnostic one? If we restrict the meaning of "gnostic" to "having to do with secret knowledge of the mind and

[52] W. F. Albright, *New Horizons*, p. 46.

[53] R. E. Brown, *The Gospel according to John I–XII*, p. LV.

[54] K. Rudolph, *Die Mandäer* I, p. 266; 'War der Verfasser', p. 555: '. . . der "qumränische" Dualismus auf dem Wege zum gnostischen ist. . . .'

[55] K. G. Kuhn, 'Die in Palästina gefunden hebräischen Texte und das Neue Testament', *ZThK* 47 (1950), p. 205.

[56] *Trajectories*, p. 380; *cf.* p. 266.

[57] B. Reicke, 'Traces of Gnosticism in the Dead Sea Scrolls?' *NTS* 1 (1954–1955), p. 141.

will of God", perhaps we may be led to answer yes. But if we are looking for a way of salvation expressed in terms of some kind of knowledge apart from Torah and "deeds in Torah", or for the presence and activity of a redeemer–revealer figure, historical or mythological, or indeed an emphasis on knowledge in its own right, we shall have to say no.'[58]

Indeed, a close study of the very elements which have been cited as providing parallels with Gnosticism – the emphasis on knowledge and dualism – reveals the differences between Qumran and true Gnosticism. Reicke concludes that the epistemology of the Qumran congregation as represented by the *Manual of Discipline* 'does not show any direct traces of gnostic mysticism'. Furthermore, 'the expression *da^cat* is not to be identified with the gnostic term "gnosis"'.[59] Davies, while acknowledging that the Qumran community placed a greater emphasis upon the concept of knowledge than other Jewish circles, stresses the difference between the eschatological 'knowledge' of the Dead Sea Scrolls and the *gnōsis* of Hellenism.[60]

In contrast with Rudolph, who considers Qumranian dualism as being 'on the way' to Gnostic dualism, on the basis of Schubert's identification of the *Manual of Discipline* iii. 13–iv. 28 as an early proof of Jewish Gnosticism, M. Black finds that the author of this particular passage 'stands in the Hebrew and Biblical, not the Greek tradition, though in comparison with the New Testament his speculative interest is slightly more pronounced: but it is in no way comparable to the later speculations and mythological systems of Gnosticism'.[61] Schubert himself, in an article written ten years after the one cited by Rudolph, strongly underscores the contrast between the ethical and eschatological dualism of Qumran and the absolute and cosmic dualism of Gnosticism.[62]

One of the most striking evidences to indicate that the

[58] M. Wilcox, 'Dualism, Gnosticism, and Other Elements in the Pre-Pauline Tradition', in M. Black (ed.), *The Scrolls and Christianity* (1969), p. 92.
[59] B. Reicke, 'Traces of Gnosticism', p. 140. *Cf.* B. Reicke, 'Da'at and Gnosis in Intertestamental Literature', in E. Ellis and M. Wilcox (eds), *Neotestamentica et Semitica* (1969), pp. 245–255.
[60] W. D. Davies, 'Knowledge in the Dead Sea Scrolls', pp. 131, 135.
[61] M. Black, *The Dead Sea Scrolls and Christian Origins* (1961), p. 134.
[62] K. Schubert, 'Jüdischer Hellenismus', p. 456.

Qumran documents do not really present us with Gnostic elements, as many in the first flush of enthusiasm over the newly published texts claimed, is the reversal of position in this regard on the part of two noted scholars. K. G. Kuhn, a student of Bultmann's, as we have already noted, hailed the Qumran texts as a 'Vorform' of Gnosticism in an article published in 1950. In an article written but two years later, Kuhn abandoned his earlier position and associated the ethical dualism of Qumran with Iranian influence rather than with Gnosticism.[63] H.-J. Schoeps in 1954 accepted the existence of a pre-Christian Jewish Gnosticism on the basis of the Scrolls.[64] In a work published two years later he maintains a sharp distinction between Gnosticism and Judaism – Christianity. 'Gnosticism is never anything other than pagan Gnosticism.'[65] Ideas similar to those in Gnosticism which appear in Judaism belong to heterodox Judaism rather than to Gnostic Judaism. Such syncretism is simply not the same as Gnosticism.[66]

Other scholars agree that the Scrolls are not Gnostic. Scholem wrote: 'As a careful reader of these texts (the Scrolls) I have not been able to detect those special terms and shades of meaning, read into them by K. G. Kuhn, that give them a specifically Gnostic or pre-Gnostic character.'[67] Jonas says, '. . . I do not think that any of the Qumran texts, even with what there is of dualism in them, qualifies for inclusion in the gnostic category.'[68] Ringgren outlines the basic differences between Qumran and Gnosticism as follows:

'1. The God of Qumran is the God of the O.T., who is himself the creator; there is no creator of lower rank, or demiurge.

2. God has created good *and* evil; matter is not evil in itself; and there is no series of aeons between the spiritual (divine) world and the material world.

3. Man, as he is, is totally sinful and corrupt, and there is no hint at his origin in the spiritual world or his having a spark of eternal light within him, or the like.

[63] K. G. Kuhn, 'Die Sektenschrift', p. 315.
[64] H.-J. Schoeps, 'Das gnostische Judentum in den Dead Sea Scrolls', *ZRGG* 6 (1954), pp. 276–279.
[65] H.-J. Schoeps, *Urgemeinde-Judenchristentum-Gnosis* (1956), p. 39.
[66] Schoeps in *OG*, p. 535.
[67] G. Scholem, *Jewish Gnosticism*, p. 3.
[68] *OG*, p. 104.

4. The typically Gnostic language with terms such as sleep, intoxication, call, awakening, etc., is absent from the Qumran writings.

5. Predestination is known by some Gnostics; there are also traits of fatalism in some Gnostic circles. But *heimarmene* as something to be saved from is unknown in Qumran, for predestination rests on God's rāṣōn or good pleasure. In Gnosticism fate is something negative, in Qumran it has a positive value as deriving from God.'[69]

MacRae concludes: 'The Scrolls do not contain Gnostic ideas, although they do belong to the broader movement of apocalyptic Judaism which may well have been a forerunner of Gnosticism.'[70]

VII. APOCALYPTICISM

Bultmann was of the opinion that 'the syncretistic apocalypticism of Judaism stands under the influence of Gnostic mythology'.[71] Some recent attempts have been made to trace the origins of Gnosticism to the Jewish apocalyptic movement, of which the Qumran community was a part.[72] Apocalyptic texts, written in the first two centuries BC and the first century AD, are writings 'of the oppressed who saw no hope for the nation simply in terms of politics or on the plane of human history'.[73] The apocalyptists looked beyond history to the miraculous intervention of God, who would vindicate his people Israel.

There are to be sure certain broad similarities between the Gnostics and the apocalyptists. Both groups maintained a negative attitude towards the present world, and both entertained the notion of secret knowledge. Both were keenly interested in angelology. But upon further examination, we see that these similarities conceal essential differences. The dualism of apocalyptic literature was eschatologically conditioned, whereas the dualism of the Gnostics was cosmologically conditioned. Whereas the Gnostic wanted to flee from

[69] H. Ringgren, 'Qumran and Gnosticism', in *OG*, pp. 382–383; cf. M. Mansoor, 'The Nature of Gnosticism in Qumran', in *OG*, pp. 389–400.

[70] G. W. MacRae, 'Gnosticism and New Testament Studies', p. 2629.

[71] R. Bultmann, *Das Evangelium des Johannes*, p. 12.

[72] Cf. J. Daniélou, 'Judéo-christianisme et gnose', p. 139.

[73] D. S. Russell, *The Method and Message of Jewish Apocalyptic*, p. 17.

the world, the apocalyptist hoped for a new world. Whereas in Gnosticism knowledge meant salvation itself, in such apocalyptic groups as at Qumran knowledge meant the proper interpretation of the Old Testament prophecies.[74]

Robert M. Grant has set forth the thesis that it may have been the sharp disappointment which the Jewish apocalyptists experienced with the fall of Jerusalem in AD 70 which turned some of them in bitterness to an anticosmic attitude leading to Gnosticism. 'Out of such shaking, we should claim, came the impetus toward Gnostic ways of thinking, doubtless not for the first time with the fall of Jerusalem but reinforced by this catastrophe.'[75] As a modern parallel Grant adduces the disorientation of the Plains Indians in nineteenth-century America.

Grant's proposal has met with sharp criticism. Pétrement points out that the catastrophe of 70, the destruction of the temple, plays no role in Gnostic teachings.[76] According to Robinson, the emergence of Gnosticism cannot 'be explained simply in inner-Jewish or inner-Christian terms, e.g. as the effect of the collapse of Jewish apocalypticism's imminent hope in a final military deliverance . . .'.[77] Jonas notes that the historical sources picture a different response:

'But as a Jewish response to the catastrophe of the year 70 we have, in the next generation, the uprisings in Cyrenaica, Egypt, on Cyprus, and finally Bar Kochba and Rabbi Akiba. Jewish apocalyptics were a hardy breed, and their response to the historical adversity of their fortunes bespeaks a very different psychological condition from the one which the hypothesis of an inner-Jewish reaction resulting in gnosticism must assume.'[78]

Moreover, Jonas argues that in the Gnostic derogations of the demiurge, he is represented as the effective ruler of this world; he is not shown as a god who could not control the course of events.

Haardt also points out the fact that even after the catastrophe of 70 we have the apocalyptic works of the Syrian *Baruch* and

---

[74] K. Schubert, 'Jüdischer Hellenismus', pp. 455ff.; cf. also 'Gnosticism, Jewish', pp. 529ff.

[75] R. M. Grant, *Gnosticism and Early Christianity*, p. 34; cf. 'Les êtres intermédiaires dans le judaïsme tardif', in *OG*, p. 154.

[76] S. Pétrement, 'Le Colloque de Messine', p. 357.

[77] *Trajectories*, p. 15.

[78] *OG*, p. 457.

4 Ezra.[79] In addition Russell lists as coming after AD 70 the Greek *Apocalypse of Baruch*, and the *Apocalypse of Abraham*.[80] It is pointed out by Haardt that even after the later catastrophe of the Bar Kochba revolt, a strong apocalyptic expectation was still expressed by certain rabbis – though the sense of imminence is lost and the predictions of the coming Messiah are placed in the distant future.[81]

VIII. THE MAGHARIYAH

To support the thesis of a Jewish origin of Gnosticism some have sought to find Jewish evidence for the notion that the world was not created by God but by a demiurge, perhaps by some angelic being. Philo, for example, taught that the irrational soul of man and his body were made by angels. Justin Martyr implies that some Jews taught that the human body was the creation of angels.

The clearest attestation that there were Jews who believed in both a high God and an angelic creator of the world is to be found in late Arabic texts describing the quasi-Jewish sect of the Maghariyah or Magharians. The best description is in al-Qirqisānī (AD 925), and supplementary accounts are to be found in al-Bīrūnī (AD 973–1048) and al-Shahrastānī (AD 1076–1153). These writers describe a group who were called Magharians after the Arabic word for *maġār* 'cave' as their books were found in caves. Although some have compared them to the sect from Qumran, the two groups agree only in one point – in the prohibition of foolish laughter.

According to Qirqisānī ,'they referred all anthropomorphic passages in the Bible to an angel rather than to God himself, and claimed that it was this angel who created the world'.[82] Wolfson has suggested that the Gnostics may have derived their concept of an angelic demiurge from this Jewish sect.[83]

---

[79] R. Haardt, 'Erlösung durch Erkenntnis: Probleme und Ergebnisse der Gnosis-Forschung', *Wort und Wahrheit* 16 (1961), p. 849.

[80] D. S. Russell, *op. cit.*, pp. 60, 65.

[81] A. H. Silver, *A History of Messianic Speculation in Israel* (1927; repr. 1959), pp. 24ff.

[82] N. Golb, 'Who Were the Maġārīya?' *JAOS* 80 (1960), p. 348.

[83] H. Wolfson. 'The Pre-existent Angel of the Magharians and al-Nahāwandi', *Jewish Quarterly Review* 11 (1960), p. 97.

This view has been endorsed by Quispel, who would specifically associate the Magharian doctrine with Cerinthus, whom he regards as a Jewish Christian. He further argues: 'I think we must suppose that such a group (the Magharians) did exist before the Christian era in Palestine.'[84] He then concludes that the concept of the demiurge, 'the characteristic feature, which distinguishes Gnosticism from Gnosis in a general sense, originated in Palestine among rebellious and heterodox Jews'.[85]

Even if we can disregard the fact that our evidence for the Magharians is found in sources that date to the tenth century AD and later, we are still faced with a number of problems with Quispel's reconstruction. In the first place, there is no evidence that such a group lived in Palestine, or that they existed in the pre-Christian era. Golb, after a detailed study of the Arabic sources, concludes that the Magharians were 'Jewish gnostics of an ascetic character who flourished in Egypt during the first few centuries of the present era, and who had access to Philonic writings or ideas . . .'.[86]

Grant, who does not agree that the Magharians were Gnostics, writes:

'Unfortunately for those who desire to discover a Jewish Gnosticism, that which Qirqisani says on the subject of their teaching about the moon shows that they could not have been Gnostics. "They affirm that all things have been created complete and perfect. . . ." But if all has been created complete and perfect, the angelic creator was himself complete and perfect; he was not evil. Among the Magharians we find then realized the possibility for Jewish heterodoxy, that an angel created the world, but we also find confirmed there the impossibility – for Jewish thought – that he was evil.'[87]

IX. ANTI-JEWISH SENTIMENTS AND A JEWISH ORIGIN OF GNOSTICISM

When we consider the presence of Jewish elements in Gnosticism, we are faced with the paradox that these elements are

[84] G. Quispel, 'The Origins of the Gnostic Demiurge', in Granfield and Jungman (eds), *Kyriakon* I, p. 273.
[85] *Ibid.*, p. 276.
[86] N. Golb, *op. cit.*, p. 358.
[87] R. M. Grant, 'Les êtres intermédiaires', p. 149.

used in a decidedly anti-Jewish fashion. Some scholars, such as MacRae, believe that the origins of Gnosticism must still go back to an inner Jewish origin though they concede that nothing within Judaism itself can account for the basic anti-cosmic attitude of Gnosticism.[88]

On the other hand, van Unnik minimizes the importance of the Jewish element and holds that one cannot speak of a direct influence of Judaism.[89] Pétrement suggests that the Gnostics absorbed the Jewish elements through the mediation of Christianity.[90] Adam, who holds to a pre-Christian origin of Gnosticism, believes that the anti-Jewish slant of Gnosticism prohibits a direct derivation from Judaism. He suggests that an Aramaic wisdom school in Mesopotamia may have absorbed elements of the Old Testament from Israelite exiles.[91]

Jonas, while admitting that Gnosticism indicates a reaction against Judaism and while conceding that it may be possible that Gnosticism arose out of such a reaction, objects to the theory that Gnosticism was created by the Jews themselves.[92] Though this last suggestion cannot be ruled out *a priori*, it lacks support in independent evidence and in psychological verisimilitude. Jonas would suggest that it would be safer to hold 'that Gnosticism originated in *close vicinity* and in partial reaction to Judaism'.[93] Schenke goes so far as to suggest that there was no real border-line between Judaism and non-Judaism, and that in some no man's land of syncretistic Judaism Gnosticism was able to gain a foothold.[94]

But the fact of the matter is that the gap between the Jewish view of a monotheistic God who created a good world, and the Gnostic view of a lower demiurge who created an evil world cannot be bridged by any known evidence but only by conjecture. A split in the deity is unheard of in Judaism and

---

[88] G. W. MacRae, 'The Jewish Background', p. 101.
[89] W. C. van Unnik, 'Die jüdische Komponente', p. 81.
[90] S. Pétrement, 'La notion de gnosticisme', p. 389; 'Le Colloque de Messine', p. 359.
[91] A. Adam, 'Ist die Gnosis in aram. Weisheitsschulen entstanden?', p. 300.
[92] In J. P. Hyatt (ed.), *The Bible in Modern Scholarship*, pp. 288–289.
[93] *OG*, p. 102.
[94] H.-M. Schenke, 'Das Problem der Beziehung', p. 133.

even in Samaritanism. When Rudolph proposes that the scepticism of the Jewish wisdom school led to a pessimistic view of the divine Providence and thence outside of official Judaism to Gnosticism, he is simply expressing 'a conclusion based solely on a comparative examination according to Motivgeschichte' of the discredited Religionsgeschichtliche Schule.[95]

X. JEWISH GNOSTICISM

What then is meant by the frequently used term 'Jewish Gnosticism'? And how early and sound are the evidences for its existence? According to Rudolph an early Jewish Gnosticism was the source of the parallel and concurrent streams of Gnosticism and of Christianity.[96] Elsewhere he admits that this conviction is based only on hypotheses and is difficult to prove.[97]

On the other hand, as Daniélou uses the term Jewish Gnosticism he is referring to a Jewish gnosis which was not characterized by the radical dualism. He writes:

'The original gnosis is the theology of Jewish Christianity, and is found in the works so far examined. The Gnostic dualists borrowed the symbolism of this Jewish Christian gnosis . . . but they adapted their borrowings to the demands of their own dualist system, and it is this system which constitutes Gnosticism properly so-called.'[98]

He also holds that 'Gnosticism as a system is fundamentally foreign both to Judaism and to Christianity . . .'[99] and also affirms that 'gnosis' but not 'Gnosticism' is to be found in the writings of Paul.[100]

When we review the evidences which have been adduced to prove the existence of a truly dualistic Jewish Gnosticism, we find that the sources are either ambiguous or late, or both. For example, such early sources as the Apocrypha, Philo, the Dead Sea Scrolls, and the New Testament itself do not reveal

[95] H. J. W. Drijvers, 'The Origins of Gnosticism', p. 349.
[96] K. Rudolph in his review of Colpe, *Die religionsges. Schule*, in *ThLZ* 88 (1963), col. 32.
[97] Rudolph, 'Randerscheinungen', p. 114.
[98] J. Daniélou, *The Theology of Jewish Christianity*, p. 54.
[99] *Ibid.*, p. 70.
[100] *OG*, p. 550.

clear-cut cases of Gnosticism. The Colossian heresy clearly betrays Jewish elements, but it cannot be shown to be Gnostic beyond dispute. This does not, of course, deny the possibility or even the probability that such Jewish-tinged Gnosticism may have existed. What is not proven, however, is a full-fledged pre-Christian Jewish Gnosticism. As Wilson summarizes the situation:

> 'The fact that so often it is difficult to decide whether some feature is Gnostic or Jewish, and the marked Jewish element in later Gnostic thinking, may suggest that there was a Jewish Gnosticism before there was a Christian, and hence that the origins of Gnosticism proper go back to the pre-Christian period; but here we are moving beyond what can be established on the basis of the New Testament evidence into the realm of conjecture.' [101]

[101] R. McL. Wilson, *Gnosis and the New Testament*, p. 59.

CHAPTER TEN

THE PRE-CHRISTIAN REDEEMER MYTH

I. REITZENSTEIN'S AND BULTMANN'S PRE-CHRISTIAN REDEEMER MYTH

As we have pointed out earlier (chapters 1 and 2) the keystone of the hypothesis of a pre-Christian Gnosticism as developed by Reitzenstein and by Bultmann has been the teaching of the Redeemed Redeemer myth combined with the Primal Man myth, which was then historicized by Christianity. This myth supposes the existence of a Primal Man, a figure of light, who was torn asunder and divided into particles of light, which were then distributed in the world as human souls. The powers of darkness attempt to prevent these souls from realizing their heavenly origins. God then sent a Redeemer in corporeal form to awaken these souls, to liberate them from their bodies, and to gather them back to their heavenly home. Bultmann set forth to prove that the Gospel of John presupposed this Redeemer myth and could only be understood in the light of the myth.

There are, of course, still scholars who steadfastly maintain their conviction in the pre-Christian existence of the Primal Man–Redeemer myth, though no longer basing themselves upon the same Iranian sources upon which Reitzenstein relied. Rudolph, for example, recently wrote:

'I am hence of the well-grounded conviction that the gnostic redeemer myth is of pre-Christian origin. . . . In my opinion Paul and the anonymous author of the Gospel of John presuppose a gnostic-type doctrine of the redeemer; they use its terminology, but also oppose it. For them the mythological redeemer or revealer has been transcended by the historical redeemer Jesus Christ.

'An irreproachable proof for our view is provided, apart from segments of Hermetic Gnosticism and the "Hymn of the Pearl", by Mandaean literature. It is derived from a non-Christian gnostic sect, which has demonized Christ as redeemer.'[1]

[1] K. Rudolph, 'Stand und Aufgaben', p. 97, as translated and cited in

But when we realize that *all* of the evidences cited by Rudolph as irreproachable proof – the Hermetica, the Hymn of the Pearl, the Mandaic literature – are of clearly post-Christian date, we have grave doubts as to the strength of his case.

Some scholars have posited a pre-Christian development of the myth on the assumption of a development in Judaism prior to Christianity. Whereas Bultmann had assumed that the Gnostic Redeemer figure had influenced the concepts of Sophia, Anthropos, and Logos, Käsemann has come to the reverse conclusion. He suggests that the concepts of Sophia, Anthropos, and Logos in pre-Christian Judaism came together to make up the Gnostic Redeemer.[2] Sanders, for one, does not think it likely that Christianity would have invented the cosmic dimensions of its Christology without a prior myth in Judaism. But as no pre-Christian Jewish text presents us with an unambiguous Gnostic Redeemer myth, the chief arguments for this hypothesis remain logical ones which take what is common to the figures of Logos, Anthropos, Sophia, and the Christology of the New Testament and presuppose a common ancestor.[3]

II. A POST-CHRISTIAN DEVELOPMENT OF THE REDEEMER MYTH

When even such an ardent advocate of pre-Christian Gnosticism as Schmithals admits that by the end of the first century the Gnostic Redeemer myth no longer appears anywhere in its 'pure' form, one is tempted to ask with Wilson whether the postulated Redeemer myth is anything other than a scholar's reconstruction.[4] Neill is even more emphatically sceptical:

'One question calls urgently for an answer. Where do we find the evidence for pre-Christian belief in a Redeemer, who descended into

---

Trajectories, pp. 263–264. In a portion of the original article which is not cited, Rudolph goes on to say that even if it be disputed that the old Mandaic texts provide us with a certain proof for the pre-Christian existence of Gnosticism, they at least give us witnesses for Gnostic teachings which are not dependent upon Christianity.

[2] J. T. Sanders, *The New Testament Christological Hymn*, p. 80.

[3] *Ibid.*, pp. 96ff.

[4] R. McL. Wilson, 'Some Recent Studies in Gnosticism', *NTS* 6 (1959–1960), p. 43.

the world of darkness in order to redeem the sons of light? Where is the early evidence for the redeemed Redeemer, who himself has to be delivered from death? The surprising answer is that there is precisely no evidence at all. The idea that such a belief existed in pre-Christian times is simply a hypothesis and rests on nothing more than highly precarious inferences backwards from a number of documents which themselves are known to be of considerably later origin.'[5]

Indeed, an impressive array of scholars both in the past and in more recent times have come to the conclusion that the Gnostic Redeemer figure as described by Reitzenstein and Bultmann, and as attested in the Hymn of the Pearl, the Manichaean and the Mandaean texts is simply a post-Christian development dependent upon the figure of Christ, rather than a pre-Christian myth upon which the New Testament figure of Christ depends.

As early as 1930 Carl Kraeling, who had done a careful study of the Anthropos figure, rejected Bultmann's formulation: 'Whatever the origin of the Johannine christology may be, it is almost certainly not to be found in the redeemed redeemer in whom we see rather the end than the beginning of syncretistic Oriental soteriology.'[6] Percy, who also opposed Bultmann's reconstruction, argued that apart from the Mandaean and Hermetic literature, the figure of the Gnostic Redeemer rested upon a syncretistic concept of the Christian Saviour.[7] Dodd pointed out that the Mandaean figure of Enosh-Uthra was clearly based upon the Christ of Christian Gnosticism. He wrote:

'But if that is so, then the only appearance of an historical redeemer in the Mandaean literature is due to Christian influence. . . . Mandaism offers no real exception to the dictum of Edwyn Bevan that the idea of a personal redeemer of mankind is always the result of Christian influence.'[8]

It is especially significant that in recent years a number of the leading scholars of Gnosticism, who have worked first-hand with the sources, have come to deny emphatically the existence of a pre-Christian Redeemer myth. Haardt, who

[5] S. Neill, *The Interpretation of the New Testament*, pp. 179–180.
[6] C. H. Kraeling, 'The Fourth Gospel and Contemporary Religious Thought', *JBL* 49 (1930), p. 146.
[7] E. Percy, *Untersuchungen*, pp. 287–299.
[8] C. H. Dodd, *The Interpretation of the Fourth Gospel*, p. 127.

does not think that the existence of a pre-Christian Gnosticism has been proved, writes that this is even less certain for the figure of the hypothetical pre-Christian Gnostic Redeemer.[9] Wilson states: 'The myth of the Urmensch-Redeemer has been adequately examined by others, and the view that such a myth, if it ever existed, exercised a formative influence on the early Church is now generally rejected.'[10] According to Grant:

'In pre-Christian Graeco-Roman religion there was no redeemer or saviour of a Gnostic type. . . . The most obvious explanation of the origin of the Gnostic redeemer is that he was modelled after the Christian conception of Jesus. It seems significant that there is no redeemer before Jesus, while we encounter other redeemers (Simon Magus, Menander) immediately after his time.'[11]

Especially influential on this score have been the studies of Quispel and of Colpe. In his important study published in 1953, Quispel concluded: 'And finally, Gnosticism, so far as we have come to know it up to the present, did not have a redeemer figure; it is incorrect to picture the Anthropos, Adam, Poimandres, as a redeemer. Even if perhaps there was a pre-Christian Gnosis, still there was never a pre-Christian Gnostic redeemer.'[12] Even if at a later date the Anthropos or other related figure appeared in Valentinianism as a redeemer, this merely shows that Gnosticism, which was originally and principally a religion of self-redemption, later came under the influence of Christianity.[13] Elsewhere Quispel writes:

'There would appear to be good grounds for supposing that it was from Christianity that the conception of redemption and the figure of the Redeemer were taken over into Gnosticism. A pre-Christian re-

[9] R. Haardt, 'Erlösung durch Erkenntnis', p. 850.
[10] R. McL. Wilson, *The Gnostic Problem*, p. 220.
[11] R. M. Grant, *Gnosticism, A Sourcebook*, p. 18. Elsewhere in *A Historical Introduction to the New Testament* (1963), p. 203, Grant says:

'There seems to be no evidence for the existence of a Gnostic redeemer-revealer before the rise of Christianity. It is therefore probable that Christianity was an important factor in producing Gnostic systems. Again, there seems to be no evidence for the existence of Gnostic systems before the end of the first century.'

[12] G. Quispel, 'Der gnostische Anthropos', p. 224.
[13] *Ibid.*, p. 234.

deemer and an Iranian mystery of redemption perhaps never existed.'[14]

Although Colpe would concede that there may have been other redeemer figures in systems developed outside of Christianity, he contends that the Redeemer myth is not understandable apart from the Docetic interpretation of Christ.[15] He has argued that the Adam-Christ parallel in Paul's writings is not an attestation of a pre-Christian Gnostic Redeemer myth but is Paul's own interpretation of an originally Jewish concept for his Hellenistic readers. This was only later developed into the Gnostic myth.[16] He has also affirmed that the Logos doctrine in the Gospel of John is not, as Bultmann saw it, the temporalization and historization of the Gnostic Redeemer myth. 'It is, first and foremost, something substantially and phenomenologically new, something totally inadequate to the old material of conceptions and imaginations.'[17]

In a similar vein Schenke has shown that the Gnostic Anthropos doctrine originated from speculations on Genesis 1 : 26f., and that there was no Redeemer myth in the full sense before Manichaeism. The myth represented but the climax of a long process of development and not its original starting-point.[18]

The impact of all of these studies which have denied the existence of the pre-Christian Redeemer myth as it has usually been conceived has been such that it has forced Schmithals, Bultmann's student and the leading proponent of a pre-Christian Gnostic interpretation of the New Testament, to make some major modifications. He now regards what he calls the 'historical envoy' – the messenger who appears in the guise of a specific historical man – to be atypical of Gnosticism rather than the normal type as had been presupposed in earlier studies.[19] With respect to this figure of the historical envoy, Schmithals is prepared to concur with Quispel's

[14] In F. L. Cross (ed.), *The Jung Codex*, p. 78.

[15] 'Gnosis', in *RGG*[3], II, p. 1652.

[16] C. Colpe, 'Zur Leib-Christi-Vorstellung in Epheserbrief' in W. Eltester (ed.), *Judentum, Urchristentum, Kirche (Festschrift für Joachim Jeremias)* (1960), pp. 186–187.

[17] C. Colpe, 'New Testament and Gnostic Christology', p. 237.

[18] H.-M. Schenke, *Der Gott 'Mensch' in der Gnosis: Ein religionsgeschichtlicher Beitrag zur Diskussion über die paulinische Anschauung von der Kirche als Leib Christi* (1962), p. 148.

[19] W. Schmithals, *The Office of Apostle*, p. 132.

opinion that this figure was dependent upon Christianity rather than the reverse.[20] He writes:

> 'The judgment of Bultmann (*Das Evangelium Johannes*, p. 10): "However, the idea of the incarnation of the redeemer did not somehow penetrate Gnosticism from Christianity, but is originally Gnostic", appears to me accordingly to need correcting. The redeemer myth is undoubtedly Gnostic, but the special form of the myth which speaks of the incarnation of the redeemer in a concrete historical person is not proved in the pre-Christian era, not even in the documentation cited by Bultmann. . . .'[21]

What Schmithals would maintain is that there were other figures in pre-Christian Gnosticism, who though they were not 'historical' emissaries, none the less functioned as 'redeemers' in the broad sense of the word, bringing gnosis as messengers.[22] This, of course, is a major concession and admits that the Christian teaching of the incarnation of a historical Redeemer was a unique and original concept uninfluenced by Gnosticism.

III. GNOSTICISM WITHOUT THE REDEEMER MYTH

In opposition to Quispel, Rudolph writes that a pre-Christian Gnosticism without a Redeemer or a Gnosticism without a Redeemer myth is inconceivable.[23] But Schmithals and others have pointed out that it is still possible to conceive of Gnosticism without the specific Redeemer myth.[24] Colpe points out three types of heavenly messengers: (1) prophetic figures who are sent to proclaim the saving gnosis, as in the Hermetica; (2) the messenger who is sent through the firmaments, often in the pre-cosmic era, but who does not appear on the earth; (3) the Gnostic Redeemer who appears upon the earth in a Docetic body.[25]

Schmithals asserts: 'At the beginning of Gnosticism stands no redeemer myth, but rather the redeeming Gnosis as such.'[26]

---

[20] *Ibid.*, p. 133, n. 125.
[21] *Ibid.*, p. 134, n. 153.
[22] *Ibid.*, p. 148.
[23] K. Rudolph, *Die Mandäer* I, p. 101, n. 4.
[24] J. Duchesne-Guillemin, *Ormazd et Ahriman* (1953), p. 111.
[25] C. Colpe, *Die religionsges. Schule*, p. 198.
[26] W. Schmithals, *The Office of Apostle*, p. 126.

He holds that: 'Especially in Jewish Gnosticism apparently a redeemer was often unknown.'[27] Schmithals distinguishes between two chief types of Gnostic Redeemers: 'the redeemer sent from heaven, and on the other side, the earthly being who fetches the Gnosis from heaven'.[28] In the former case the Redeemer is usually one, but in the latter case the number of Redeemers is in principle unlimited.[29] As an example of what he calls the 'primaeval emissary' he cites numerous Mandaean figures who are concerned with the pre-mundane victory over demons and who appear to give the primitive revelation to Adam or to Noah. Schmithals concludes:

> 'This always implies that the Gnosis is known from primeval times onward. This alone is important, and not any special form of the redeemer myth. The apostle who descends as teacher of Gnosis is one of the numerous heavenly figures who battle with the planetary deities in the Mandaean primordial history.'[30]

What shall we say about Schmithals's attempt to salvage the thesis of a pre-Christian Gnosticism by substituting non-historical Gnostic emissaries in place of Bultmann's primal man-historical redeemer? If we examine the proof-texts for Schmithals's portrayal of the figures of the 'heavenly apostle' and the 'earthly apostle' of Gnosticism,[31] we are struck by the fact that apart from a very few references to Apocryphal texts, all of the evidence – as was the case with Bultmann – comes from post-Christian sources. A good half of his citations are to Mandaic texts; the other references are to the *Odes of Solomon*, the Hymn of the Pearl, the Hermetica, the Manichaean texts, *etc.* We must therefore conclude that the case for a pre-Christian Gnosticism without the classical Redeemer myth but with non-historical emissaries is no stronger than Bultmann's original formulation.

[27] *Ibid.*, p. 116.
[28] *Ibid.*, p. 121.
[29] *Ibid.*, p. 189.
[30] *Ibid.*, p. 130.
[31] *Ibid.*, pp. 122–192.

CHAPTER ELEVEN

CRITICISMS OF METHODOLOGY

I. THE USE OF LATE SOURCES

It should be apparent that one of the most commonly expressed criticisms of the History of Religious scholars and their modern successors has been the uncritical use of late sources to postulate a system of pre-Christian Gnosticism. Peel has pointed out that the 'Achilles' heel' of the pre-Christian Gnostic view lies in Reitzenstein's original construction.[1] For like Reitzenstein, Bultmann and Schmithals have continued to use late Mandaic and Manichaean texts for their reconstructions.

Wilson points out that in the entire chapter on Gnosticism in Bultmann's *Primitive Christianity* 'there is not a single reference to any document which can be dated prior to the New Testament',[2] though Bultmann assumes that Gnosticism was a pre-Christian movement which influenced the New Testament. Wilson warns that:

> 'The assumption that the full development of later Gnosticism is already present in pre-Christian Gnosis obviously involves a begging of the question, a reading of first-century texts with second-century spectacles, and this amply justifies the reluctance of some scholars . . . to admit any widespread "Gnostic influence" in the formation stages of early Christianity.'[3]

Casey scores the 'cavalier' attitude of Reitzenstein to matters of chronology and sarcastically describes him as raising 'the subjective criticism of documents to a high imaginative art'.[4]

---

[1] M. L. Peel, 'The Epistle to Rheginos: A Study in Gnostic Eschatology and Its Use of the New Testament', PhD dissertation, Yale University (1966), p. 72.
[2] In J. P. Hyatt, *The Bible in Modern Scholarship*, p. 274.
[3] R. McL. Wilson, *Gnosis and the New Testament*, p. 24.
[4] R. P. Casey, 'Gnosis, Gnosticism', p. 53.

Nock remarks, 'Certainly it is an unsound proceeding to take Manichaean and other texts, full of echoes of the New Testament, and reconstruct from them something supposedly lying back of the New Testament.'[5] Similarly van Unnik writes: 'It is surely fundamentally erroneous, in disregard of chronology, to confuse data whose origins are different, to collect facts from here, there and everywhere and to combine them into a single picture as happens much too frequently.'[6] Colpe, describing the synthetic analysis of Hartmans, observes that the resulting syncretism is not so much that of the original documents but that of the modern scholar![7]

II. PARTS FOR THE WHOLE

One of the fallacious assumptions which seems to underlie the work of Reitzenstein, Bousset, Bultmann, Schmithals, *etc.*, is the belief that Gnosticism was a unified phenomenon through the centuries whose presence or influence can be detected by its constituent elements – *i.e.* by terms which are allegedly Gnostic technical terms. Neill complains:

'Unfortunately, some scholars are less cautious than others; there is a tendency to suppose that when any Gnostic word or phrase occurs in any document that is available to us, the whole of the Gnostic myth must have been present in the mind of the writer whoever he may have been. Clearly, this is an assumption which is more readily made than proved.'[8]

Corwin explains the reasoning of Bultmann in this regard:

'Bultmann maintains that the appearance of isolated mythological motifs is explained by the fact that something akin to a process of demythologizing was going on in the New Testament period and the years adjacent to it. It is this that explains why – with the Mandaean myth, as he believes, available – early Christian writers do not make use of the full myth but seem to strip it, taking from it elements consonant with their emerging beliefs about the salvation wrought by Christ. He assumes their knowledge of it, and their discarding of those parts of it which do not serve their purposes.'[9]

---

[5] A. D. Nock, 'Gnosticism', p. 278.
[6] In F. L. Cross, *The Jung Codex*, p. 85.
[7] C. Colpe, *Die religionsges. Schule*, p. 169.
[8] S. Neill, *Interpretation*, p. 177.
[9] V. Corwin, *St. Ignatius*, p. 128.

A specific illustration of this tendency in New Testament exegesis may be seen in the works of Schmithals and Wilckens on Paul's opponents in Corinth. Pearson, in his Harvard dissertation, writes: 'One may ask whether these two books suffer from an over-emphasis on the use of certain allegedly "gnostic" terms, and frequently fall into the trap of reading into a passage from the Corinthian letters a whole theological system or philosophical Weltanschauung just on the basis of the occurrence of certain terms – not the least of which are the terms *pneumatikos* and *psuchikos*.' [10]

With respect to Schlier's book on Ignatius, which follows the methods of Reitzenstein, Corwin comments: 'Their primary interest is in individual figures and motifs of myth, which they find in different religions, but a difficulty arises because they tend to assume that the whole myth was known whenever a phrase suggests an aspect of it.' [11] Concerning the alleged Gnostic character of the *Odes of Solomon*, Charlesworth remarks: 'In light of these phenomena during the early Christian centuries, it is important to recognize that it is not the presence of such terms as light, darkness, truth, sleep, knowledge, etc., which characterizes Gnosticism; rather it is the interpretation of these terms and the metaphysical framework in which they are given expression which is uniquely gnostic!' [12] In a similar vein, van Baaren underscores the limitations of the phenomenological investigation of motifs:

'It is, moreover, a fallacy to speak of gnostic elements in describing elements found elsewhere which are found in gnosticism too, unless there is a demonstrable, or, at least, probable, historic relation, because, as said before, gnosticism is only partly determined by the elements it contains, but mostly by the way in which they function together forming an integrated whole.' [13]

These warnings are particularly appropriate in view of our increasing knowledge of the great variety of Gnostic systems of thought. In 1960 Corwin wrote: 'We may well be cautious about granting the availability of any single myth, and even

[10] B. A. Pearson, 'The *Pneumatikos-Psuchikos* Terminology', p. 4.
[11] Corwin, *op. cit.*, p. 12.
[12] J. H. Charlesworth, 'The Odes of Solomon', p. 365. *Cf.* Bianchi, 'Le problème des origines', p. 163.
[13] T. P. van Baaren, *OG*, p. 175.

of a dominant cosmic dualism. Even gnostic speculation seems to have been more fluid in those years than some of the German scholars associated with the religious-historical movement have been willing to grant.'[14] In the ensuing decade with the publication of more and more of the Coptic Nag Hammadi documents, this fluidity and variety have become even clearer, as pointed out by Peel:

> 'Unfortunately, it has often been supposed that this "idealized form" of Gnosticism could be found from Philo to late Manichaeanism and that wherever any particular theologumenon could be detected in a writing, one might assume the presence of others – even though unmentioned. . . . Such a presupposition appears to take too little into account both the considerable time lapse between the earliest and latest of these writings and the fact that even "proto-Gnosticism" was a growing, changing entity. And, as Nag Hammadi is reminding us with ever increasing emphasis, nuances in historical development – even in Gnosticism – are important!'[15]

From all of this, Drijvers concludes that 'we should on no account fill up gaps in our knowledge of one system with what we know of other systems, purely on the grounds of a common Gnosticism we attribute to them'.[16]

III. THE NEW TESTAMENT ITSELF AS EVIDENCE

It has been noted earlier that the evidences adduced for the existence of pre-Christian Gnosticism are either late or ambiguous, or both. The New Testament itself is an early but ambiguous source of evidence which has been used, *e.g.* by Bultmann. Bultmann presupposed that there was a Gnosticism behind the Gospel of John and then used John as his main source for reconstructing this Gnosticism.

This circular reasoning is explicitly justified as an unavoidable 'hermeneutical circle' by Schmithals as follows. He suggests that there are only three possible relationships between Gnosticism and the New Testament: (1) Gnosticism can be presupposed for the explanation of New Testament Christianity. (2) New Testament Christianity can be presupposed

---

[14] Corwin, *op. cit.*, p. 188.
[15] M. Peel, 'Gnostic Eschatology and the New Testament', *NovTest* 12 (1970), p. 164.
[16] H. J. W. Drijvers, 'The Origins of Gnosticism', p. 330.

for the explanation of Gnosticism. (3) There are no causal relationships between the New Testament and Gnosticism.[17] Schmithals considers the second and third alternatives impossible, and argues that the first relationship is supported by the indisputable existence of a pure Jewish Gnosticism, by the early western origin of the Mandaean Gnosticism, and by the patristic notices concerning Simon and other heretics – though we do not possess any Gnostic sources which can be certainly dated to the pre-Christian period.[18] He therefore concludes that the New Testament exegete ought in any case first to presuppose Gnosticism in his interpretation of individual passages, just as he himself has done. He asserts, 'we must reconstruct the Gnosticism which stands in the background of the New Testament from the New Testament texts themselves . . .'.[19]

It is somewhat of an ironic situation that a 'circular' appeal for support with respect to pre-Christian Gnosticism exists in the relationship between New Testament scholars and Mandaean scholars – though no-one seems to have noticed this. We have seen that New Testament scholars like Bultmann, Schmithals, Schlier, Bornkamm, Robinson, *etc.*, have appealed to the Mandaean evidence. What is not so well known is that Mandaean scholars have in turn appealed to the studies of Bultmannian scholars for a major source of their conviction that the Mandaean texts represent an early Gnosticism.

Rudolph, for example, cites Bultmann as demonstrating the undeniable contacts between Mandaica and the Johannine corpus.[20] He writes furthermore as follows:

'The existence of a pre-Christian Gnostic tendency in sectarian Judaism can therefore no longer be denied. The best evidence for this is the polemic of certain writings of the New Testament, as the Gospel of John, of Paul (in the Corinthian and Galatian letters), of Colossians and Ephesians.'[21]

Rudolph refers to New Testament scholars who have demonstrated the dependence of the New Testament upon

[17] W. Schmithals, 'Das Verhältnis von Gnosis', p. 378.
[18] *Ibid.*, p. 379.
[19] *Ibid.*, p. 380.
[20] K. Rudolph, 'War der Verfasser', p. 554.
[21] Rudolph, 'Stand und Aufgaben', p. 93.

Gnosticism, although he recognizes that they have not always worked with assured premises and that they have sometimes overshot the mark. In Rudolph's opinion, however, they have none the less proved beyond objection that the Gnostic movement, including the Redeemer myth, is not dependent upon Christianity, but the reverse. He cites as examples of this type of research the works of Bauer, Bultmann, Schlier, Käsemann, Bornkamm, Becker, Schmithals, and Haenchen.[22]

Macuch, after discussing the legendary *Haran Gawaita* as a possible evidence for the alleged Palestinian origins of the Mandaeans, concedes that a pre-Christian origin for the Mandaeans, as far as he is concerned, does not rest upon such a legendary account: 'There origin betrays itself *alone* in their oldest liturgical literature, and is thereby so strongly assured, that the confusion of Mandaean legends over their Palestinian beginnings, their poor transmission of Palestinian names and the ignorance of Palestinian topography cannot refute this.'[23] (Italics ours.) Instead, his conviction rests upon the harmony of the oldest Mandaic hymns with early Palestinian texts. And what are these early Palestinian parallels that supply the evidence of the origin of Mandaeism? Why, the Gospel of John, in particular. Macuch is convinced that the prologue of John's Gospel fairly teems with Mandaean concepts.[24]

In a critique of Macuch's position, I suggested that for those of us who are not Bultmannians, it would be necessary to prove the validity of the Mandaic parallels to John by a demonstration of the pre-Christian age of the Mandaeans and *not* to prove the pre-Christian age of the Mandaeans by the Mandaic parallels to John.[25] In response to this criticism, Professor Macuch has written to me as follows:

'There is no necessity of proving something which cries, and of which the denial is not possible, even if there is no other evidence apart from the NT, because logical conclusions are authorised to play their rôle in the research, even if there is only scanty external evidence. But in this case the evidence not only is not scanty but, on the contrary, it is very impressive and persuasive, and I do not follow the belief propagated by you that people who would like to deny this evidence would be in a

[22] *Ibid.*, pp. 97–100.
[23] R. Macuch, 'Anfänge der Mandäer', p. 125.
[24] *Ibid.*, p. 109.
[25] *GEMO*, p. 71.

better position to interpret the NT than those who, with open eyes, use the only possible working hypothesis. . . .'[26]

Thus, it would seem that there is a great gulf between German scholars who feel that it is valid to use 'logical' deductions even in the absence of early objective evidence, and English-speaking scholars who would decry such arguments as subjective and speculative. Alan Richardson, for example, writes:

'. . . when scholars like Bultmann describe a Gnostic doctrine they take their first-century "evidence" from the New Testament itself. But this is a question-begging proceeding, since the New Testament is susceptible of a very different interpretation.

'. . . those scholars who readily find Gnostic influences at work in the New Testament argue that the beginnings of this type of thought must have been fairly well defined in the first century; they then set out to look for evidences of it in the New Testament, and are then in peril of interpreting the earlier by means of the later writings.'[27]

IV. PARALLELS AND DEPENDENCE

One of the most common methods of logical 'proof' used by the German scholars who favour the dependence of Christianity upon a pre-Christian Gnosticism is to set up parallels and argue that there are only two or three possibilities. Reitzenstein, for example, argued that because of the parallels between Christian and Mandaean baptism we are faced with the following alternatives: (1) Christian baptism was the prototype for Mandaean baptism; (2) Mandaean baptism was the prototype for Christian baptism; (3) both rites had different origins.[28] Inevitably the possibility of independent development is rejected, and the case for a dependence of Christianity upon the Gnostic example is urged.[29]

In a similar fashion Schmithals compares the office of the apostles in the early church and in later Gnostic texts and comes quite logically to the utterly unlikely conclusion that the church borrowed this office from the Gnostics:

'In my opinion, after what has been said, there can be no doubt that the primitive Christian apostolate was an appropriation of the mission-

---

[26] In a personal letter of 28 June 1971.
[27] A. Richardson, *Introduction to the Theology of the New Testament* (1958), pp. 41ff.
[28] R. Reitzenstein, *Die Vorgeschichte*, p. 152.   [29] *Ibid.*, p. 158.

ary office of Jewish or Jewish-Christian Gnosticism native to the same Syrian region in which the church's apostolate is at home. The original relationship of the two "offices" is evident, and the comparison which was carried through above shows with utter clarity that the dependence lies on the side of the church's apostles.'[30]

Schmithals also maintains that it is irrefutable 'that the Gnostic terminology in Paul cannot have first created the Gnostic myth, but presupposes it!' He thus assumes the existence of Gnostic communities for the early period of Christianity. Despite the complete lack of early, unambiguous texts for Gnosticism in the pre-Christian period and his use of much later texts to fill this void, Schmithals says: 'Without labeling the contesting of this presupposition as unscientific, I think I may claim for its champions at least the same scientific seriousness as for its opponents.'[31]

Schweizer and other Bultmannians have argued for the dependence of New Testament passages upon Gnostic prototypes by citing Mandaean parallels to them. But it is quite unwarranted to take Mandaic texts and then by comparing them with New Testament parallels to conclude that the Mandaic texts are logically prior, unless one can prove that Mandaeism historically antedated the New Testament. Speaking of the parallels between John and the Mandaean texts and the *Odes of Solomon* cited by Becker, Smith comments:

'That such parallels exist and that they can be shown to stand in close relationship to John's discourses does not, however, mean that John used such a non-Christian document (or a Christian one, for that matter) as the basis for his own gospel. What is more, such parallels do not give one the right, certainly they do not compel one, to hypothesize that John used such a written source, in the belief that such a hypothesis, once adopted, could be vindicated in the course of literary analysis.'[32]

Vincent Taylor, for one, was convinced that the Mandaean parallels to John are not the result of dependence in one direction or the other but of independent development:

'*The Johannine sayings are not directly dependent on the Mandaean sayings, and the latter are not directly dependent on the Fourth Gospel.* Striking as the parallels sometimes are, they are not close enough to suggest dependence;

[30] W. Schmithals, *The Office of Apostle*, p. 229.
[31] *Ibid.*, p. 115, n. 72.
[32] D. M. Smith, *The Composition*, p. 82.

they are not verbal correspondences, but analogues which imply the same forms, figures and symbols, and in some cases similar religious conceptions.'[33]

We must be careful in distinguishing between mere parallels, and parallels which are evidence of dependence. Though late documents may preserve earlier materials, it is hazardous in comparisons to disregard chronology. As Wilson warns us:

'When we are studying the phenomena we have to note the similarities, the typical features, but these similarities do not necessarily guarantee any historical continuity, a point that has not always been borne in mind. From the phenomenological point of view it may be perfectly legitimate to group religious movements together on the basis of their common elements; but this does not necessarily mean that these movements stand in any genetic relationship, or that there is any direct connection between the earlier and the later.'[34]

One real pitfall in comparing parallels is that parallels are inevitably confined to elements extracted out of context. We need to have in mind the original settings of the elements, otherwise we may be dazzled only by the similarities and may be oblivious to the real and usually enormous differences which the larger contexts betray. Corwin, remarking on the comparisons of Reitzenstein and Schlier, comments: 'When one reads uncritically long pages of such parallels, there is an extraordinary cumulative effect. It is not sustained, however, for at least one reader, when each step in the series is evaluated, and inquiry is made whether the conclusions reached necessarily follow.'[35] Elsewhere she writes:

'Parallels become less convincing when they exist only in documents which in their present form come from a considerably later period and which must undergo drastic source analysis to establish an "early" stratum, and this difficulty emerges in many of Schlier's examples (in his work on Ignatius). Furthermore, the method is almost by definition atomistic, presenting concepts, isolated from the total scheme in which alone they have meaning.'[36]

Drijvers, in his work on Bardaisan, chose not to list paral-

---

[33] V. Taylor, 'The Mandaeans and the Fourth Gospel', *Hibbert Journal* (1929–1930), pp. 544–545.
[34] R. McL. Wilson, *Gnosis and the New Testament*, p. 7.
[35] V. Corwin, *op. cit.*, p. 203.
[36] *Ibid.*, p. 12.

lels in the mode of the Religionsgeschichtliche Schule for the following reasons:

'In doing this there is a considerable temptation to cite numerous parallels from more or less related systems, and to dissect the whole into many fragments of different origin, Jewish, Iranian, Chaldaean, Christian, Stoic, etc. By such means the unity of the system is lost, however, while the parallels themselves shed little or no light, as roughly identical concepts often function in a totally different manner within the various systems.'[37]

When one compares not isolated phrases and elements with their parallels in the New Testament, but Gnostic systems and the New Testament as a whole, one is struck not so much with the similarities as with the profound differences. As Laeuchli concludes:

'To speak of Gnostic language in the New Testament is therefore misleading. We can recognize Gnostic elements in a broad sense, yet we have such Gnostic elements in countless documents far removed from any historical Gnosticism. What distinguishes biblical speech from Gnostic speech is nothing less than its very center. . . . To designate both biblical and Gnostic language as "syncretistic" obscures the extent of two opposed atmospheres and misses the emphasis within the two: the dominant "Hebraic" language, used to describe incarnation and redemption, is replaced in Gnosticism by a language or languages of equal value.'[38]

V. THE APPEAL TO AUTHORITY

In surveying the works on Gnosticism and the New Testament one is struck with the frequency of statements, particularly in German works, which appeal to the authority of Reitzenstein and Bultmann for the assumption that the case for a pre-Christian Gnosticism has been proved beyond cavil. This mood of confidence in the assured results of the Religionsgeschichtliche Schule seems to pervade the studies written from the 1930s through the 1950s.

Jonas, writing in 1934, assumed the results of previous scholars as established and intentionally renounced any further 'religionsgeschichtliche' or historical work on the texts in favour of a philosophical–phenomenological analysis of

[37] H. J. W. Drijvers, *Bardaiṣan*, p. 213.
[38] S. Laeuchli, *The Language of Faith*, p. 90.

Gnosticism as a unity.[39] Over two decades later he was to recall: 'When, many years ago, under the guidance of Rudolf Bultmann, I first approached the study of Gnosticism, the field was rich with the solid fruit of philology and the bewildering harvest of the genetic method. To these I neither presumed nor intended to add.'[40] Regarding Jonas's position, Munck caustically observed: 'The author is under the delusion that the so-called "philological" research is at an end, and that the time has come for philosophy to explore and put in order the ground already won.'[41]

Bornkamm in his 1933 study of the apocryphal *Acts of Thomas* wrote that no one any longer contested the Gnostic interpretation of the Hymn of the Pearl thanks to the works of Bousset and Reitzenstein.[42] In an essay on Colossians published in 1958 he still felt that there could be no doubt possible as to the relationship between Gnosticism and the ancient Indo-Aryan cosmology as proved by Reitzenstein.[43]

Sometimes an appeal is made to authorities who in turn appeal ultimately to the earlier works of Reitzenstein for evidence of pre-Christian Gnostic concepts. For example, Martin[44] appeals to S. Mowinckel[45] to support the position that 'a widespread myth of the Primal Man in the pre-Christian Near East seems very possible'. But when one examines Mowinckel's work one discovers that he in turn relies for his support on the works of Bousset and Reitzenstein.[46]

Even fairly recent German studies continue to express the unperturbed conviction that pre-Christian Gnosticism is an established fact without any reference to the questions raised by British and American scholars. Krause, for example, writes: 'It is now generally accepted that Gnosticism was already of pre-Christian origin.'[47]

Rudolph states: 'It is, in my opinion, today the consensus

---

[39] H. Jonas, *Gnosis und spätantiker Geist* I, pp. 83–84.
[40] Jonas, *The Gnostic Religion*, p. xvii.
[41] J. Munck, 'The New Testament and Gnosticism', p. 228.
[42] G. Bornkamm, *Mythos und Legende*, pp. 111, 113, n. 1.
[43] Bornkamm, *Das Ende des Gesetzes*, p. 142, n. 9.
[44] R. P. Martin, *Carmen Christi*, p. 160, n. 3.
[45] S. Mowinckel, *He That Cometh* (1959), pp. 420–437.
[46] *Ibid.*, p. 422, n. 2.
[47] M. Krause, 'Das literarische Verhältnis', p. 223.

of scholarship that the Gnostic redeemer belief (to which the Mandaean belief belongs) is pre-Christian and is presupposed by primitive Christianity.'[48] Rudolph assumes, for the basis of his own investigations of the Mandaean texts and for his conviction that they include pre-Christian materials, the demonstration of the pre-Christian origin of the Urmensch-Redeemer myth by Reitzenstein and Widengren.[49] With respect to Rudolph's arguments for the pre-Christian nature of Mandaeism built on such a foundation, Peel writes: 'We have grave doubts about this type of architectonic methodology, especially when it involves Reitzenstein and Jonas as foundation stones.'[50]

It is now apparent, however, especially in the light of Colpe's devastating criticism of the Religionsgeschichtliche Schule and its purported proofs of pre-Christian Gnosticism that it is no longer legitimate merely to appeal to authoritative names for evidence. Even James Robinson, who states that he is involved in the 'indigenization of the Bultmann tradition on American soil',[51] recognizes this fact when he criticizes Schmithals as follows:

'Unfortunately Schmithals, like Baur before him, overdoes his case and thus tends to discredit the truth in his position. In the first place, he presupposes in an uncritical way the Bultmannian solution of the gnostic problem, centered in the pre-Christian origin of the gnostic redeemer myth. But the time is past even in Germany when this can be presupposed without further ado simply by allusion to Reitzenstein.'[52]

VI. NON-CHRISTIAN THEREFORE PRE-CHRISTIAN?

The discovery of purportedly non-Christian texts from the Nag Hammadi library – such as the *Apocalypse of Adam*, the *Letter of Eugnostos*, and the *Paraphrase of Shem* – has led some to conclude that here at long last is evidence of a pre-Christian Gnosticism. But as Quispel has remarked: 'It is becoming increasingly clear

[48] K. Rudolph, *Die Mandäer* I, p. 101. In a footnote on the page he cites as his authorities: Bultmann 'die auf Bousset und Reitzenstein aufbauen', Bornkamm, Schmithals, Haenchen, Jonas, Widengren, and Schlier.

[49] *Ibid.*, pp. 150ff., 159f., 169ff.

[50] M. L. Peel, 'The Epistle to Rheginos', p. 62.

[51] *Trajectories*, p. 1.

[52] J. M. Robinson, 'Basic Shifts', p. 80.

that Gnosis in its essential being is *non*-Christian; the view that it is also *pre*-Christian must still be proven.'[53] In other words, it does not necessarily follow that non-Christian Gnosticism was also pre-Christian Gnosticism.

Many have cited Krause's demonstration that the *Sophia of Jesus Christ* represents a Christianizing of the *Eugnostos* materials as proof of a non-Christian Gnosticism, and by implication a pre-Christian Gnosticism. Krause did say, 'In this tractate are found isolated Jewish, but no Christian concepts.'[54] But in attempting to explain the Christianization of *Eugnostos* by the Gnostics as a device designed to convert more orthodox Christians, Krause cites Epiphanius's description of Gnostic conventicles in upper Egypt who posed a threat to the church in the fourth century AD.[55] Doresse, who was the first to suggest that the *Sophia* was a Christianized edition of *Eugnostos*,[56] also believes that the Gnostics Christianized *Eugnostos* for a missionary purpose. This does not mean, however, that he is assuming a pre-Christian date for the non-Christian Gnosticism of *Eugnostos*. On the contrary, Doresse suggests as the occasion for this transformation the Constantinian conversion of the Roman Empire to Christianity in the fourth century:

> 'Does not this hasty and artificial Christianizing of texts by the Gnostics, texts which they had earlier put forward as revelations of the Magi or as philosophical treatises with no mention of Christianity correspond, considering its fairly precise date, to the fact that the victory then won by the Church over the Paganism that was persecuting her, incited the sects to hide their doctrines under Christian disguises which were henceforth to be the fashion?'[57]

Schenke, who does believe in the establishment of Gnosticism independently of Christianity 'not long before the establishment of Christianity or at the same time as Christianity',[58] none the less considers Eugnostos to be a late product of Valentinianism and therefore not to be dated before the late second century.[59]

[53] G. Quispel, *Gnosis als Weltreligion*, p. 5.
[54] M. Krause, 'Das literarische Verhältnis', p. 222.
[55] *Ibid.*, p. 223.
[56] J. Doresse, 'Trois livres gnostiques inédits'.
[57] In Bleeker and Widengren, p. 549.
[58] Schenke, 'Hauptprobleme der Gnosis', p. 118.
[59] H.-M. Schenke, 'Nag-Hamadi Studien II', p. 266.

Although, as we have pointed out earlier, we do not agree with Böhlig's analysis of the Coptic *Apocalypse of Adam* as a document of non-Christian Gnosticism untouched by any influence of Christianity, let us for the sake of argument accept his proposition. We must still ask whether this means that the non-Christian Gnosticism of the *Apocalypse* was also pre-Christian? Some who have cited Böhlig's work seem to believe that here is evidence for this position. They seem to have over-looked the fact, not made very clear in the first place by Böhlig, that this is not exactly what he meant. In a later work he explained 'that the designation "pre-Christian Gnos-ticism" is not to be equated with a Gnosticism before the birth of Christ, but a Gnosticism out of which developed the Christian Gnosticism of the second century'.[60]

There are a number of scholars who concede the non-Christian Gnostic character of the *Apocalypse of Adam* but who maintain that the *Apocalypse* dates from a post-Christian period. Kasser, for example, thinks that the work may go back to one of 'the most obscure (periods) of primitive Christianity', by which he means the end of the first or beginning of the second century AD.[61] Schotroff likewise holds that the *Apocalypse of Adam* is non-Christian but not pre-Christian.[62] Ménard be-lieves that certain Nag Hammadi tracts have shown that 'Gnosticism was at first pagan, then Christian, without, however, having been pre-Christian'.[63]

Not only is there the possibility of a parallel development of non-Christian Gnosticism, but there is also the possibility suggested by Schenke of a de-Christianization or paganization of a prior Christian Gnosticism.[64] This possibility has been argued in particular by Pétrement. She points to the analogy of Christians who disguised their Christianity in Judaism or in paganism for missionary purposes, and cites the examples of the *Testaments of the Twelve Patriarchs*, the *Ascension of Isaiah*, the *Odes of Solomon*, and certain Sibylline books which are Christian

[60] A. Böhlig, 'Christentum und Gnosis im Ägypterevangelium', in W. Eltester (ed.), *Christentum und Gnosis* (1969), p. 2, n. 5.

[61] R. Kasser, 'Bibliotèque gnostique', pp. 317–318.

[62] L. Schottroff, 'Animae naturaliter salvandae', in Eltester, *Christen-tum und Gnosis*, p. 83.

[63] J.-É. Ménard, 'Le "Chant de la perle"', p. 290.

[64] *Cf.* Wilson, *Gnosis and the New Testament*, p. 117.

documents without open Christian references. She suggests that the Christian Gnostics might have done the same in such works as the *Apocalypse of Adam*. 'When our scholars believe that they can explain such works by actually pre-Christian traditions, they simply enter into the play of the Gnostics, they construct a myth of which one can say that it is the same as a Gnostic myth.'[65] As further examples of non-Christian Gnostic documents which are patently post-Christian, she cites the Hermetica, the Chaldean Oracles, and the teachings of Numenius – all dating from the second century AD or later.[66]

Not many scholars would go as far as Pétrement in saying: 'The sole decisive proof, the discovery of a pagan Gnosticism in texts anterior to Christianity, has always been lacking and will always be lacking.'[67] But as long as such texts are lacking, elaborate attempts to prove pre-Christian Gnosticism on the basis of post-Christian evidences must be viewed with critical suspicion. Drijvers concludes as follows:

> 'We can reduce this whole complex of relations to two questions; was there a pre-Christian Gnosticism, and were there forms of Gnosticism that are non-Christian? For non-Christian does not automatically mean pre-Christian. In spite of all the suppositions in this field, we know nothing of a pre-Christian Gnostic system.'[68]

VII. CONCLUSIONS

In conclusion, we have seen how the imposing scholarly edifice of Reitzenstein's and Bultmann's pre-Christian Gnosticism is but little more than an elaborate multi-storied, many-roomed house of cards, whose foundations have been shaken, some of whose structures need buttressing and others have

---

[65] S. Pétrement, 'Le Colloque de Messine', p. 371.

[66] *Ibid.*, p. 370; 'La notion de gnosticisme', p. 418. *Cf.* C. Colpe, 'Die Thomaspsalmen als chronologischer Fixpunkt . . .', pp. 92–93, with respect to the development of Mandaeism and of Manichaeism: 'Wir haben ihre Entwicklung in Manichäismus und Mandäertum als eine rein endogene verständlich machen können und brauchten keinerlei christologische Voraussetzungen zu Hilfe zu nehmen. Damit stellt sie sich uns inhaltlich als nicht christlich dar. Chronologisch gesehen aber ist sie nachchristlich.'

[67] S. Pétrement, 'La notion de gnosticisme', p. 387.

[68] H. J. W. Drijvers, 'The Origins of Gnosticism', p. 339.

collapsed, leaving a mass of debris with but few solid timbers fit for use in reconstruction.

At this point, it would seem best to follow Wilson in accepting the presence of an incipient Gnosticism slightly later than the genesis of Christianity. As Wilson points out, 'It therefore seems a legitimate inference that the origins of Gnosticism proper are pre-Johannine, although here we are moving into the shadowy no-man's land between Gnosticism proper and vaguer Gnosis.'[69]

Schlier has described Gnosticism as the twin brother of Christianity.[70] Such a vivid description, however, gives more credit to the originality of Gnosticism than it deserves. As both Rudolph and Bianchi have noted, Gnosticism always appears as a parasite. 'Nowhere do we find a pure form of Gnosticism, always it is built on earlier, pre-existing religions or on their traditions.'[71]

Even if we may admit that Paul and John interacted with and combated a rudimentary form of Gnosticism, there is no convincing evidence to uphold the view that Christianity derived as much from Gnosticism as Gnosticism derived from Christianity. As MacRae points out, 'Whatever their debt to nascent Gnosticism, both Paul and John evolved doctrines of Christian Gnosis that could well have been partly inspired by elements current in the syncretistic world about them but are certainly original because they focus on the person of Christ.'[72]

For some scholars, such as Jonas, the priority of Christianity or of Gnosticism may not be a matter of much importance.[73] For the Christian New Testament scholar it is of considerable importance because of the possibility of influence or dependence.[74] No one, of course, can rule out *a priori* the possibility of the adaptation of a pre-existing pagan or Jewish Gnosticism by the early Christians. It seems fairly clear that some of the

[69] Wilson, *Gnosis and the New Testament*, p. 48; cf. *The Gnostic Problem*, pp. 68f.; 'Some Recent Studies in Gnosticism', p. 35.
[70] H. Schlier, 'Das Denken der frühchristlichen Gnosis (Irenäus Adv. Haer. I, 23. 24)', in *Neutestamentliche Studien für Rudolf Bultmann zu seinem siebzigsten Geburtstag am 20. August 1954* (1954; 2nd ed. 1957), p. 81.
[71] H. J. W. Drijvers, 'The Origins of Gnosticism', p. 331.
[72] G. W. MacRae, 'Gnosis, Christian', p. 522.
[73] *OG*, p. 103.
[74] Wilson, *Gnosis and the New Testament*, p. 24.

Psalms of the Old Testament, for example, made use of demy-thologized Ugaritic literary motifs without any reflection upon the essence of Jehovah's revelation. There is no inherent reason why the New Testament writers could not have used non-Christian materials also. But in the case of the Old Testament we have Ugaritic texts which are indisputably older. In the case of the New Testament texts we have no Gnostic texts which are older, and the evidences which have been adduced to prove the priority of Gnosticism over Christianity have been weighed in this study and found wanting.

BIBLIOGRAPHY

The following is a selected bibliography of books, articles, and reviews which have been cited two or more times. The reviews are listed under the author's name rather than the reviewer's.

Adam, A., 'Ist die Gnosis in aramäischen Weisheitsschulen entstanden?' *OG*, pp. 291–301.

Adam, A., *Die Psalmen des Thomas und das Perlenlied als Zeugnisse vorchristlicher Gnosis* (1959).
   Review by A. F. J. Klijn in *BiOr* 19 (1962), pp. 94–95.

Albright, W. F., *New Horizons in Biblical Research* (1966).

Baaren, T. P. van, 'Towards a Definition of Gnosticism', in *OG*, pp. 174–180.

Barth, M., 'A Chapter on the Church – the Body of Christ', *Interpretation* 12. 2 (1958), pp. 131–156.

Bauer, W., *Orthodoxy and Heresy in Earliest Christianity* (1971).

Bauer, W., *Rechtgläubigkeit und Ketzerei im ältesten Christentum* (1934; 2nd ed. 1964).

Becker, H., *Die Reden des Johannesevangeliums und der Stil der gnostischen Offenbarungsreden* (1956).

Betz, O., 'Was am Anfang geschah: Das jüdische Erbe in den neugefundenen koptischen-gnostischen Schriften', *Abraham unser Vater: Juden und Christen im Gespräch über die Bibel*, ed. O. Betz et al. (1963), pp. 24–43.

Beyschlag, K., 'Zur Simon-Magus-Frage', *ZThK* 68 (1971), pp. 395–426.

Bianchi, U. (ed.), *Le Origini dello Gnosticismo* (1967).
   Review by G. Quispel in *JAOS* 90 (1970), pp. 321–322.

Bianchi, U., 'Le problème des origines du gnosticisme et l'histoire des religions', *Numen* 12 (1965), pp. 161–178.

Bianchi, U. (ed.), *Studi di Storia Religiosa della tarda antichità* (1968).

Bivar, A. D., and Shaked, S., 'The Inscriptions at Shīmbār', *Bulletin of the School of Oriental and African Studies* 27 (1964), pp. 265–290.

Black, M., *The Dead Sea Scrolls and Christian Origins* (1961).

Bleeker, C. J., and Widengren, G. (eds), *Historia Religionum* I: *Religions of the Past* (1969).

Böhlig, A., 'Die Adamsapokalypse aus Codex V von Nag Hammadi als Zeugnis jüdisch-iranischer Gnosis', *Oriens Christianus* 48 (1964), pp. 44–49.

Böhlig, A., *Mysterion und Wahrheit* (1968).

Böhlig, A., and Labib, P., *Koptisch-gnostische Apocalypsen aus Codex V von Nag Hammadi im Koptischen Museum zu Alt-Kairo* (1963).

Bornkamm, G., *Das Ende des Gesetzes: Paulusstudien* (1958).

Bornkamm, G., *Mythos und Legende in den apokryphen Thomas-Akten* (1933).

Borsch, F. H., *The Christian and Gnostic Son of Man* (1970).

Bousset, W., *Kyrios Christos* (1970).

Brown, R. E., *The Gospel according to John I–XII* (1966).

Bultmann, R., 'Die Bedeutung der neuerschlossenen mandäischen und manichäischen Quellen für das Verständnis des Johannesevangeliums', *ZNW* 24 (1925), pp. 100–146.

Bultmann, R., *Das Evangeliums des Johannes* (1941; repr. 1968).

Bultmann, R., *The Gospel of John: A Commentary* (1971).

Bultmann, R., *Primitive Christianity in Its Contemporary Setting* (1956).

Bultmann, R., *Theology of the New Testament* I and II (1952 and 1955).

Casey, R. P., 'Gnosis, Gnosticism and the New Testament', *The Background of the New Testament and Its Eschatology*, ed. W. D. Davies and D. Daube (1956), pp. 52–80.

Cerfaux, L., 'Gnose préchrétienne et biblique', *Dictionnaire de la Bible*, Supplément III (1938), cols 659–701.

Charlesworth, J. H., 'The Odes of Solomon – Not Gnostic', *CBQ* 31 (1969), pp. 357–369.

Colpe, C., 'New Testament and Gnostic Christology', *Studies in the History of Religions* XIV, ed. J. Neusner (1968), pp. 227–243.

Colpe, C., *Die religionsgeschichtliche Schule: Darstellung und Kritik ihres Bildes vom gnostischen Erlösermythus* (1961).

Colpe, C., 'Die Thomaspsalmen als chronologischer Fixpunkt in der Geschichte der orientalischen Gnosis', *Jahrbuch für Antike und Christentum* 7 (1964), pp. 77–93.

'Coptic Gnostic Library', *NovTest* 12 (1970), pp. 81–85.

Corwin, V., *St. Ignatius and Christianity in Antioch* (1960).

Coxon, P. W., 'Script Analysis and Mandaean Origins', *Journal of Semitic Studies* 15 (1970), pp. 16–30.

Cross, F. L. (ed.), *The Jung Codex* (1955).

Cullmann, O., *Le problème littéraire et historique du roman pseudo-Clémentin: Étude sur le rapport entre le gnosticisme et le judèo-christianisme* (1930).

Daniélou, J., 'Judéo-christianisme et gnose', *Aspects du judéo-christianisme* (1965), pp. 139–166.

Daniélou, J., *The Theology of Jewish Christianity* (1964).

Davies, W. D., 'Knowledge in the Dead Sea Scrolls and Matthew 11:25–30', *HTR* 46 (1953), pp. 113–139.

Dinkler, E. (ed.), *Exegetica: Aufsätze zur Erforschung des Neuen Testaments* (1967).

Dinkler, E. (ed.), *Zeit und Geschichte: Dankesgabe an Rudolf Bultmann zum 80. Geburtstag* (1964).

Dodd, C. H., *The Bible and the Greeks* (1935; repr. 1964).

Dodd, C. H., *The Interpretation of the Fourth Gospel* (1953; repr. 1968).

Doresse, J., *The Secret Books of the Egyptian Gnostics* (1960).

Doresse, J., 'Trois livres gnostiques inédits: Évangile des Égyptiens, Epître d'Eugnoste, Sagasse de Jésus Christ', *VigChr* 2 (1948), pp. 137–160.

Drijvers, H. J. W., *Bardaiṣan of Edessa* (1966).

Drijvers, H. J. W., 'Edessa und das jüdische Christentum', *VigChr* 24 (1970), pp. 4–33.

Drijvers, H. J. W., 'The Origins of Gnosticism as a Religious and Historical Problem', *Nederlands Theologisch Tijdschrift* 22 (1968), pp. 321–351.

Drower, E. S., *The Canonical Prayerbook of the Mandaeans* (1959).

Drower, E. S., *Diwan Abatur or Progress through the Purgatories* (1950).

Drower, E. S., *The Haran Gawaita and the Baptism of Hibil-Ziwa* (1953).

Drower, E. S., 'Mandaean Polemic', *Bulletin of the School of Oriental and African Studies* 25 (1962), pp. 438–448.

Drower, E. S., *The Secret Adam* (1960).

Ehlers, B., 'Kann das Thomasevangelium aus Edessa stammen?' *NovTest* 12 (1970), pp. 284–317.

Eltester, W. (ed.), *Christentum und Gnosis* (1969).

Feine, P., Behm, J., and Kümmel, W. G., *Introduction to the New Testament* (14th ed., 1966).

Frye, R. N., *The Heritage of Persia* (1963).

Frye, R. N., 'Reitzenstein and Qumrân Revisited by an Iranian', *HTR* 55 (1962), pp. 261–268.

Gibson, J. C. L., 'From Qumran to Edessa', *Annual of Leeds University Oriental Society* 5 (1963–1965), pp. 24–39.

Giversen, S., 'The Apocryphon of John and Genesis', *StTh* 17 (1963), pp. 60–76.

Golb, N., 'Who Were the Maġārīya?' *JAOS* 80 (1960), pp. 347–359.

Grant, R. M., 'The Earliest Christian Gnosticism', *Church History* 22 (1953), pp. 81–98.

Grant, R. M., 'Les êtres intermédiaires dans le judaïsme tardif', in *OG*, pp. 141–157.

Grant, R. M., *Gnosticism: A Sourcebook of Heretical Writings from the Early Christian Period* (1961).

Grant, R. M., *Gnosticism and Early Christianity* (1959; 2nd ed. 1966).

Haardt, R., 'Erlösung durch Erkenntnis: Probleme und Ergebnisse der Gnosis-Forschung', *Wort und Wahrheit* 16 (1961), pp. 848–852.

Haardt, R., 'Gnosticism', *Sacramentum Mundi* II (1968), pp. 379–381.

Haenchen, E., 'Gab es eine vorchristliche Gnosis?' *ZThK* 49 (1952), pp. 316–349.

Hennecke, E., and Schneemelcher, W. (eds), *New Testament Apocrypha* I and II (1963 and 1965).

Henning, W. B. 'The Monuments and Inscriptions of Tang-i Sarvak', *Asia Major* n.s. 2 (1952), pp. 151–178.

Henrichs, A., and Koenen, L., 'Eine alte griechische Mani Schrift', *Zeitschrift für Papyrologie und Epigraphik* 5 (1970), pp. 97–216, plates IV–VI.

Huth, O., 'Das Mandäerproblem – das Neue Testament im Lichte der mandäischen und essenischen Quellen', *Symbolon* 3 (1962), pp. 18–38.

Hyatt, J. P. (ed.), *The Bible in Modern Scholarship* (1965).

Jonas, H., *Gnosis und spätantiker Geist* I: *Die mythologische Gnosis* (1934).

Jonas, H., *The Gnostic Religion* (1958; 2nd ed. 1963).

Käsemann, E., *Essays on New Testament Themes* (1964).

Käsemann, E., *Exegetische Versuche und Besinnung* I (1960).

Kasser, R., 'Bibliothèque gnostique V: Apocalypse d'Adam', *RThPh* 16 (1967), pp. 316–333.

Klijn, A. F. J., *The Acts of Thomas* (1962).

Klijn, A. F. J., 'The Influence of Jewish Theology on the Odes of Solomon and the Acts of Thomas', *Aspects du Judéo-Christianisme* (1965), pp. 167–179.

Koester, H., 'The Purpose of the Polemic of a Pauline Fragment (Phil. 3)', *NTS* 8 (1961–1962), pp. 317–332.

Kraeling, C. H., *Anthropos and Son of Man* (1927).

Krause, M., 'Das literarische Verhältnis des Eugnostosbriefes zur Sophia Jesu Christi', *Mullus (Festschrift, T. Klauser)* (1964), pp. 215–223.

Kuhn, K. G., 'Die Sektenschrift und die iranische Religion', *ZThK* 49 (1952), pp. 296–314.

Laeuchli, S., *The Language of Faith: An Introduction to the Semantic Dilemma of the Early Church* (1962).

Lidzbarski, M., *Ginza: Das grosse Buch der Mandäer* (1925).

Lidzbarski, M., *Mandäische Liturgien* (1920; repr. 1962).

MacRae, G. W., 'The Coptic-Gnostic Apocalypse of Adam', *Heythrop Journal* 6 (1965), pp. 27–35.

MacRae, G. W., 'Gnosis, Christian', and 'Gnosticism', *New Catholic Encyclopedia* VI (1967), pp. 522–523, 523–528.

MacRae, G. W., 'Gnosticism and New Testament Studies', *Bible Today* 38 (1968), pp. 2623–2630.

MacRae, G. W., 'The Jewish Background of the Gnostic Sophia Myth', *NovTest* 12 (1970), pp. 86–101.

Macuch, R. 'Alter und Heimat des Mandäismus nach neuerschlossenen Quellen', *ThLZ* 82 (1957), cols 401–408.

Macuch, R., 'Altmandäische Bleirollen', *Die Araber in der Alten Welt*, ed. F. Altheim and R. Stiehl. Vol. IV (1967), pp. 91–203, plates pp. 626–631; vol. V (1968), pp. 34–72, plates pp. 454–468.

Macuch, R., 'Anfänge der Mandäer', *Die Araber in der Alten Welt*, ed. F. Altheim and R. Stiehl. Vol. II (1965), pp. 76–190.

Macuch, R., 'Der gegenwärtige Stand der Mandäerforschung und ihre Aufgaben', *OLZ* 63. 1–2 (1968), cols 6–14.

Macuch, R., *Handbook of Classical and Modern Mandaic* (1965).

Martin, R. P., *Carmen Chrisi: Philippians ii. 5–11 in Recent Interpretation and in the Setting of Early Christian Worship* (1967).

Meeks, W., *The Prophet-King: Moses Traditions and the Johannine Christology* (1967).

Ménard, J.-É., 'Le "Chant de la perle" ', *RevSR* 42 (1968), pp. 289–325.

Mowinckel, S., *He That Cometh* (1959).

Munck, J., 'The New Testament and Gnosticism', *Current Issues in New Testament Interpretation*, ed. W. Klassen and G. Snyder (1962), pp. 224–238.

Murphy-O'Connor, J. (ed.), *Paul and Qumran* (1968).

Naveh, J., 'The Origin of the Mandaic Script', *Bulletin of the American Schools of Oriental Research* no. 198 (1970), pp. 32–37.

Neill, S., *The Interpretation of the New Testament 1861–1961* (1964).

Neusner, J., *A History of the Jews in Babylonia* I: *The Parthian Period* (1969).

Neusner, J., 'Jews and Judaism under Iranian Rule: Bibliographical Reflections', *History of Religions* 8 (1968), pp. 159–177.

Nock, A. D., 'Gnosticism', *HTR* 57 (1964), pp. 255–279.

Nodelman, S. A., 'A Preliminary History of Characene', *Berytus* 13 (1960), pp. 83–121.

Oden, T. C., 'From Event to Language: The Church's Use of Gnostic Mythology', *Religion in Life* 36 (1967), pp. 92–99.

Pallis, S. A., *Mandaean Studies* (1926).

Pearson, B. A., 'The *Pneumatikos-Psuchikos* Terminology in 1 Corinthians: A Study in the Theology of the Corinthian Opponents of Paul and Its Relation to Gnosticism'. PhD dissertation, Harvard University (1968).

Peel, M. L., 'The Epistle to Rheginos: A Study in Gnostic Eschatology and Its Use of the New Testament'. PhD dissertation, Yale University (1966).

Percy, E., *Untersuchungen über den Ursprung der johanneischen Theologie* (1939).

Pétrement, S., 'Le Colloque de Messine et le problème du gnosticisme', *Revue de Métaphysique et de Morale* 72 (1967), pp. 344–373.

Pétrement, S., 'La notion de gnosticisme', *ibid.* 65 (1960), pp. 385–421.

Pokorný, P., *Die Epheserbrief und die Gnosis: Die Bedeutung des Haupt-Glieder-Gedankens in der entstehenden Kirche* (1965).

Quispel, G., 'The Discussion of Judaic Christianity', *VigChr* 22 (1968), pp. 81–93.

Quispel, G., 'Gnosis', *Vox Theologica* 39 (1969), pp. 27–35.

Quispel, G., *Gnosis als Weltreligion* (1951).

Quispel, G., 'Gnosticism and the New Testament', *The Bible in Modern Scholarship*, ed. J. P. Hyatt (1965), pp. 252–271.

Quispel, G., 'Der gnostische Anthropos und die jüdische Tradition', *Eranos Jahrbuch* 22 (1953), pp. 195–234.

Quispel, G., *Makarius, das Thomasevangelium und das Lied von der Perle* (1967).

Quispel, G., 'The Origins of the Gnostic Demiurge', *Kyriakon (Festschrift Johannes Quasten)*, ed. P. Granfield and J. A. Jungmann (1970), I, pp. 271–276.

Quispel, G., 'Das Thomasevangelium und das Alte Testament', *Neotestamentica et Patristica*, ed. W. C. van Unnik (1962), pp. 243–248.

Reicke, B., *The Epistles of James, Peter, and Jude* (1964).

Reicke, B., 'Traces of Gnosticism in the Dead Sea Scrolls?', *NTS* 1 (1954–55), pp. 137–141.

Reitzenstein, R., *Poimandres: Studien zur griechisch-ägyptischen und früh-christlichen Literatur* (1904; repr. 1966).

Reitzenstein, R., *Die Vorgeschichte der christlichen Taufe* (1929; repr. 1967).

Robinson, J. M., 'Basic Shifts in German Theology', *Interpretation* 16 (1962), pp. 76–97.

Robinson, J. M., 'The Coptic Gnostic Library Today', *NTS* 14 (1968), pp. 356–401.

Robinson, J. M., and Koester, H., *Trajectories through Early Christianity* (1971).

Rudolph, K., 'Gnosis und Gnostizismus, ein Forschungsbericht', *ThR* 34. 2 (1969), pp. 121–175; 34. 3 (1969), pp. 181–231; 36. 2 (1971), pp. 89–124.

Rudolph, K., 'Ein Grundtyp gnostischer Urmensch-Adam-Spekulation', *ZRGG* 9 (1957), pp. 1–20.

Rudolph, K., *Die Mandäer* I and II (1960 and 1961).

Rudolph, K., 'Problems of a History of the Development of the Mandaean Religion', *History of Religions* 8 (1969), pp. 210–235.

Rudolph, K., 'Randerscheinungen des Judentums und das Problem der Entstehung des Gnostizismus', *Kairos* 9 (1967), pp. 105–123.

Rudolph, K., 'Stand und Aufgaben in der Erforschung des Gnostizismus', *Tagung für allgemeine Religionsgeschichte 1963, Sonderheft der Wissen-schaftliche Zeitschrift der Friedrich-Schiller-Universität Jena*, pp. 89–102.

Rudolph, K., *Theogonie, Kosmogonie und Anthropogonie in den mandäischen Schriften* (1965).

Rudolph, K., 'War der Verfasser der Oden Salomos ein "Qumran-Christ"?', *Revue de Qumran* 4 (1964), pp. 523–555.

Russell, D. S., *The Method and Message of Jewish Apocalyptic* (1964).

Salles-Dabadie, J. M. A., *Recherches sur Simon le Mage* I: '*L'Apophasis Megalè*' (1969).

Sanders, J. T., *The New Testament Christological Hymn* (1971).

Säve-Söderbergh, T., *Studies in the Coptic Manichaean Psalm Book: Prosody and Mandaean Parallels* (1949).

Schenke, H.-M., 'Die Gnosis', *Umwelt des Christentums* I, ed. J. Leipoldt and W. Grundmann (1965), pp. 371–415.

Schenke, H.-M., 'Hauptprobleme der Gnosis', *Kairos* 7 (1965), pp. 114–123.

Schenke, H.-M., 'Nag-Hamadi Studien II: Das System der Sophia Jesu Christi', *ZRGG* 14 (1962), pp. 263–278.

Schenke, H.-M., 'Das Problem der Beziehung zwischen Judentum und Gnosis', *Kairos* 7 (1965), pp. 124–133.

Schlier, H., *Religionsgeschichtliche Untersuchungen zu den Ignatiusbriefen* (1929).

Schmithals, W., *Gnostics in Corinth* (1971).

Schmithals, W., *The Office of Apostle in the Early Church* (1969).

Schmithals, W., *Paulus und die Gnostiker: Untersuchungen zu den kleinen Paulusbriefen* (1965).

Schmithals, W., 'Das Verhältnis von Gnosis und Neuem Testament als methodisches Problem', *NTS* 16 (1970), pp. 373–383.

Schoeps, H.-J., 'Judenchristentum und Gnosis', in *OG*, pp. 528–537.

Scholem, G., *Jewish Gnosticism, Merkabah Mysticism, and Talmudic Tradition* (1960).

Scholem, G., *Major Trends in Jewish Mysticism* (1961).

Schubert, K., 'Gnosticism, Jewish', *New Catholic Encyclopedia* VI (1967), pp. 528–533.

Schubert, K., 'Jüdischer Hellenismus und jüdische Gnosis', *Wort und Wahrheit* 18 (1963), pp. 455–461.

Schulz, S., 'Die Bedeutung neuer Gnosisfunde für die neutestamentlich Wissenschaft', *ThR* 26 (1960), pp. 209–266, 301–334.

Schweizer, E., *Ego Eimi: Die religionsgeschichtliche Herkunft und theologische Bedeutung der joh. Bildreden* (1939; repr. 1964).

Segal, J. B., *Edessa 'The Blessed City'* (1970).

Segelberg, E., 'Old and New Testament Figures in Mandaean Version', *Syncretism*, ed. S. Hartman (1969), pp. 228–239.

Smalley, S. S., 'Diversity and Development in John', *NTS* 17 (1971), pp. 276–292.

Smith, D. M., *The Composition and Order of the Fourth Gospel: Bultmann's Literary Theory* (1965).

Talbert, C. H., *Luke and the Gnostics* (1966).

Till, W., *Die gnostischen Schriften des koptischen Papyrus Berolinensis 8502* (1955).

Turner, H. E. W., *The Pattern of Christian Truth* (1954).

Unnik, W. C. van., 'Die jüdische Komponente in der Entstehung der Gnosis', *VigChr* 15 (1961), pp. 65–82.

Vermaseren, M. J., *Corpus Inscriptionum et Monumentorum Religionis Mithriacae* (1956).

Widengren, G., 'Der iranische Hintergrund der Gnosis', *ZRGG* 4 (1952), pp. 97–114.

Widengren, G., 'Die Mandäer', *Handbuch der Orientalistik* VIII. 2, ed. B. Spuler (1961), pp. 83–101.

Widengren, G., *Mani and Manichaeism* (1965).

Wilckens, U., *Weisheit und Torheit* (1959).

Wilson, R. McL., *Gnosis and the New Testament* (1968).

Wilson, R. McL., *The Gnostic Problem* (1958).

Wilson, R. McL., 'Gnostics – in Galatia?', *Studia Evangelica* IV. 1 (1968), pp. 358–367.

Wilson, R. McL., 'Simon, Dositheus and the Dead Sea Scrolls', *ZRGG* 9 (1957), pp. 21–30.

Wilson, R. McL., 'Some Recent Studies in Gnosticism', *NTS* 6 (1959–1960), pp. 32–44.

Wisse, F., 'The Redeemer Figure in the Paraphrase of Shem', *NovTest* 12 (1970), pp. 130–140.

Yamauchi, E. M., 'Aramaic Magic Bowls', *JAOS* 85 (1965), pp. 511–523.

Yamauchi, E. M., *Gnostic Ethics and Mandaean Origins* (1970).

Yamauchi, E. M., *Mandaic Incantation Texts* (1967).

Yamauchi, E. M., 'A Mandaic Magic Bowl from the Yale Babylonian Collection', *Berytus* 17 (1967), pp. 49–63.

Yamauchi, E. M., 'The Present Status of Mandaean Studies', *Journal of Near Eastern Studies* 25 (1966), pp. 88–96.

Zaehner, R. C., *The Dawn and Twilight of Zoroastrianism* (1961).

INDEX OF SUBJECTS

INDEX OF MODERN AUTHORS

INDEX OF SCRIPTURES